Secret Passions,
Secret Remedies

Secret Passions, Secret Remedies

NARCOTIC DRUGS IN
BRITISH SOCIETY
1820–1930

Terry M. Parssinen

A Publication of the
Institute for the Study of Human Issues
Philadelphia

Manufactured in the United States of America

1 2 3 4 5 6   88 87 86 85 84 83

Publication of this book was assisted by a grant from the
National Institute on Drug Abuse, an independent federal
agency.

Library of Congress Cataloging in Publication Data

Parssinen, Terry M.
    Secret passions, secret remedies.

    Includes bibliographical references and index.
    1. Drug abuse—Great Britain—History.   I. Title.
HV5840.G7P37   1983   362.2′93′0942   82-15571
ISBN 0-89727-043-6

For information, write:

Director of Publications
ISHI
3401 Science Center
Philadelphia, Pennsylvania 19104
U.S.A.

For Carol

Publisher's Note

Academic publishing is a celebration of scholarly accomplishment, and as a publisher we take pride in each new book we produce. Of the present volume, however, we are especially proud. It is a major product of our research program in the history of opiate production, trade and use. As a research institute we fostered the investigation that generated this work, and now as a publisher we bring forth the product of that investigation. We hope you will indulge us in our pride in this volume and in the work of our research program. We hope as well that the work lives up to any expectations that pride engenders. We would like to thank the National Institute on Drug Abuse for its support of both the research and this publication. In particular we wish to acknowledge the wise and patient counsel of the late Eleanor Carroll, the project's program officer. Eleanor was an inspiration and a bulwark for all who seek to understand the social character of drug use and abuse. We wish to acknowledge as well the efforts of her colleagues, Louise Richards and Dan Lettieri, in guiding this study to completion.

Betty Crapivinsky-Jutkowitz
Director of Publications

Acknowledgments

Many persons contributed to the making of this book. My colleagues at the Institute for the Study of Human Issues deserve special mention. David Feingold encouraged me to start the project and offered helpful criticism at its various stages. Karen Kerner was the Co-Principal Investigator on the project and the co-author of two published articles. While her research concentrated on opiate use in Scotland, I benefited enormously from our many conversations about general problems. Joel Jutkowitz initiated me into the mysteries of constructing a budget. Maria Sanchez offered her good humor and secretarial skills as we wrote many drafts of grant proposals and reports, and Elaine Berman contributed her considerable research skills. The Director of ISHI Publications, Betty Crapivinsky-Jutkowitz, and editors Doug Gordon and Brad Fisher helped me put the manuscript in publishable form.

Financial support was provided by several institutions. A grant from the National Institute on Drug Abuse allowed me to live in Britain for two years while I did most of the research. Smaller grants from ISHI and the Temple University Faculty Senate supported shorter research trips.

Many of my colleagues in the history department at Temple University gave encouragement at various times. I am particularly grateful to those who were willing to read and criticize chapters which touched on their special areas: Mark Haller,

S. M. Chiu, Rod McGrew, Shumpei Okamoto, Waldo Heinrichs, Allen Davis, and Herb Bass.

Other scholars with an interest in the history of narcotic drugs read parts of the manuscript and offered thoughtful suggestions. David Courtwright's insightful comments saved me from some awful errors and pointed me in new directions. Eric Josephson provided me with a forum to try out early drafts of some chapters and brought his sociological perspective to bear on the project. David Musto offered help and encouragement, especially at the beginning of my work. John Crellin, Michael Durey, and John Frisch gave intelligent criticism on various parts of the manuscript.

I owe thanks to a legion of British and American librarians and archivists who helped me locate the materials out of which this book was formed. Miss Jones, a fount of knowledge about things historical at the Pharmaceutical Society Library (London), and Christine Ruggere, Head of the Historical Section of the College of Physicians (Philadelphia) deserve special mention.

Gloria Basmajian and Daria Kravchenko transformed my scribblings into a readable typescript through their wondrous word processor.

I am grateful to the editors of *Medical History* and the *Journal of Drug Issues* for allowing me to reprint material, in Chapters Seven and Ten, which previously appeared as articles in their respective journals.

No one deserves more heartfelt thanks than Carol Parssinen. She did much of the research and some of the writing on the literary topics, and she edited the entire manuscript. Moreover, she was willing to share bed and board with me while I went through the depressions, frustrations, anxieties and elations that were part of my life while I worked on this project. In retrospect it seems like a miracle that we are still married, but a miracle for which I am profoundly grateful.

T.M.P.

Introduction

From reading biographies and novels of the period, one can easily become persuaded that British society between 1820 and 1930 was completely narcotized. The literature runs over with opium-addicted poets, laudanum-swilling churchmen, morphia-crazed gentlewomen, opium-smoking Chinese, and cocaine-sniffing showgirls. These literary depictions of narcotic drug use first aroused my curiosity: Were they typical British drug users? In attempting to answer this question, I went to those sources—statistics, parliamentary blue books, periodical articles, manuscripts—by which the social historian tries to reconstruct the past. Most of the book is derived from these traditional materials. Nevertheless, my interest in the literature remained strong and I continued to be fascinated by the relationship between the literary world and the real world of narcotic drug use. That original inquiry has given this book one of its themes. Other themes appeared as I did research and wrote preliminary drafts of several chapters: the changing role of narcotic drugs in medicine; the importance of professional concerns in shaping legislation; and the relationship between regulation and consumption patterns of narcotic drug use. These themes are woven into the text, connecting one chapter to another, hopefully giving the book some continuity.

Finding a structure for a topic on which there had been little previous research presented a serious problem. After con-

sidering several alternatives, I decided to give the book a traditional, chronological structure. First, as to beginnings and end-
ings. Social history is rarely delineated by exact dates. At best
one can talk about a particular decade, rather than a particular
year, as a beginning, a turning point, or an end. Accordingly, I
have begun with the 1820s because it was then, in the wake of
the publication of Thomas De Quincey's *Confessions of an English
Opium-Eater* (1821), that opium and its effects first became a
topic of concern in nineteenth-century Britain. At the other end
of the study, I have concluded with the 1920s. The decade began with the passage of the Dangerous Drugs Act (1920) and an
uproar of concern about the illicit use of narcotic drugs. But by
the end of the decade, narcotic drug use and concern about it
were both fading fast.

Turning points were more difficult. After mucking around
in the sources for a few years (for if the truth be told, most
historians work less like a scientist testing a hypothesis than like a
small boy fondling sea shells), I began to see the outline of a
pattern. From the 1820s through the 1860s, opiates were freely
available, used regularly and increasingly, for a variety of reasons, by a great many Victorians. Insofar as these early Victorians thought and wrote about opiates at all (which, for the most
part, they did not), they thought that they were relatively harmless. From the 1870s through the first decade of the twentieth
century there was a growing concern of alarm about the dangers
of opiates (and later cocaine) from different quarters. And, in
the two decades between 1910 and 1930, narcotic drugs were
perceived as a social menace, even though the *number* of persons
who used them was diminishing. Admittedly, this outline is un-
tidy. The Poisons and Pharmacy Act of 1868, for example, was
passed on the wrong side of 1870. And common opiates, like
laudanum, continued to be freely and unselfconsciously used by
many Britons up through the Great War, long after medical
men had begun to worry about them. But if one allows for a
degree of flexibility, I believe that the outline represents the
major changes in the social history of narcotic drugs in Britain.

The historian is obliged not only to tell his readers how

things changed; he must also provide them with an explanation. To use Robin Winks' apt description, the historian is a detective. He must first locate the body, then find out whodunit and why. The search for explanations has taken me in different directions and turned up disparate pieces of evidence. The argument in Part Two, for example, rests on material as diverse as popular novels, poisoning statistics, and articles published in arcane medical journals. One must be willing to cross traditional disciplinary boundaries in order to understand why the attitudes of later Victorians toward narcotic drugs began to change.

I have written an afterword comparing the history of narcotic drugs in Britain and America from the 1860s through the 1920s. While I was doing my research, I read the work of historians who either had done or were doing comparable research on the history of narcotic drugs in American society: David Courtwright, John Frisch, H. Wayne Morgan, John Kramer, and David Musto. I wondered why the American experience with narcotic drugs had been so different from the British. I have tried to answer that by gleaning what I could from the American historians' books and articles, and setting it alongside my own work. The afterword is unashamedly speculative, and is based, at least on the American side, on secondary sources.

I believe that history does not have to illuminate present problems in order to justify its existence, so it is with some hesitation that I claim that this book does. It makes a small contribution to a debate that is current among narcotic drug policymakers as to whether the U.S. should adopt the British medical model of dealing with drug addiction. That, too, is a part of the afterword.

A Note on Abbreviations

Because of the frequency with which they are cited in the text and notes, certain publications will often be referred to in an abbreviated form. These include the *British Medical Journal* (or *BMJ*), *Chemist and Druggist* (or *C&D*), the British *Parliamentary Papers* (or *PP*), and the *Pharmaceutical Journal* (or *Pharm. J.*). References to government documents make use of standard abbreviations such as PRO (Public Record Office), HO (Home Office), FO (Foreign Office), and MH (Ministry of Health).

Contents

A picture section appears between pages 128 and 129.

Secret Passions,
Secret Remedies

PART ONE

The Great Victorian Drug Bazaar, 1820–1870

CHAPTER ONE

The Oriental Dream

In 1821, the *London Magazine* published a piece of literature that was extravagant, even as measured by the criteria of that extravagant age. In the *Confessions of an English Opium-Eater,* Thomas De Quincey used autobiography to explore a subject which was, in 1821, unknown to all but a handful of Englishmen: opium addiction. "Not the opium-eater, but the opium is the true hero of the tale," wrote De Quincey, as he concluded the *Confessions.* "The object was to display the marvelous agency of opium, whether for pleasure or for pain."[1]

Contrary to De Quincey's claim, the great appeal of the *Confessions* is that the opium and the opium-eater are inextricable. The narrative organization is frankly autobiographical, and the phenomena De Quincey records in "The Pleasures of Opium" and "The Pains of Opium" lose much of their meaning without the chronicle of his early years recorded in the "Preliminary Confessions." This account of a precocious, but solitary and dreaming boy, whose childhood was repeatedly shattered by the loss of loved ones, provides a crucial explanation for De Quincey's attraction to opium and the experiences he had while under its influence.

De Quincey himself makes it clear that opium can only reorder what is already in the dreamer's mind; it cannot create anything new: "If a man 'whose talk is of oxen' should become an opium-eater, the probability is that (if he is not too dull to dream at all) he will dream about oxen. . . ."[2] De Quincey, however, had

3

a philosopher's mind, stocked with images from many years of intensive reading, and a "constitutional determination to reverie." He found in opium a release from pain, elevation of spirits, feelings of kinship with other men, and the exquisite sensual pleasure of visits to the opera:

> Here were the hopes which blossom in the paths of life, reconciled with the peace which is in the grave; motions of the intellect as unwearied as the heavens, yet for all anxieties a halcyon calm; a tranquillity that seemed no product of inertia, but as if resulting from mighty and equal antagonisms; infinite activities, infinite repose.[3]

"The Pains of Opium" presents the dark side of opium's effects, but De Quincey makes even his suffering seem grand and alluring. He does begin with a sincere lament for the intellectual torpor and "infantile feebleness" he experienced in trying to carry out any project: "[The Opium Eater's] intellectual apprehension of what is possible infinitely outruns his power, not of execution only, but even of power to attempt."[4] The cause of his "acutest suffering," however, was what took place in his dreams.

De Quincey outlines four qualities of his dreams: the transmutation of daydreams into the dreams of sleep; anxiety, melancholy, and gloom; the infinite extension of space and time; and the recollection of minute incidents from past experience. Throughout, De Quincey's language suggests how his dreams have set him apart, allowing him glimpses of "gorgeous spectacles," "insufferable splendor," "feelings representative . . . of duration far beyond the limits of any human experience;" the rending of the veil "when the obscuring daylight shall have withdrawn."[5] Whatever the pains of these phenomena might have been, they are surely presented as worth the suffering. Even De Quincey's famous "Oriental dream" has the sinister lure of the otherworldly:

> Under the connecting feeling of tropical heat and vertical sunlights I brought together all creatures, birds, beasts, reptiles, all trees and plants, usages and appearances that are found in all

tropical regions, and assembled them together in China or Indostan. From kindred feelings I soon brought Egypt and all her gods under the same law. I was stared at, hooted at, grinned at, chattered at by monkeys, by parakeets, by cockatoos. I ran into pagodas and was fixed for centuries at the summit or in secret rooms; I was the idol; I was the priest; I was worshipped; I was sacrificed. I fled from the wrath of Brahma through all the forests of Asia; Vishnu hated me; Siva laid wait for me. I came suddenly upon Isis and Osiris; I had done a deed, they said, which the ibis and the crocodile trembled at. I was buried for a thousand years, in stone coffins, with mummies and sphinxes, in narrow chambers at the heart of eternal pyramids. I was kissed, with cancerous kisses, by crocodiles and laid, confounded with all unutterable slimy things, amongst reeds and Nilotic mud.[6]

The *Confessions,* then, is not a cautionary tale. Rather, De Quincey emerges as a noble self-experimenter, one whose life and personal qualities have enabled him to experience opium's power to the fullest. "This is the doctrine of the true church on the subject of opium, of which church I acknowledge myself to be the only member."[7]

The *Confessions,* which first appeared anonymously, caused an immediate sensation and catapulted its author into the literary foreground. The editors of the *London Magazine,* Taylor and Hessey, who publicly dedicated their journal to "Principles of Sound Philosophy in Questions of Taste, Morals, and Politics," drew on a distinguished company of writers.[8] Charles Lamb, William Hazlitt, and the poet John Clare were among their regular contributors, and pieces by Byron, Shelley, and Sir Walter Scott appeared from time to time. Even in this company, however, the opium-eater was set apart. His biographer David Masson writes:

> There was something almost staggering in the act of self-exposure by which man consented to be known as 'The Opium-Eater,' not figuratively or fictitiously, as some at first supposed, but with the most positive assurances that his revelations were real excerpts from his life.[9]

Not only did the opium-eater make startling revelations, but

he did so in "impassioned prose," De Quincey's designation for
writing which has the power to move, as well as to teach.[10] Taylor and Hessey recognized his genius and introduced the second
installment of the *Confessions* with unaccustomed praise:

> We are not often in the habit of eulogizing our own work, but we
> cannot neglect calling the attention of our readers to the deep,
> eloquent, and masterly paper which stands first in our present
> Number. Such *Confessions*, so powerfully uttered, cannot fail to do
> more than interest the reader.[11]

A third part of the *Confessions* was listed as a principal attraction for the coming year in December, 1821, but De Quincey,
distracted and in pain with the effort to break his habit, never
wrote it. Instead he added an appendix to the *Confessions*, detail-
ing the program to reduce his daily dose of opium.[12] Unlike the
"Pains of Opium," which De Quincey makes darkly appealing,
his withdrawal is presented in graphic physical terms:

> . . . unceasing restlessness night and day; sleep—I scarcely knew
> what it was—three hours out of the twenty-four was the utmost I
> had, and that so agitated and shallow that I heard every sound
> that was near me; lower jaw constantly swelling, mouth ulcerated;
> and many other distressing symptoms. . . .[13]

Since De Quincey had intended the thid part to correct what his
readers felt was an "overbalance on the side of the *pleasures* of
opium," he had in fact fulfilled his intention.[14]

Throughout 1823 and 1824, De Quincey continued to write
for the *London Magazine* under the signature of the "Opium-
Eater" on a wide variety of subjects. Of particular interest is a
series he entitled "Letters to a Young Man Whose Education has
been Neglected."[15] These explorations of language, literature,
and philosophy are delivered with such scholarly self-assurance
and magisterial dignity that one is hard pressed to remember
that the voice belongs to the same man who has confessed himself enslaved by a drug. Even though the opium-eater's signature was doubtless a way to draw readers, Taylor and Hessey
apparently had no reservations about allowing De Quincey to

offer academic advice or moral counsel. J. R. Findlay draws an instructive conclusion: "It was impossible to deal with or judge De Quincey by ordinary standards—not even his publishers did so."[16]

The perspective of nineteenth-century literary periodicals varied widely, and the image of the opium-eater presented in them is as complex as his multiple personae. He is sometimes the laudable, if pedantic, scholar, or literary star, as well as the fascinating initiate into the mysteries of opium. But De Quincey is never presented as an evil influence or moral pariah. Hazlitt accused De Quincey of plagiarizing material for an essay on Malthus from him, but the argument is entirely academic and no mention is made of De Quincey's addiction.[17]

Blackwood's Edinburgh Magazine mentions the opium-eater in "Noctes Ambrosianae," a monthly column of satire in dialogue on contemporary figures by John Wilson. Wilson calls him "a man in a million," and the opium-eater later appears frequently as a character in the dialogues. His position among the speakers is that of pedantic intellectual, but although other characters are often mercilessly ridiculed, the opium-eater is, at worst, presented as an absent-minded professor.[18]

Certainly the *Confessions* was satirized. "The Confessions of an English Glutton" (also in *Blackwood's*) is clearly a parody of De Quincey's work, but of his confessional style rather than what the opium-eater reveals about his use of drugs.[19] By reducing the confession to one of gluttony, the author suggests that only De Quincey's inflated prose has made his addiction seem important. By contrast, *Belgravia* published "The Confessions of a Chloral-Eater" in 1875, in which De Quincey's format and style have provided a pattern for a discussion of the uses and dangers of chloral.[20] The date of publication is significant for two reasons. The fact that a satire could appear over fifty years after the original attests to the continuing influence of De Quincey's *Confessions* throughout the century. And the fact that it was not De Quincey's style but his subject that was satirized demonstrates the changed view of drug addiction by the last quarter of the century.

In revealing his opium habit, De Quincey introduced the

subject of drug addiction to nineteenth-century Englishmen in a way which was both personal and intense. He made it clear that opium may have elevated his consciousness, but it had crippled his life. Yet the reaction of his contemporaries to this unique confession was benign, even bemused. De Quincey's career did not suffer from his revelation. To the contrary, the *Confessions* was the springboard to success and even a modest prosperity. The reaction to De Quincey is indicative of the early Victorian attitude toward opium and opium addiction generally. It was, for the most part, a nonissue. Medical men wrote about it rarely; popular writers almost never. And when people thought about it at all, they thought that addiction was a relatively infrequent, if unfortunate, by-product of the therapeutic use of an important drug.

This very lack of concern and paucity of writing about opium ensured that De Quincey continued to be regarded as the expert on the subject, at least by the nonmedical public. De Quincey and opium—the two were linked together in the popular consciousness long after his death. His experiences, and even his literary inventions, established a standard for writing about opium that persisted well into the twentieth century.

Notes

1. Thomas De Quincey, *Confessions of an English Opium-Eater and Other Writings*, ed. Aileen Ward (New York: Signet, 1966), p. 100. Referred to hereafter as *Confessions*. The best introduction to opium and Victorian literature is Alethea Hayter, *Opium and the Romantic Imagination* (Berkeley: University of California Press, 1970).

2. *Confessions*, p. 26.

3. *Confessions*, p. 71.

4. *Confessions*, p. 89.

5. *Confessions*, pp. 90–91.

6. *Confessions*, pp. 95–96.

7. *Confessions*, p. 64.

8. "Prospectus," *London Magazine, 1*, 1 (January 1820), iv.

9. David Masson, *De Quincey* (London, 1881) p. 76.

10. Thomas De Quincey, "The Literature of Knowledge and the Literature of Power," in *Confessions*, pp. 329–334.

11. *London Magazine, 4*, 22 (October 1821), 351.

12. "Appendix to the *Confessions of an English Opium-Eater*," *London Magazine, 6*, 36 (December 1822), 512–517.

13. *Confessions*, p. 105.

14. "To the Editor of the *London Magazine*," *London Magazine, 4*, 24 (December 1821), 585.

15. *London Magazine, 7*, 37–43 (January–July 1823).

16. J. R. Findlay, "The Life and Writings of De Quincey," in John Downie, ed., *De Quincey's 'Confessions of an English Opium-Eater'* (London, 1901), p. xx.

17. "To the Editor of the *London Magazine*," *London Magazine, 8*, 47 (November 1823), 448–452.

18. *Blackwood's Edinburgh Magazine, 18*, 105 (October 1825), 508.

19. *Blackwood's Edinburgh Magazine, 13*, 71 (January 1823), 86–93.

20. *Belgravia, A London Magazine, 26*, (April 1875), 179–190.

CHAPTER TWO

The International Opium Trade

De Quincey's *Confessions*, despite its popularity, did not lead to an epidemic of opium taking in Britain. However, there was an expansion of opium consumption. The per capita amount of opium imported into Britain for domestic consumption grew at the rate of just over 2 percent per year between 1831 and 1859 (see Fig. 1). It is reasonable to believe that this steady rate of growth continued, at least through the 1870s.[1] Meanwhile, the amount of *all* opium imported into Britain grew enormously. In the early 1830s, opium imports averaged 91,000 pounds per annum; by the late 1860s, they averaged 280,000 pounds. Opium imports continued to expand, although at a reduced rate, through the next four decades. Re-exports (imports which were exported without being processed) also expanded, from an average of 41,000 pounds per annum in the early 1830s, to an average of 151,000 pounds in the late 1860s. Opium re-exports generally followed the same upward path as did imports for the next four decades, although they began to decline fifteen years earlier than did imports (see Fig. 2). Re-exports were shipped all over the world, but America was by far the largest single customer: About half of all opium re-exports were sent to the United States. The high figures for both imports and re-exports from the late 1860s through the second decade of the twentieth century are indicative of Britain's predominance in the world market for drugs in general, and opium in particular, during that period.

Drugs were only one of many commodities—like tea or cotton—which were grown in the less-developed lands of the southern hemisphere, consumed and sometimes processed by Europeans, and then often exported in manufactured form back to the areas whence they had come. This commerce had gone on for centuries. By 1800, however, the sources of supply had come to be controlled more directly by Europeans, either by direct political intervention, or by a more efficient economic penetration. Britain used both means to extend her control over most of the world's opium supply. In India, the East India Company fell heir to the opium-producing monopoly of the Mogul emperors. The Company extended it, made it more efficient, cultivated outlets for opium among Chinese smokers, and connived with smugglers and corrupt officials to move it illicitly into Chinese markets. Quantities and profits were immense. At the height of the traffic, in the late nineteenth century, the Indian opium monopoly exported to China 14 million pounds per annum, which generated 18 percent of the total revenues of the Government of India.[2]

Despite the opium-producing resources of India, most of the opium that was consumed in nineteenth-century Britain was grown in Turkey. Although highly prized by Chinese smokers, Indian opium had a low morphia content (4–6%), which made it uneconomic for pharmaceutical uses in Britain. Sporadic experiments in domestic opium production were carried out from the 1740s through the 1830s, but ultimately the poppies proved to need a more hospitable climate and more intensive labor than was available in Britain.[3] Turkish opium, however, was perfectly suited to the British market. It had a high morphia content (10–13%); it could be cheaply produced by Turkish peasants; and its production was centralized around the Anatolian town of Afiun ("opium" in Turkish), only fifty miles inland from the port of Smyrna. Furthermore, vigilant Ottoman inspectors kept adulteration—always a problem in the opium trade—to manageable levels, which gave Turkish opium a good reputation in the London market.

While Britain did not control Turkey politically, she nevertheless had long-standing strategic and economic interests in the

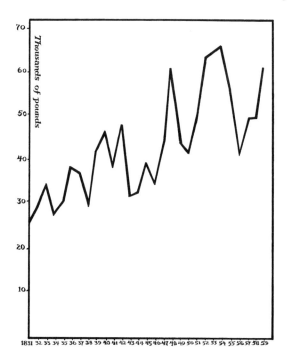

Figure 1.
Opium imports entered for home consumption, 1831–1859.
(Source: Annual Accounts of Trade and Navigation,
Parliamentary Papers.)

country. The ailing Ottoman Empire, long known as "the sick
man of Europe," was in a critical geographical position to safeguard British interests in the eastern Mediterranean. The Ottoman Empire straddled the narrow Bosphorus and Dardanelles,
which connected the Black Sea to the Mediterranean. As long as
Turkish sovereignty over these straits could be maintained, the
Russian warm water fleet remained bottled up in the Black Sea,
thus assuring that British trade routes through the Mediterranean to the East would not be threatened. Additionally, the
Ottoman Empire provided a nearly perfect trading partner for
Britain, a fact which had been recognized as early as 1581, when

Figure 2.
Import and re-export of opium in five-year averages.
(Source: Annual Accounts of Trade and Navigation,
Parliamentary Papers.)

the Levant Company was founded. By 1800, the Levant Company was moribund, and by 1825 it had been disbanded; but not before it had established Smyrna as a major port, and had provided a network of connections for British traders.[4]

The trade between Britain and Turkey expanded rapidly after the Napoleonic Wars, and particularly after the Treaty of Balta Limon (1838). This secured "most favored nation" status for Britain by reducing the Turkish export duties; by removing restrictions on access to the interior by British merchants; and by abolishing permits, monopolies, and interior taxes on produce for export. After Balta Limon, export and tariff rates were set

uniformly at 12 percent.[5] The results were dramatic. Exports to
Turkey from Britain rose from £2.25 million in 1827 to £12
million in 1849.[6] The Ottoman Empire became the fourth
largest market in the world for British cotton goods and, in turn,
supplied Britain with a variety of agricultural products, including opium.[7] In 1860, for example, the major British imports
from Turkey, in order of value, were corn (£825,000), madder
root, goat's wool, valonia, sponge, opium (£187,000), silk, and
raisins.[8] Another spur to the rise of opium imports was the
gradual decline and then elimination of the British import duty
on opium, as well as on many other goods in the early
nineteenth century. In 1826, the duty per pound of opium was
set at 9s., which decreased to 4s. in 1838, and then to 1s. in 1841
before being eliminated altogether in 1860.[9] British firms, based
in Smyrna, controlled virtually the entire trade in opium until
the later nineteenth century, when they began to be challenged
by Americans.

Until the 1870's, over 85 percent of the opium imported
into Britain came from Turkey.[10] Turkish growers expanded
their opium crop through the middle decades of the nineteenth
century to keep pace with increasing demand. In the long run,
the price of Turkish opium remained fairly stable from the end
of the Napoleonic Wars through the early 1880s (see Table 1 in
the Appendix). There were, however, short-term fluctuations of
considerable magnitude. In 1868, for example, the price of
opium in Smyrna reached 390 piastres per pound, an increase
of more than 100 percent over the previous year's highest price.
In other years, a variation of 25 to 50 percent was not unusual
(see Table 2 in the Appendix). There were several factors which
accounted for short-term fluctuations. The first, and most important, was the great variability of production from year to
year. The delicate opium poppies are particularly susceptible to
extremes of moisture and heat. Heavy rainfall, a prolonged
drought, an early frost, or a scorching autumn were all potential
disasters which could greatly reduce the size of the crop. Turkish production in the years 1880 to 1882, which yielded successive crops of 2,100, 11,000 and 4,500 baskets, illustrates the
vagaries of opium-growing (see Table 2).

In addition to the size of the crop, the opium trade was influenced by speculators at three key points in the market chain: in the Anatolian interior, where the crop was purchased from Turkish peasants by Greek and Armenian merchants who often kept them in debt-slavery; in Smyrna, where European drug traders purchased the opium from merchants; and in London, where wholesale drug dealers, and later pharmaceutical manufacturers, bought opium at auction. At each point, traders bought and sold, held or depleted stocks according to their assessment of future price changes and their ability to manipulate the market. Many European traders in Smyrna had operated there for decades. But there were also spot buyers—mostly Americans—who were in and out of the market from one season to the next, and occasionally even government departments, such as the Dutch Colonial Office, which for some years in the late nineteenth century bought directly at Smyrna rather than in London.[11]

Usually, the trade was sufficiently fragmented to inhibit really successful speculative ventures. That is, there was usually enough opium in different hands to ensure that when speculators forced up the price by cornering a large share of the year's crop, a release of opium stocks was triggered and drove the price back down again. A notable exception was 1868, when an extremely small crop was controlled by a few speculators, which sent the price of opium to record highs (see Table 2).

Although Southampton and the ports of the southeast had been important entrepôts in the Middle Ages, by the late seventeenth century over 95 percent of drug imports came through London.[12] In the nineteenth century, London developed into the center of the international drug trade. At least through the 1870s, most of the world's supply of raw drugs was brought to auction in London's Mincing Lane. In part, London's preeminence was the result of its commercial advantages as the center of international shipping, finance, and insurance.[13] In addition, as a result of her imperial expansion in the eighteenth century, Britain controlled the sources of many drugs—as well as other raw materials—and through the Navigation Acts of the seventeenth century insured that the trade in colonial goods would be channeled through London. London's natural advantages were enhanced even further by the creation of a dock police in 1800, and by the passage of the Warehousing Act of 1803, which allowed for the creation of bonded warehouses where dutiable goods could be stored and duty paid only when they were taken out to be sold. These measures greatly reduced pilferage of cargoes, and eliminated the need for shippers to pay duty and then claim rebates on goods which entered the port and were later re-exported. Opium and other drugs which entered the port were warehoused at the London and East India docks, where they were classified, sorted, and samples prepared for auction.[14]

Mincing Lane became commercially important in the late sixteenth century, and by the eighteenth century it had become synonymous with the drug trade. By the mid-eighteenth century, drugs were auctioned at Garraway's Coffee House "by the candle." A one-inch candle was lit at the beginning of the auction, and bids entertained until it had burned out, the highest prevailing bid at that moment taking the lot. In 1811, the traders moved the venue of their auctions, first to the Commercial Sale Rooms, then to the New Corn Exchange Hotel, and finally back to the rebuilt Commercial Sale Rooms in the 1890s. The auctions themselves were highly ritualized. About one hundred traders—drug brokers, representing importers, and drug buyers—gathered fortnightly, for sessions that began at 10:30 a.m., and continued until all the parcels had been disposed of late in the afternoon.[15]

The drug trade was a high-risk, high-profit business. At the beginning of the nineteenth century, a survey of British commerce noted of the drug trade: "This is a very profitable business, the returns sometimes cent. [i.e., 100] percent., and seldom less than fifty; but it requires a capital of from £500 to £2000."[16] The risk came from the extreme fluctuation in drug prices, and the increasing competition as London became the center of the international trade.

Connections between wholesalers and retailers were immensely improved in the early nineteenth century by several factors. The coming of the penny post and railways made ordering and dispatching both cheaper and faster. The time elapsed between an order being sent and received by a chemist was reduced from several weeks to a few days. In addition, wholesalers began to issue monthly "prices current," reflecting the sharp changes in market prices of drugs, which allowed retailers to shop around for the best deals, and to capitalize on temporarily lowered prices for certain drugs.[17]

The rationalization of the entire drug trade, from the point of production to the point of sale, steadily lowered the prices of drugs throughout the century. A chemist, writing in 1909, claimed that

> a pharmacist in 1810 purchasing equal quantities of 155 drugs and chemicals, paid on an average 11s.6d. per lb., while the pharmacist of 1909, purchasing equal quantities of the same 155 articles, pays an average 5s.7d. per lb., or less than half the sum.[18]

One could, by working from a different base year, and by calculating along different lines, produce an even greater contrast. A columnist for the *Chemist and Druggist* compared the prices of twenty-five drugs from "Prince's Price Current" for 1817 to prices prevailing for the same drugs in 1907 and concluded: "In 1817 the twenty-five purchases would have run to £164 19s. 4d., in 1907 to £33 13s.8d., or just about one-fifth. Customs duties accounted for £50 16s. 6d. of the higher price, averaging about 30 per cent."[19] In addition to the dropping of customs duties on drugs, another factor that brought prices down was the more efficient management of both the supply and transportation of drugs. As international demand increased, drugs ceased to be simply an ancillary commodity to be bought and sold irregularly by persons who traded in other goods. Regular and efficient international trade networks were established, and governments encouraged the growth of commercial drug crops, since they produced more income for their peasants, and more taxes for themselves.

In contrast to the downward trend of drug prices generally, the wholesale price of opium remained fairly stable for most of the century. From the Napoleonic Wars through the 1870s, the wholesale price of opium hovered within a few shillings of 22s.

per pound. Not until the 1880s did the wholesale price drop permanently (see Table 1). The retail price of opiates was even more regular. Through the 1870s, laudanum generally sold for 8d. per ounce, while the more concentrated Battley's Syrup fetched 2s.6d. per ounce. From the 1880s, retail prices began to follow wholesale prices downward (see Table 3 in the Appendix).

By the 1870s, then, Britain had become the center of the international traffic in opium. The India-China trade in smoking opium continued unabated, while medicinal opium from Turkey came into British ports before being sent to other parts of the world. Meanwhile, a steadily increasing amount of Turkish opium was retained for consumption in Britain.

Notes

1. Beginning in 1831, the British Customs Office recorded the amount of opium imported into Britain "for home consumption." In 1860, when opium was removed from the list of dutiable items, this category was eliminated. Thus there is no way of determining, after 1859, how much of the imported opium was retained for home consumption and how much was manufactured and exported. Between 1831–35 and 1855–59, the amount of opium imports retained for home consumption, and adjusted for population growth, increased by 70 percent.

2. Maurice Collins, *Foreign Mud: Being an Account of the Opium Imbroglio at Canton in the 1830s and the Anglo-Chinese War that Followed* (London: Faber & Faber, 1946), pp. 76, 309; see also Arthur D. Waley, *The Opium War Through Chinese Eyes* (London: Allen & Unwin, 1958), David E. Owen, *British Opium Policy in China and India* (New Haven: Yale University Press, 1934), Brian Inglis, *The Opium War* (London: Hodder & Stoughton, 1976).

3. "Opium Production in England." *Pharm. J.*, April 25, 1925, 467–468; "The Winslow Opium: British Production in the Early Eighteens," *Pharm. J.*, February 28, 1948, 151; V. Berridge, "Our Own Opium: Cultivation of the Opium Poppy in Britain, 1740–1823," *British Journal of Addiction*, 72 (1977), 90–94.

4. Alfred C. Wood, *A History of the Levant Company* (London: Oxford

University Press, 1935); Ina S. Russell, "The Later History of the Levant Company 1753–1825," D. Phil. thesis, University of Manchester, 1935.

5. J. B. Williams, *Commercial Policy and Trade Expansion, 1750–1850* (Oxford: The Clarendon Press, 1972), pp. 295–296; V. J. Puryear, *International Economics and Diplomacy in the Near East. A Study of British Commercial Policy in the Levant, 1834–1853* (Palo Alto: Stanford University Press, 1935), pp. 124–125.

6. Puryear, pp. 108–109.

7. Arthur Redford, *Manchester Merchants and Foreign Trade, 1794–1939,* (Manchester: Manchester University Press, 1934) I, pp. 243–245.

8. Charles Capper, *The Port and Trade of London* (London: Smith, Elder, 1862), p. 291.

9. "Opium," *Pharm. J.,* April 1, 1851, 524. As long as there was an import duty, there was inevitably a certain amount of smuggling, especially of a commodity like opium, which had a high value relative to bulk. In the eighteenth century, when the duty on opium was high, there were occasional reports of opium smuggling, largely by ships' captains, who simply did not declare all that they were carrying. See, for example, Russell, pp. 158–160. As the duty was progressively lowered in the nineteenth century, the incentive to smuggle was diminished. There is, of course, no way to estimate the extent of smuggling, but after 1841, when the duty was lowered to only 1s. per pound, it must have been insignificant.

10. Calculated from "Annual Accounts of Trade and Navigation," *PP.* From the 1870s onward, Britain began to import substantial quantities of opium from Persia. According to late nineteenth-century reports, opium became a major Persian export crop by the 1880s due to the buoyant prices then being paid for it in Hong Kong and London. British merchants, however, controlled only 20 to 25 percent of this trade. "Persian Opium," *Pharm. J.,* May 7, 1887, 904.

11. There are market reports on Turkish opium in nearly every issue of *Chemist and Druggist,* and in many issues of the *Pharmaceutical Journal.* The most extensive and informed discussions of the production and marketing of middle eastern opium are E. R. Heffler, "Notes on the Culture and Commerce in Opium in Asia Minor," *Pharm. J.,* January 1869, 434–437; "The Poppy in Persia," *Pharm. J.,* June 20, 1885, 1051–1052; "The Opium Trade In Persia," *C&D,*

July 15, 1880, 229; Karl von Scherzer, "Commercial Notes on Opium," *Pharm. J.*, April 9, 1881, 835–836; and Joaquin Marti y Artis, "The Smyrna Markets: Opium and its Cultivation," *C&D*, September 15, 1880, 392–393. Of special interest is Col. Fayk Bey, *Monographie des opiums de l'Empire Ottoman* (Paris, 1867). There is a copy of this very rare pamphlet in the Pharmaceutical Society Library, London. Occasional attempts were made to introduce poppy cultivation into areas where labor was cheap and the climate was suitable. However, as the poppy required experienced labor, and as the risks were so great, most of these did not succeed. One of the most spectacular failures was a heavily capitalized attempt, in the 1870s, to introduce opium into Mozambique. In one year, a crop which had cost £10,000 to plant returned a harvest worth £100. See also "Opium Production in Africa," *Pharm. J.*, June 15, 1878, 1007–1008; "Poppy Cultivation and Manufacture of Opium in Mozambique," *Pharm. J.*, August 2, 1890, 87; "Opium Cultivation in Mexico," *C&D*, September 20, 1890, 396; "Notes on the Cultivation of the Opium Poppy in Australia," *Pharm. J.*, October 1, 1870, 272–274; "Preparation of Opium in France," *Pharm. J.*, February 8, 1859, 229–230; "Opium in Russia," *Pharm. J.*, January 13, 1912, 52; and C. O. Harz, "Opium Production in Europe," *Pharm. J.*, September 16, 1871, 223–224.

12. R. S. Roberts, "The Early History of the Import of Drugs into Britain," in F. N. L. Poynter, ed., *The Evolution of the Pharmacy in Britain* (London: Pitman, 1965), p. 171.

13. Stephen Miall, *A History of the British Chemical Industry* (London: Ernest Benn, 1931), p. 119; "London's Position as a Drug Market," *Pharm. J.*, Feb. 25, 1905, 263–264.

14. A. W. Kirkaldy, *British Shipping: Its History, Organization, and Importance* (reprint of 1914 edition: Newton Abbey, Devon: David & Charles, 1970), pp. 495, 506; Joseph Broadbank, *The History of the Port of London* (London: Daniel O'Connor, 1921), I, pp. 89–90, 109–110.

15. "London's Drug Market and the Romance of Mincing Lane," *C&D*, June 30, 1928, pp. 851–867; "A Century of Commerce in Drugs," *C&D*, November 10, 1959, 160–166; "The Drug Sales," *C&D*, August 21, 1886, 230–232.

16. Joshua Montefiore, *The Trader's and Manufacturer's Compendium: Containing the Laws, Customs and Regulations Relative to Trade; In-*

tended for the use of Wholesale and Retail Dealers (London, 1804), p. 286.

17. "The Drug Trade in the Victorian Era," *C&D*, June 19, 1897, 973.

18. "The Average Prices of Drugs," *C&D*, July 31, 1909, 206.

19. "Observations and Reflections by Xrayser," *C&D*, March 9, 1907, 369.

CHAPTER THREE

The Magical Healer:
Opium as Therapeutic Agent

Opium's healing powers were seemingly magical. The drug could kill pain, bring sleep, ease rumbling stomachs, and stop runny bowels. This assured its growing use by healers, both inside and outside the medical profession. Opium had been known to the English medical profession since the seventeenth century. Indeed, it had been so highly praised by Dr. Thomas Sydenham that it had earned him the sobriquet "Opiophilos." His widely publicized formula for tincture of opium continued to be known as "Sydenham's Laudanum" well into the nineteenth century.[1] Opium had been the subject of papers by both toxicologists and clinicians throughout the eighteenth and early nineteenth centuries.[2] Furthermore, opium was an integral part of the great medical systems of the eighteenth-century thinkers like John Brown and Benjamin Rush.[3] Yet it was not until the 1830s and 1840s that opium assumed a crucial therapeutic role in English medicine. Medical journals were flooded with articles touting its expanded use. Jonathan Pereira, in his influential textbook on medicine and therapeutics, echoed the dominant professional opinion when he claimed that

> opium is undoubtedly the most important and valuable remedy of the whole Materia Medica. We have, for other medicines, one or more substitutes; but for opium we have none. . . . Its good

effects are not, as is the case with some valuable medicines, remote and contingent, but they are immediate, direct, and obvious; and its operation is not attended with pain or discomfort.[1]

Opium had a wide variety of therapeutic uses, most notably as an analgesic, a febrifuge, a sedative, and as a specific for gastrointestinal difficulty, especially diarrhea. Since most medical men still prepared their own medicines, opium was available in the doctor's surgery as well as in the local pharmacy. It was compounded in prescriptions with other elements, and it was prepared on its own, in powder, in pills, or in liquid, most commonly as laudanum—tincture of opium. By the 1840s, opium had become one of the most important staples of English therapeutics.

What accounts for the increased popularity of opium in English medicine at mid-century? One factor which played a role was the influence of former East India Company medical men. Opium had long been a staple of Indian therapeutics, and was used in the treatment of cholera, which was endemic to India. When the cholera broke out in Britain (1831–2, 1848–9, and 1853–4), they promoted its use. Opium mixed with calomel was one of the most frequently used and successful cholera remedies in nineteenth-century Britain.[5]

A second factor was the challenge to orthodox therapeutics. The early nineteenth century was a period of prolonged crisis in English medicine. Orthodox medical men were threatened by the sudden emergence of irregular practitioners in the 1830s and 1840s: homeopaths, hydropaths, "galvanic" healers, and mesmerists. Unlike such older rivals as herbalists, white witches, and bonesetters, these new "quacks" had many of the trappings of orthodoxy, from well-appointed consulting rooms and medical degrees to entire philosophies derived from medical thinkers like Hahnemann or Mesmer. They often succeeded in attracting the wealthy urban patients who were in too short supply in early Victorian Britain.[6] The success of these irregular practitioners is easily explained. Despite the demise of the humoral etiology in the late eighteenth century, the heroic therapies which were based on it continued to be practiced by orthodox medical men well into the nineteenth century. These included such painful and unpleasant measures as bleeding, blistering, and dosing with large amounts of harsh drugs like calomel. Understandably, some patients felt that they might be better off without the attendance of orthodox medical men. Irregular practitioners benefited from this reaction since they offered therapies which were relatively painless and harmless. At first, orthodox medical men reacted angrily, claiming that mesmerists, homeopaths, and hydropaths were merely providing placebos. Eventually, however, some medical men admitted that the success of irregular practitioners was, in effect, a public rejection of the heroic therapies they had been so dependent on early in the century. This line of argument dealt the deathblow to heroic therapies by mid-century.

If medical men were no longer to bleed and blister their patients, how would they treat them? Until the revolution in therapeutics in the early twentieth century, physicians did not so much cure diseases as manage their symptoms. Given this fundamental limitation in nineteenth-century medical practice, opium was invaluable. Along with alcohol, opium became an important part of the treatment plan of noninterventionist medical practice, which urged doctors to let disease run its natural course while monitoring and managing its symptoms. Opium offered the orthodox medical man a gentle and effective means of alleviating some of his patients' most common forms of distress: pain, fever, and diarrhea. But as important as opium was in orthodox medical practice, it was even more important in the tradition of self-medication.

Until the nineteenth century, self-medication in Britain meant reliance upon the pharmacy of the woods and fields. The folk tradition of gathering, preparing, and using herbs commonly available in the English countryside dates back to at least Anglo-Saxon times, and probably much earlier.[7] In the seventeenth century, a number of classic "herbals" were published, most notably Nicholas Culpepper's *Physicall Directory* (1649), which continued to be sold and used well into the nineteenth century. One also finds evidence of the herbalist tradition in the manuscript "receipt" books that have survived from the seven-

teenth and eighteenth centuries. Typically, these are compila-
tions of cookery, medical, and household recipes, gathered from
eclectic sources, and added to over the years. Often the distinction between a cookery and a medical recipe is unclear, indicat-
ing how often foods were used as medicaments.

Implicit in such receipt books, and explicit in published
works, such as John Hill's many popular herbals and John Wesley's *Primitive Physic* (1747) is a distinct antipathy to orthodox
pharmacy and medicine. "There is," according to John Hill, "no
form of medicine sent from the apothecary which may not be
prepared from the herbs of our own growth in the same manner
as from foreign drugs." Wesley distrusted physicians and
apothecaries, believing, with many of his contemporaries, that
their fees were exorbitant and their knowledge was deficient.
Every man, with the resources of the countryside and the aid of
a readable guide, could be his own doctor. Even the Scottish
physician William Buchan drew his colleagues' scorn and anger
for "laying Medicine more open to Mankind," the announced
purpose of his *Domestic Medicine* (1769).[8]

Opium, as an imported and relatively expensive drug, did
not figure prominently in the herbalist literature. While opium
was mentioned in many of the eighteenth-century treatises on
domestic medicine, and it occasionally appears in receipt books,
it clearly did not occupy as central a position in self-medication
practices in the eighteenth century as it did in the nineteenth.

The herbalist tradition, both oral and written, had an important, though declining influence well into the nineteenth
century. On one level, it continued as a part of the mix of good
sense, empiricism, and superstition that made up village folk
medicine. "A Village Chemist," writing in 1874, revealed a thriving trade in herbs around Manchester which was so large that it
had both wholesale and retail dealers.[9] This Lancashire trade
was clearly a part of a surviving tradition, for the "Village Chemist" places herbalism in the context of a continuing belief in the
"doctrine of the signatures," and in the efficacy of charms and
amulets.[10]

On a somewhat different level, herbalism had a Victorian
revival in the form of the system of "botanic medicine" of the

American, Samuel Thomson. Thomson's disciple, A. I. Coffin, introduced it into England with his "Botanic Guide to Health," which, by 1852, had gone through twenty-five editions. In 1864, Coffin and his associates founded the National Institute of Medical Herbalists, and conferred certificates upon its graduates.[11] Coffin's botanic medicine resembled the other medical sects of early Victorian Britain—mesmerism, homeopathy, and hydropathy—in that it was based on a medico-scientific system, it differentiated between professionals and amateurs, and it acquired some of the trappings of orthodox medicine. But herbalism, whether of the village or scientific variety, was clearly a marginal phenomenon in late nineteenth-century Britain.[12] The real legacy of herbalism lay in the sense of medical self-reliance which it fostered, and which continued to thrive long after the doctrines of herbalism had disappeared.

Herbalism was the predominant form of self-medication so long as most Britons lived in villages and small towns, close to the countryside and attuned to rural folk traditions. Rapid urbanization changed that. By mid-century, the majority of the population lived in cities, cut off both from physical proximity to wild herbs, and from the culture which encouraged their use. At the same time, the population density of urban areas brought many more people into contact with chemists' shops than previously. While self-medication continued to thrive in Victorian Britain, the forms that it assumed changed significantly.[13]

Victorians were no less reluctant than their grandparents had been to consult medical men. Although physicians' fees fell in the course of the century, they still stood at 5s. (or 2s. 6d. for a poor person) for a consultation with a general practitioner at the end of the nineteenth century. With the weekly wages of an unskilled laborer at 18s. to 25s., he would think twice before knocking on the doctor's surgery, especially for treatment of a minor problem. Where did the urbanized Victorian go to obtain relief from the ordinary aches and pains of life? There were, by the late nineteenth century, a number of clinics that treated poor patients at greatly reduced cost, or gratis. In addition, some medical men set aside one morning a week to see charity cases. But Victorian working people were often reluctant to use

these services, both because they found it degrading to be patronized as a pauper, and because the inevitable wait to see a
doctor could deprive a man of a half day's pay. One of the most
popular sources of cheap advice and medication was the local
chemist. The customer would describe his symptoms and the
chemist, on the basis of his practical knowledge of therapeutics
acquired over years of trade, would suggest a remedy, sometimes a patent medicine, but more often a compound of his own
devising. Often the customer, on the basis of previous experience, already knew what drug or mixture he wanted. But
whether or not he asked for the chemist's advice, the customer
paid only for the medicine, which could usually be purchased in
quantities as small as a pennyworth.[14]

Medical men denounced these "prescribing chemists" as
dangerous, untrained practitioners, and tried several times in
the course of the century to force them to desist.[15] But the
chemists replied that they provided an essential service to persons whose simple complaints did not warrant a medical man's
attention. At the times when prosecutions mounted by the Society of Apothecaries (the general practitioners' body) brought the
issue to public prominence, the newspapers almost always sided
with the chemists. In a typical comment, the *Birmingham Daily
Post* published an editorial on the subject in 1878 which concluded that "it would be a great hardship, not only upon chemists, but upon poor persons, if it were made compulsory in every
case where a man has a toothache, a gumboil, or a cold in the
head, to pay a doctor's fee in order to obtain the necessary
medicine."[16]

The significance of chemists' counter-practice in poor
neighborhoods was graphically described by an East End chemist in 1868:

On Saturday I made an account of the customers served from
eight o'clock, a.m. until twelve p.m. The amount was 400 persons:–
209 Penny Customers
12 at 1s.
Patent Medicines 3s. 4½d.

. . . The chief part of a druggist's business in this neighborhood is prescribing for the poor.[17]

Some chemists even achieved local fame, not unlike the fame achieved in rural areas by a particularly successful bonesetter, white witch, or herbalist. One such case came to light at an inquest, held in Bermondsey in 1898, into the death of an elderly hoopmaker. The wife of the deceased testified that her husband, "seized with diarrhea and sickness," went to his local chemist, "Dr." Wiggins, and brought two bottles of Wiggins' diarrhea mixture. When asked by the coroner why her husband did not call in a doctor, the witness replied: "He would not have one. Over and over again I advised him to have a doctor, but he refused. He had a great faith in 'Dr.' Wiggins' mixtures." A medical witness at first tried to suggest that death was caused by the mixture. But when the wife testified that the deceased had been drinking heavily, the doctor admitted that this, rather than the mixture, was probably the immediate cause of death. The coroner's jury, after formally exonerating Wiggins from any blame, praised him individually. One elderly juror rose and said emphatically, "I beg to say that I have had Mr. Wiggins' mixture for fourteen years, and I have never had to have a doctor." Wiggins himself ended the proceeding by crowing a bit at the expense of the local doctors. The *Chemist and Druggist* concluded laconically that

> Mr. Wiggins, who has a very large connection in the district, has called forth much opposition from medical men through the wide circulation of a self-prescribing list, by the aid of which the most ignorant can physic themselves for any particular complaint. It is headed:—Treat (by the aid of this) your Ills, and so save Doctors' Visiting Bills.[18]

Since there was no significant restriction on the drugs that could be sold over the druggist's counter until 1916, narcotics of all types were dispensed through counter-practice. Opium, because of its effectiveness, was certainly the most important single drug sold by chemists. In addition to the standard version of laudanum, opium was also sold in countless local mixtures, some

of which, like "Battley's Syrup" or "Black Drop," achieved such a
wide popularity that they were eventually incorporated into the
official British pharmacopoeia.[19]

In 1857, a Select Committee of the House of Lords held
hearings on a Sale of Poisons Bill, which produced a great deal
of information about the sale and consumption of poisonous
drugs, including opiates. Jacob Bell, the founder of the Pharmaceutical Society of Great Britain, testified that restrictions on
the sale of opiates "would be almost impossible to carry . . . into
effect in many country districts, where pennyworths of
laudanum and opium are very often sold, and habitually taken
by the public at large."[20] He was supported by subsequent witnesses. W. T. Brade, Professor of Chemistry at the Royal Institution, testified that "there are a number of persons who are in the
habit of keeping laudanum by them; they take 10 or 20 drops of
laudanum when their bowels get out of order, or when they are
apprehensive of cholera, or disorders of that kind. [21] Mr.
W. Herapath, a senior magistrate from Bristol, pointed out that
chemists sell opium so frequently that it is unrealistic to ask them
to keep the bottle under lock and key in a special cabinet. When
questioned further, Herapath estimated that in large towns,
chemists might make 100 sales of opium per day.[22] Even John
Hammill, a police magistrate distressed by the frequent use of
opiates in suicides and homicides, conceded that its widespread
use as a popular medicine militated against its effective regulation.[23]

Sixty years later not much had changed. An attempt by the
General Medical Council, in 1914, to restrict the sale of
laudanum brought forth a flurry of letters from chemists testify-
ing to the importance of laudanum to their business. According
to "W. S.,"

> In my business, it is safe to say that not a single half-hour passes
> during business hours that a sale is not made. And of these sales I
> am satisfied that only one customer has it to indulge the 'opium
> habit.' The rest have it for liniments, cough mixtures, and tooth-
> aches, but most of all for application to small cuts and wounds.[24]

Mr. Brackenbury, of Middlesborough, reported that "last week I kept account of all my sales, and found they numbered roughly a hundred; 75 percent were for quantities not exceeding two-pennyworth, and the bulk was supplied to messengers sent for laudanum specifically, or with recipes containing it."[25] And, as late as 1916, the opiate paregoric could be purchased by the cupful at grocers' shops. The medical officer at an inquest that year said that although the sale of opium was supposedly restricted by the Poisons' Act, "taking it in the form of paregoric was a well-known habit among many poor women."[26]

Opium was not only effective, it was also cheap. Syrup of White Poppies, a mild opiate used as an anodyne and sedative for infants and children, sold for only 3d. per ounce (see Table 3). Put another way, a penny would buy one-third of an ounce, enough for twenty-five to thirty doses. For working-class mothers, the cost of this medicine, as against a minimum fee of 2s. 6d. for a consultation and 1s. 6d. for a prescription from a general practitioner, must have inclined them to use it in all but the most serious cases of childhood illness. Laudanum, the most common form in which opium was consumed by adults, could be had for 8d. an ounce through the 1870s; 6d. an ounce through the mid-1880s; and 3½ or 4d. an ounce after that.

For a person who used it in doses of twenty to forty drops, for the occasional headache or stomach ailment, laudanum was a very good value. But a person addicted to, say, two ounces per day would spend 8d. to a shilling on it, a very high cost for a working-class person. In 1881, one George Dilley, a railway carpenter from Bedfordshire earning 28s. per week, tried to have his wife committed to the workhouse. To support her habit, she had sold everything in the house, even the bedclothes. He could not provide for his children, he said, while his wife had her freedom.[27]

The cheapness of opium was a factor which contributed to its widespread use by all segments of the population. When used therapeutically, and in moderation, opium was well within the means of most Victorian families. Indeed, opium represented a real health bargain. However, when an occasional user became a regular user, even of modest proportions, the economics turned around: addiction was ruinously expensive, especially for working-class families.

A second form of Victorian self-medication was the patent or proprietary medicine, the actual ingredients of which were secret.[28] The first patent for a medicine was issued in 1698, but proprietary medicines, or secret nostrums, had existed for centuries.[29] In 1748, the author of an article that appeared in *Gentleman's Magazine* was able to list over two hundred readily available patent medicines.[30] In 1783, the Government instituted a stamp duty on all patent medicines, equal to about 12 percent of an item's sale price. From revenue figures, one can appreciate how rapidly sales accelerated in the late nineteenth century (see Fig. 3). From 1855 to 1905, the period of greatest growth, sales of patent medicines increased nearly tenfold, while the population just about doubled.

The line between counter-practice and patent medicine sales was very thin indeed. The profit to the chemist on the sale of a patent medicine was always small, but especially so from the 1870s when cooperative stores and grocers began to sell patent medicines at a penny or a half-penny over wholesale cost. In 1897, the *Chemist and Druggist* lamented that a chemist who sold two thousand stamped medicines per year would realize a net profit of about £10.[31] Why then did chemists continue to sell patent medicines? First, they brought customers into the shop who might then be sold perfumes, soaps, and other sundries that the chemist stocked. Second, the chemist could often switch the customer to his own compound—"It's just as good, sir, but only half the cost; there's no advertising, you see." "Substitution" was widely practiced by chemists. It accounts, on the one hand, for the dire warnings to the potential buyer on so many patent medicine advertisements not to be talked into an imitation; and on the other, for the analyses of the formulas of popular patent medicines published in the pharmaceutical press in the late nineteenth century.[32] In fact, the economics of the patent medicine trade made substitution inevitable. The *Chemist and Druggist* estimated that manufacturing costs of a bottle of medicine designed to sell retail at 1s. 1½d. were as follows:

2d.   materials (incl. medicine, bottle, label, wrapper)
1½d.   government stamp
3d.   advertising
1½d.   gross profit (incl. labour & overhead)
8d.   wholesale selling price[33]

The retail chemist, having neither advertising nor stamp expenses, could reproduce the patent medicine—if he knew its
formula—at greater profit to himself and lower cost to his customer. Thus the patent medicine trade, far from decreasing
counter-practice, undoubtedly enhanced it.

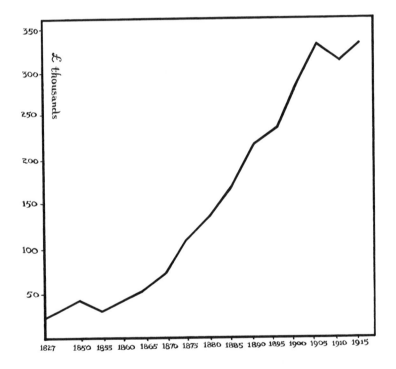

Figure 3.
Revenue from patent medicine stamp duty, 1827–1915.
(*Source:* Adapted from S. Chapman, *Jesse Boots of Boots the Chemist,*
London: Hodder & Stoughton, 1974.)

The medicines offered for sale to the Victorian public ranged from headache powders and digestive aids to cures for cancer and thinly disguised abortifacients.[34] Some were perfectly harmless, containing little more than glucose, coloring, and flavoring. Others actually contained a moderate amount of active ingredients which did in fact produce their advertised effects upon the purchaser. Still others contained powerful drugs, including narcotics, in dangerous concentrations. British Medical Association analysis of thirteen patent medicines showed that they contained varying amounts of morphine, prussic acid, strychnine, and aconite. Only four were labeled "poison" as the law required, and none, of course, actually listed the ingredients on the bottle.[35] Even more dangerous for consumers was the fact that there was no consistency in the proportions among similar medicines. Of the seven samples that contained morphia, for example, the proportion varied from 0.2 to 3.11 grains per fluid ounce. Thus a patent medicine user, accustomed to a relatively mild opiate in one ounce of "Brand X" sleeping draught, could unexpectedly receive an intoxicating, or even lethal, dose in one ounce of the more concentrated "Brand Y" sleeping draught. The dangers of an accidental toxic dose were even greater when the manufacturer changed the morphia content of his medicine. From analyses carried out over a period of years on "Mrs. Winslow's Soothing Syrup," an infants' sedative popular in both Britain and America, it is clear that the morphia content varied from nil to one grain per fluid ounce.[36]

Opium was not unknown in eighteenth-century patent medicines. Indeed, "Dover's Powders," one of the most famous, was a compound of ipecacuanha and opium.[37] But opium and its derivatives came to be the most important single ingredient in Victorian patents. One of the earliest was "Godfrey's Cordial," the forerunner of all the "soothing syrups," which was recommended for infants' "colicky pains, flatus, and restlessness."[38] Godfrey's was basically tincture of opium in a thick, sweet syrup to make it palatable to children. It became so popular that the name lost its specific designation and came to stand for any such preparation. At an inquest in 1873, a chemist in rural Yorkshire testified that he "sold about half a gallon of Godfrey's Cordial

per week, and the greater portion went out in cups, which he did
not label. . . . Every druggist had a formula of his own for what
he called Godfrey's Cordial."[39] This particular chemist proudly
boasted that *his* Godfrey's contained no opiates whatsoever,
which was fine, of course, until his customers, accustomed to
swilling pints of his mixture with no ill effects, ordered Godfrey's from a chemist who used a more conventional formula.
Besides Godfrey's, virtually all soothing syrups, such as
"Mother's Friend" or the ominously named "Quietness," contained opiates. Opiates were also the main ingredient in many
sedatives, cough syrups, and diarrhea remedies.[40]

In the 1880s two new kinds of patent medicines came onto
the market. The justifiable concern about opiate addiction produced various proprietary "cures" for "opiomania," 95 percent
of which, according to one analysis, contained opium.[41] One of
these, "Eucomen," was discovered to contain 41 percent alcohol
and 1½ percent morphia.[42] The "St. George's Association" marketed "Orphine," a "permanent cure for drug addiction," which,
if taken as directed, would result in a daily dose of 8 grains of
morphia.[43] Even more popular were the medicated wines, such
as "Hall's Coca Wine" or "Vin Mariani," which contained
cocaine. These were usually advertised as "pick-me-ups" or
"nerve tonics" for persons who were not necessarily suffering
from any specific complaint, but who felt the need of something
to raise the spirits.

However, the Victorian patent medicine *par excellence,*
which still survives in vestigial form as "Collis Browne's Mixture," is chlorodyne. The mixture was invented by Dr. J. Collis
Browne, an army surgeon serving in India, as a cholera remedy.
In 1856, Browne sold the formula to a pharmacist, J. T. Davenport, who became the sole manufacturer of "J. Collis Browne's
Chlorodyne."[44] Despite Davenport's many warnings to the
public to beware of imitations, he continued to be plagued by
competitors. "Towle's Chlorodyne" and "Teasdale's Chlorodyne" were sold as patent medicines, and virtually every
chemist in Britain made his own version. The "trial size" bottle
of Collis Browne's sold for 7½d., and larger sizes sold for 1s.
1½d. and 2s. 9d., standard prices for Victorian patents. The

product was advertised as a cure for a panoply of minor, nagging ills: "Coughs, Colds, Colic, Cramp, Spasms, Stomach Ache, Bowel Pains, Diarrhoea, [and] Sleeplessness."[45] It worked. Chlorodyne brought sleep to the sleepless, cleared heads to the clogged, and relief to those with rumbling stomachs. Each ounce contained two full grains of morphia, and lesser amounts of chloral and tincture of cannabis indica. This formula, which made chlorodyne such an effective medicine, also made it potentially lethal. Victorian inquest records are filled with its victims: suicides, accidental overdoses, and chlorodyne addicts.

Chlorodyne was widely available without restriction. In the wake of a poisoning case, a physician sent his 11-year-old daughter "on an experimental tour round his neighborhood where he resides." She was unhesitatingly sold chlorodyne at chemists', grocers', and drapers' shops, with no warning about its dangers, and in bottles that were not labeled "poison."[46] In 1892, the Pharmaceutical Society prosecuted the manufacturer of "Collis Browne's" for selling his product in violation of the Poisons and Pharmacy Act of 1868, which required that compounds containing listed poisons—including opiates—be labeled as such and that their sale be restricted to registered pharmacists. Despite the 13 percent drop in sales of "Collis Browne's," little was accomplished by this ruling (see Table 4). Full-strength, opium-based patent medicines continued to be sold to both adults and children. Poisoning by, and addiction to, chlorodyne and similar preparations was a common occurrence in Victorian Britain. Until the passage of the Dangerous Drugs Act in 1920, which forced manufacturers to lower significantly the morphia content of their remedies, the only minimal safeguard on the abuse of chlorodyne was the discretion of the chemist, who might limit the sale to a single bottle per customer.[47]

It is difficult to exaggerate the importance of opium in Victorian healing. For most Britons it was invaluable. In an age in which diarrhea was one of the leading killers of children and infants; in which dehydrating diseases such as cholera were epidemic; in which overcrowding, primitive sanitation, and adulterated food produced chronic gastrointestinal problems for a large part of the population, opium was a source of cheap and effective relief. Opium was the Victorian's aspirin, Lomotil, Valium, and Nyquil, which could be bought at the local chemist's for as little as a penny.

Notes

1. Joseph F. Payne, *Thomas Sydenham* (London: T. Fisher Unwin, 1900), p. 182.

2. Melvin Earles, "Studies in the Development of Experimental Pharmacology in the 18th and Early 19th Centuries," unpublished Ph.D. thesis, University of London, 1961.

3. Lester King, *The Medical World of the Eighteenth Century* (Chicago: University of Chicago Press, 1958); John C. Kramer, "Opium Rampant: Medical Use, Misuse and Abuse in Britain and the West in the 17th and 18th Centuries," *British Journal of Addiction, 74* (1979), 377–89.

4. Jonathan Pereira, *The Elements of Materia Medica and Therapeutics* (Philadelphia: Lea & Blanchard, 1843), II, p. 703. A sample of articles published at mid-century suggesting new therapeutic uses for opium and morphia includes W. F. Bow, "On the Beneficial Effects of the External Application of Opium in Inflammatory Diseases," *London Medical and Physical Journal* (1831), 23–29; W. F. Bow, "External Applications of Opium in Inflammatory Diseases, but Especially in Bronchitis and Croup," *Lancet* (1836–7), 896–98; Montgomery Robertson, "On the Medicinal Effects of the Salts of Morphia, Especially the Muriate, with a New Mode of Preparing It," *Edinburgh Medical and Surgical Journal, 37* (1832), 278–95; "Treatment of Tetanus by Morphia to Blistered Surfaces," *Liverpool Medical Gazette, 1* (September 1833), 439–40; Dr. Rees, "On the Treatment of Diabetes Mellitus," *Medical Gazette,* August 27, 1847, 48–49; "Opium in Uterine Hemorrhage," *Half-Yearly Abstract of Medical Science, 7* (1848), 325; "Cold Applications, with Opium and Quinine, in Acute Rheumatism," *Medical Gazette,* August 27, 1847, p. 79; Edward Smith, "On the Efficacy of Small Doses of Morphia (as Opposed to the Use of Expectorants) in the Treatment of Whooping-Cough, Chronic Bronchitis, and Phthisis," *Edinburgh Medical Journal, 1* (1855–6), 1001–10; and Richard Oliver, "On the Use of Large Doses of Opium in Cases of Mania and Dementia," *Medical Times and Gazette, 7* (July–December 1853), 73–76. Even

during this period of opium's great popularity, there were a few
medical men who pointed to its dangers. The famous toxicologist,
Robert Christison, argued that the regular use of opium shortened
life expectancy through chronic poisoning. Other reports warned
that opium was an intoxicant, an acute poison, and a substance all
too readily adulterated. See, respectively, R. Christison, "On the
Effects of Opium-Eating on Health and Longevity," *Edinburgh
Medical and Surgical Journal, 37* (1832), 123–35; James Bower Harrison, "The Psychology of Opium Eating," *Journal of Psychological
Medicine and Mental Pathology, 7* (1854), 240–52; Dr. Soltau, "Remarks on Delerium Tremens," *Half-Yearly Abstract of Medical Science, 6* (1847), 20–24; and Analytical Sanitary Commission,
"Opium," *Lancet* (1853), 64–65, 116–17, 251–53.

5. Michael Durey, *The Return of the Plague: British Society and the Cholera
   1831–2* (London: Gill & Macmillan, 1979), pp. 109–11, 126–28;
   and Norman Howard-Jones, "Cholera Therapy in the Nineteenth
   Century," *Journal of the History of Medicine* (October 1972), 380.

6. See, for example, Terry M. Parssinen, "Professional Deviants and
   the History of Medicine: Medical Mesmerists in Victorian Britain,"
   in Roy Wallis, ed., *On the Margins of Science: The Social Construction of
   Rejected Knowledge*, Sociological Review Monographs, no. 27 (University of Keele, 1979), pp. 103–120.

7. Wilfrid Bonser, *The Medical Background of Anglo-Saxon England*
   (London: Wellcome Historical Medical Library, 1963).

8. Quoted in C. G. Drummond, "Pharmaceutical 'Opposition' in the
   Eighteenth Century," *Pharm. J.*, December 26, 1964, 644. "Sir"
   John Hill—with a Swedish M.D. and a self-conferred title—
   published 76 books in his lifetime. His most popular herbals were
   The Useful Family Herbal (2nd. ed., 1755), *The Family Practice of Physic*
   (1769), and *Virtues of British Herbs* (1771). Other popular herbals
   included Hugh Smythson, *Compleat Family Physician* (1785), William
   Meyrick, *The New Family Herbal* (1790), and Edward Baylis, *A New
   and Complete Body of Practical Botanic Physic* (1791). Herbalism was
   part of a larger literature on domestic medicine and pharmacy. See,
   for example, "Eighteenth Century Domestic Medicine," *C&D*, June
   29, 1935, 799–802; S. R. Hunt, "Domestic Pharmacy in Eighteenth
   Century England," *Pharm. J.*, December 21 and 28, 1974, 611–13;
   C. J. Lawrence, "William Buchan: Medicine Laid Open," *Medical
   History, 19* (1975), 20–35; and John B. Blake, "'The Compleat
   Housewife,'" *Bulletin of the History of Medicine, 49* (1975), 30–42.

9. "Herbalists and their Practice," *C&D*, March 14, 1874, 86.

10. "On Superstitious Methods for Curing Diseases," *C&D*, January 15, 1874, 14–15. The "doctrine of the signatures" was a belief that God had created plants in a shape which so obviously proclaimed their purpose that even the unlettered could discern them. Thus a plant which was good for diseases of the heart, for example, was shaped like a heart, and so on.

11. R. R. Trail, *The History of the Popular Medicine of England* (Cambridge: Papworth Industries, 1965), p. 38.

12. In 1868, the *Chemist and Druggist* published an interesting five-part series, "Report on the Conditions and Practices of the Various Classes Connected with the Drug Trade": "I. The Veritable Outsiders," January 15, 12–14; "II. The Medical Herbalists," February 15, 85–87; "III. Coffinites, Etc.," March 14, 148–149; "IV. The Black Sheep of the Flock," June 15, 342–343, July 15, 427–428; and "V. Prices," August 15, 483–487. See also "Eastward Ho!" *C&D*, June 14, 1884, 277–278.

13. S. Chapman analyzes the transition from folk medicine and herbalism to patent medicines in his chapter, "The Market for Medicines," in *Jesse Boots of Boots the Chemist* (London: Hodder & Stoughton, 1974), pp. 11–30.

14. The articles about counter-prescribing published in the pharmaceutical press run into the hundreds. The following is a sample: Joseph Ball, "Letter to the Editor," *C&D*, October 15, 1859, 33; "The Right of Chemists and Druggists to Prescribe," *C&D*, November 15, 1861, 313–14; "Medical Opinion on Counter-Prescribing," *C&D*, February 15, 1876, 63; "Counter-Prescribing," *C&D*, January 15, 1878, 11–12; "A Defence of Counter-Prescribing," *C&D*, December 22, 1894, 895–96; and U. A. Coates, "Reminiscences of Prescribing," *C&D*, January 2, 1937, 8–9. In 1908, the General Medical Council urged the Local Government Board to review the state of unqualified practice throughout the country, which it undertook through 1600 medical officers of health. The form of unqualified medical practice *most* regularly mentioned was prescribing by chemists. "Unqualified Medical Practice," *Pharm. J.*, December 3, 1910, 670–73.

15. Medical men were, however, vulnerable to the counter-criticism that they encroached on chemists' business by dispensing, as well as prescribing, drugs. The *Chemist and Druggist* estimated that nine-tenths of all medical men dispensed their own drugs, and that

many kept an "open shop;" that is, they sold drugs and sundries to persons other than their own patients. That figure may be slightly high, but not by much. See "Concentration in Medicine," *C&D*, November 26, 1887, 672–73; and "Shop-Keeping Doctors," *C&D*, June 15, 1875, 261–62.

16. Quoted in "The Public and Counter-Practice," *C&D*, November 15, 1878, 485.

17. "A Voice from the East," *C&D*, December 15, 1868, 812.

18. "Saving Doctors' Visiting-Bills," *C&D*, October 8, 1898, 610.

19. The term laudanum has an uncertain origin. It was probably invented by the sixteenth-century physician Paracelsus, who was responsible for the introduction of opium into medical use in Europe. The most famous formula was that devised, in the mid-seventeenth century, by the English physician Thomas Sydenham: "Strained opium (2 oz.), saffron (1 oz.), cinnamon & cloves (1 drachm each), & Canary wine (1 pint)." "Sydenham's Laudanum" continued to appear in pharmacopoeias throughout Europe well into the nineteenth century. "Black Drop," also known as Quaker's or Kendal, or Lancaster Black Drop, originated in the eighteenth century and was popular throughout the north of England. It contained opium, verjuice, nutmeg, yeast, and saffron, but no wine. It had the consistency of syrup and was three or four times stronger than ordinary laudanum. Battley's Syrup also began as a patent medicine, but was soon copied by many chemists. It was basically a tincture of opium, but about 50 percent stronger than laudanum. See A. C. Wooten, *Chronicles of Pharmacy* (London: Macmillan, 1910), II, pp. 142–146; and M. Lefebvre, *Samuel Taylor Coleridge: A Bondage of Opium* (New York: Stein & Day, 1974), pp. 493–495.

20. "Report from the Select Committee of the House of Lords on the Sale of Poisons Bill (H. L.); together with the Proceedings of the Committee, Minutes of Evidence, and Index," *PP*, 1857 (Sess. 2), XII, p. 573.

21. "Sale of Poisons Bill," p. 644.

22. "Sale of Poisons Bill," p. 607.

23. "Sale of Poisons Bill," p. 621.

24. "On the Sale of Laudanum," *Pharm. J.*, January 23, 1915, 123.

25. "Recording Sales of Laudanum," *Pharm. J.*, December 12, 1914, 831.

26. "Intelligence," *Pharm. J.*, January 1916, 82.

27. Letter from J. H. Howlett (parish priest) to Mr. Hooper, November 7, 1881, uncatalogued manuscript, Bedford County Record Office.

28. A patent medicine, strictly speaking, was a proprietary medicine on which a patent had been taken out to protect the inventor's "discovery." In fact there was little practical difference between them, especially after 1783, when the government required all medicines which claimed to cure or relieve specific ailments to bear a revenue stamp. The terms patent and proprietary medicines were used interchangeably in the nineteenth century, and were also known as "nostrums" or "secret remedies." Not until 1941 did the government force manufacturers to list the ingredients of each medicine on its bottle.

29. "The First Medicinal Patents," *C&D*, June 27, 1936, 758–60; "Proprietaries of Other Days," *C&D*, June 25, 1927, 831–40; "Pharmacy in the 18th and Early Years of the 19th Century," *Pharm. J.*, January 14, 1950, 32–33; and P. S. Brown, "Medicines Advertised in Eighteenth-Century Bath Newspapers," *Medical History*, 20 (1976), 152–68.

30. "Pharmacopoeia Empirica, or the List of Nostrums and Empirics," *Gentleman's Magazine*, XVII (1748), 346–50.

31. "What is the Patent-Medicine Trade Worth?" *C&D*, November 20, 1897, 795.

32. "The Trade in Proprietary Medicines," *C&D*, November 15, 1875, 388–89; "The Sale of Poisonous Proprietary Medicines," *C&D*, June 4, 1892, 815; "West-End Trade," *C&D*, March 6, 1886, 152–53; and "Patent Medicines," *C&D*, November 24, 1888, 733.

33. "The Patent Medicine Trade," *C&D*, December 15, 1880, 530–31.

34. Angus McLaren, "Abortion in England, 1890–1914," *Victorian Studies*, 20 (1977), 379–400.

35. "Poisonous Patent Medicines," *C&D*, November 14, 1891, 710–11.

36. "Mrs. Winslow's Soothing Syrup," *C&D*, June 15, 1872, 187–88; "Winslow's Syrup," *C&D*, March 15, 1873, 75; and "Proprietary Medicines," *C&D*, January 15, 1876, 10.

37. S. Stander, "Eighteenth Century Patent Medicines," *Historia Medica*, 7 (1976), 68–71.

38. "Godfrey's Cordial," *C&D*, December 15, 1881, 520.

39. "Godfrey's Again," *C&D*, June 15, 1873, 32–33.

40. Analyses of patent medicines include John A. Paris, *Pharmacologia* (5th ed., London, 1822), II; F. Magendie, *Formulary for the Preparation and Medical Administration of Certain New Remedies*, trans. J. M. Gully (2nd ed.; London, 1836); H. Deane and H. B. Brady, "Microscopical Research in Relation to Pharmacy," *Pharm. J.*, November 1864, 232–40; E. Smith, "Chlorodyne," *Pharm. J.*, January 1870, 417–420; British Medical Association, *Secret Remedies* (London, 1909); and *More Secret Remedies* (London, 1912).

41. "Patent and Secret Narcotic Preparations," *BMJ*, September 13, 1890, 639.

42. "Eucomen, a Cure for the Morphine Habit which Contains Morphine," *Pharm. J.*, August 16, 1913, 280.

43. "The Saint George Association Cure for the Morphia Habit," *Lancet*, May 4, 1912, 1241–42.

44. "Chlorodyne: Its History, Preparation, Therapeutic Effects, Doses, etc.," *C&D*, February 15, 1860, 115; advertisement for chlorodyne, *C&D*, March 14, 1863, 37.

45. Advertisement in Folkard's Price List 1911, p. 52; copy in the Pharmaceutical Society Library.

46. "The Sale of Patent Medicines," *C&D*, May 15, 1880, 193.

47. There is an interesting analysis, published in 1921, of the effect of the Dangerous Drugs Act on chlorodyne sales. The Act forced the manufacturers of chlorodyne to lower the morphia content to 0.2 percent or less: "The inevitable consequence is that victims who have formed the habit of taking this preparation increase their dose. It is useless for the chemist to sell, say, no more than one bottle at a time to any individual purchaser. Chemists' shops abound. In any populous district enough many be bought in ten minutes to kill anyone not absolutely 'chlorinated.' I believe that as a direct result of this law it is positively easier to buy the stuff. The chemist who did exercise a measure of control now feels freed from responsibility." ("The Sale of Chlorodyne," *Pharm. J.*, November 19, 1921, 416–417.)

CHAPTER FOUR

"Mother's Friend":
Opium as an Escape

For those at the bottom of the social pyramid, life in Victorian Britain could be nearly unendurable. The accumulated miseries of monotonous labor, filthy surroundings, infectious diseases, periodic unemployment, and too many children often drove Victorian working people to seek escape—in violence, in suicide, in the temporary stupor of drunkenness, or in the blurred reality of an opium trance.

Opium's most infamous use in nineteenth-century Britain was as an infant's quietener. "Godfrey's Cordial" was the most common form in which opium was given to children, but other children's opiates ranged from such mildly narcotic decoctions as poppyhead tea and syrup of white poppies to opiate-based patent medicines of varying strength such as carminatives, preservatives, elixirs, cordials, and soothing syrups, to ordinary full-strength laudanum. While the practice of feeding opiates to children crossed class and geographic boundaries, it appears to have been most common in those areas where women worked in factories, in cottage industries, or in agricultural gangs. It went "hand-in-hand with poverty, dirt, and vice."[1] One chemist in Nottingham reported, in 1808, that "upwards of 200 lbs. of opium, and above 600 pints of Godfrey's Cordial, are retailed to the poorer class in the year."[2] In 1862, it was estimated that in Coventry, 12,000 doses of Godfrey's were administered weekly.[3]

A "responsible chemist" in a factory district in the early 1840s testified that he sold twenty gallons per year of "comfort" (the local name for Godfrey's), while other chemists sold much more.[4] In 1871, in Long Sutton (Lincolnshire), with a population of 6,000, "one chemist alone sells 25½ gallons of Godfrey's annually; another in the same town sells six imperial pints weekly for the quietening of children."[5] A chemist in the lacemaking town of Nottingham reported, in 1841, that

> a large quantity of laudanum and other preparations of opium, such as Godfrey's Cordial, is sold by the chemists, especially in the poorer neighborhoods of the town. [He] knows a chemist who sells as much as a gallon of laudanum a week retail; and also knows that several chemists in Nottingham sell many gallons in the year.[6]

Some of these chemists' best customers were the babyminders with whom working mothers were forced to leave their infants. The situation was dictated by economic necessity. The cost of day care ranged from two to four shillings per child per week, while the wages of a female factory worker in Lancashire in the 1840s was about 15s. per week. Since the wages of male factory workers were generally low, the working mother's wage was an essential contribution to the total family income. Babyminders were notoriously careless with their charges. Whether from laziness or overwork, they frequently neglected the infants and often fed them regular doses of Godfrey's or some other opiate in order to keep them quiet.[7] "The mother can often smell laudanum on the child's breath when it comes home," wrote the *Morning Chronicle*'s reporter. "As for mothers themselves," he added, "they give the 'sleeping stuff' principally at night, to secure their own rest."[8]

The practice of drugging infants was common not only in the factory districts, but in areas, like Nottingham, where there was a heavy concentration of domestic industry. Here it was often mothers themselves, rather than nurses, who administered opium to children. In 1842, a 20-year-old Nottingham lace worker, named Mary Colton, testified that she was confined of an illegitimate child in November, 1839. When the child was a week old she gave it half a teaspoonful of Godfrey's twice a day. She could not afford to pay for the nursing of the child so gave it Godfrey's to keep it quiet, that she might not be interrupted at the lace piece; she gradually increased the quantity by a drop or two at a time until it reached a teaspoonful; when the infant was four months old it was so 'wankle' and thin that folks persuaded her to give it laudanum to bring it on, as it did other children. A halfpenny worth, which was about a teaspoonful and threequarters, was given in two days; continued to give her this quantity since February, 1840, until this last [year] past (1841), and then reduced the quantity. She now buys a halfpenny worth of laudanum and a halfpenny worth of Godfrey's mixed, which lasts her three days.[9]

Opium, as an appetite suppressant, was sometimes given to children instead of food. Not surprisingly, children who were fed opium regularly were often in desperately bad health. An observer noted "the heavy, deathlike sleep, accompanied by convulsive twitchings, the scorched, swollen eyelids, the bluish pallor of countenance and growing heaviness of expression" that characterized opium-fed infants.[10] On very rare occasions, adults were charged with causing a child's death through opium poisoning. In 1878, one Jane Newry was indicted for manslaughter in the death of her grandchild. At the coroner's inquest, she testified that she had fed the child a laudanum mixture, twice daily, for three weeks prior to the child's death. Although two years old, the child weighed only nine pounds and had never walked. The local surgeon gave evidence that just before her death, the child was "stupefied and almost pulseless."[11] The disposition of this case is not clear, but it is unlikely that the defendant was convicted. Juries almost never returned guilty verdicts against those charged with poisoning children with opiates, especially if the defendant were related to the victim. This reluctance to convict was a reflection of the widespread popular acceptance of the use of opium-based quieteners. If some children succumbed to an overdose, that was an unfortunate, but probably accidental event. Overdose deaths were the result of poverty, carelessness, and ignorance, but usually not malevolence.

Juries' verdicts notwithstanding, it is clear that opium was sometimes used to destroy unwanted children. Two chemists who appeared as witnesses before the House of Commons' Poisons Committee (1857) testified that in industrial districts opiate-based medicines were used to kill, as well as to quieten, children.[12] It was usually difficult to determine when the poisoning of a child was intentional. In a very rare public confession, a 63-year-old pauper named Sarah Brewer "stated that about 45 years before, when living at Kingston, Herefordshire, she had an illegitimate child, which she had poisoned with Godfrey's Cordial." Six years subsequently she married and poisoned her second and third children in the same way, when they were only a few weeks old. A doctor saw one of them and stated that it died of inflammation of the lungs.[13] This confession notwithstanding, the distinction between accidentally causing a child's death and deliberately killing him with opiates was blurred, certainly in the judgment of most juries, and probably even in the minds of the adults who actually fed opium to children. Yet opium was undeniably connected with the deliberate destruction of children. It was, for example, used on Victorian "baby-farms," those ill-disguised institutions of infanticide.[14] The harshness of life in early industrial Britain often gave working-class men and women an ambivalent attitude toward their infant's deaths. In 1842, a druggist from Nottingham testified that, in his district, "if a child dies [from an overdose of opium], then the general expression is, 'it is a blessing it is gone.' The general feeling on these occasions, both of the mother and the neighbors is, that it is better the child should thus die than live to the misery that awaits it."[15]

The use of opium as an infants' quietener was a part of the stark reality of working-class life in the nineteenth century. An economic system which forced women to work, usually outside the home, for twelve to fourteen hours a day created a need for narcotics like Godfrey's Cordial. For those who could afford to purchase neither adequate food nor privacy, opium was a cheap solution to their children's noisy demands. Ill-paid nurses found that they could cope with ten or more children by drugging them. Women who had been working all day found that they could buy some much-needed rest at night for a ha'penny's worth of infants' sedative. And a few desperate unmarried mothers, like Sarah Brewer, found that they could survive only by destroying their infants with large doses of narcotics.

Opium was occasionally taken as an intoxicant by adults, although it is worth stressing that such reports were comparatively rare. Given the fastidiousness with which the medical and pharmaceutical press reported such exotic indulgences as chloroform-inhaling in London, eau-de-Cologne tippling in Liverpool, and ether-drinking in Glasgow, it is unlikely that any significant outbreak of opium-taking would have gone unmentioned.[16] The professional journals rarely addressed the issue editorially, and when they did, they tended to downplay its significance. After 1900, observers who commented about opium intoxication at all thought that it was on the decline.[17]

Earlier on, however, there had been sporadic reports of opium's being used as an intoxicant. In the 1830s opium was used by prostitutes in London's East End to intoxicate their sailor clients who "are then robbed of every penny they possess."[18] In the 1840s Lancashire workingmen and women occasionally used opium in either pills or powder as a stimulant. Habitual drunkards took opium since they found it cheaper "and more intensely stimulating" than spirits. And prostitutes used it "when they get low and melancholy," and to "relieve pains in their limbs."[19] In the 1850s a witness before the Poisons' Committee testified that laudanum was taken as a "dram" by adults in Lancashire. At a later inquiry, a medical man who had been house surgeon at the Stockport Infirmary during the "cotton famine" of the early 1860s claimed that the local destitution meant that opium takers came to beg for supplies of opium which they could no longer afford to purchase. While most of these applicants had modest habits, a few "opium drunkards," who consumed four ounces of laudanum per day, experienced real suffering.[20]

In Nottingham as well as Lancashire, opium was taken as an

intoxicant by adults. A local chemist estimated, in 1801, that women users outnumbered men by three to one. The practice of laudanum drinking was especially prevalent "among a large portion of the poorest class of mechanics."[21] A female turnkey in the Kirkdale Gaol (near Liverpool) reported in 1837 that

> we have had a number of prisoners addicted to the taking of opium, and the depriving them of it was like taking a child from the breast. . . . Some of the women used to be wild for it. They tell me that out of prison their custom is to buy twopennyworth at a time and make it into pills and swallow them.[22]

In 1867, a lecturer in Leicester commented that "opium is a vice very prevalent in this town."[23] And, as late as 1902, the *Glasgow Evening News* reported that "the laudanum-drinking habit is much too prevalent locally."[24]

Laudanum habitués occasionally ran afoul of the law. In Bolton, John Albert Thornley was convicted of obtaining goods on false pretenses. He confessed that he was a habitual laudanum drinker and stole to support his habit. "It is a nauseous drug," he said, "and it has knocked all the senses out of me." The judge, unmoved by Thornley's defense of drug-induced moral befuddlement, sentenced him to a year in prison and a fine of £6.[25] In Bradford, in 1904, a 24-year-old woman who had regularly consumed 12s. worth of laudanum per week for seven years was convicted of stealing a lady's watch, a diamond ring, and £3 15s. in cash.[26]

Opium habituation cases rarely appeared in the medical press because, for the most part, neither habitués nor medical men considered the condition worthy of mention. To begin with, it was usually not noticeable. Opium, a common household drug, was taken by many, perhaps most Victorians at one time or another. Particularly if a person had a chronic painful condition, like neuralgia or rheumatism, he might well be taking opium regularly. In such circumstances, how could one tell whether opium was being used a medicine or as an intoxicant? Furthermore, when opium was taken at relatively modest levels, it did not *necessarily* lead to health problems other than mild constipation. For example, Dr. Fleming reported on a patient of his, a 67-year-old medical man who had taken one ounce of laudanum daily for an asthmatic condition for the last 47 years. He was in excellent health and carried on a strenuous practice. He could "trace no injury whatever to this moderate use" of opium.[27] Only when opium was ingested in much greater quantities did it have really deleterious effects. Finally, because opium was a popular medicine, widely available without a medical man's prescription, many persons who began taking opium became habituated, lived and died without ever consulting a medical man about it. Ordinary Victorians would no more see the need to consult a medical man about taking opium than we would about taking aspirin.

Despite the "invisibility" of opium habituation, enough case reports surfaced to allow us to draw a few conclusions about habitual opium taking. In searching through the medical and pharmaceutical literature, I found 23 cases of opium habituation. Of the 21 cases in which the sex is given, fifteen are female and six male, a trend which confirms the widely stated impression of observers that women greatly outnumbered men as opium habitués. Of the 21 cases in which dosages are known, twelve are in the range of one to two ounces of laudanum (or its equivalent in raw opium) per day. Of the twelve habitués who gave an account of how they began taking opium, only one began taking it specifically as an intoxicant. Virtually all of the others cited some medical need as the reason for their habits. The ages of the patients and the duration of their habits varied so widely that any generalization is impossible. This data, limited as it is, suggests that the typical Victorian opium habitué was a female, of uncertain age, who began taking opium for a medical problem, and whose daily dosage varied between one and two ounces of landanum.[28]

There was, all observers agreed, one corner of rural England where the consumption of opium was high by any standard. This was the Fen district, which included low-lying and marshy areas of Lincolnshire, Norfolk, and Cambridgeshire, much of which had been slowly reclaimed from the sea since the late Middle Ages.[29] The amount of opium sold in the market towns of this area, such as Louth, Wisbeach, and Holbeach, was so remarkable that Victorian observers termed it "the opium district."[30] The damp, chilly climate and the prevalence of malaria before the completion of the draining of the fens in the nineteenth century made opium a popular medicine for adults. Quinine, although an excellent antimalarial medicine, was very expensive in the early nineteenth century, and opium, at one-tenth of the cost, provided relief from fevers, ague, and related problems such as rheumatism and neuralgia.[31] In addition, the women of the area worked in agricultural "gangs," which meant that they left their infants in the care of elderly nurses. As in industrial areas, this led to the widespread quietening of children with opiates.[32] Once opium was widely used in the district as a preventive medicine, it gained popular acceptance and was often taken as an intoxicant.

The amount of opium sold was staggering. The town of Whittlesea, with a population of 3,700, supported five druggists, whose primary business was the sale of opium.[33] A druggist from Spalding testified that he had forty or fifty weekly customers for laudanum, and that he sold more laudanum in his four years in Spalding than he had sold in his previous twenty years in the trade elsewhere.[34] A chemist from Holbeach estimated that £700 to £800 was spent on laudanum each year by the working classes of a single parish.[35] Dr. Henry Julian Hunter, in his famous investigation of the district, reported that it was not uncommon for retail chemists in the Fens to sell 200 pounds of opium per year.[36] One King's Lynn chemist sold 170 pounds of solid opium, in addition to six gallons of laudanum and six gallons of Godfrey's Cordial in a single year. Such prodigious rates of consumption led Dr. Hawkins of King's Lynn, in 1867, to estimate that half of all the opium imported into England was consumed in the Fen district.[37]

Opium poppies were occasionally grown in Fenland gardens, but most opium users obtained their supplies from chemists.[38] "It is sold in pills and penny sticks," Dr. Hunter reported, "and a well-accustomed shop will serve 300 or 400 customers with the article on a Saturday night."[39] A medical man noted that the item was sold so regularly that it was not even necessary to ask for it by name: a penny placed silently on the chemist's counter brought forth a box filled with opium pills.[40] In *Alton Locke* (1850), Charles Kingsley has a fictitious fenman explain local custom to a stranger:

> 'Oh! ho! ho!—you goo into the druggist's shop o' market-day, into Cambridge, and you'll see the little boxes, doozens and doozens, a'ready on the counter, and never a venman's wife goo by, but what calls in for her pennord o' elevation, to last her out the week. Oh! ho! ho! Well it keeps women-folk quiet it do; and it's mortal good agin the ago pains.'
> 'But what is it?'
> 'Opium, bor' alive, opium!'[41]

By the middle of the nineteenth century, opium had become the all-pervasive drug of choice in the Fens. Sales were particularly heavy on Saturday nights, and at least one Fenland brewer, accommodating to local taste, put opium into his beer.[42] The quantities taken, and the costs incurred, could be high. Dr. Hawkins reported that a farmer came into a chemist's office for an ounce-and-a-half of laudanum and drank it straight off; he returned twice in the day for the same amount, and left for home with a half-pint bottle.[43] Another report from rural Lincolnshire noted that each week a farmer purchased 28 ounces of laudanum, enough for a supply of four ounces per day.[44] A medical man who had lived in the Fenland town of Whittlesea estimated that the average amount of laudanum taken by a habitual opium-eater varied from four to eight ounces per week. Many opium-eaters were limited in the quantity they took, he noted, "solely by their funds."[45] Although opium was cheap when taken in therapeutic doses, the cost to regular users of opium in the Fens, as elsewhere in Britain, could be very high. "A poor family will spend eight pence to one shilling per day for opium alone," according to an 1878 report.[46]

Dr. Hunter argued that the extremely heavy use of opiates as an infant's quietener was the most important cause of the high infant mortality rate in the Fens. Other medical men agreed.[47] Opiates led to children's deaths directly through overdosing, but also indirectly through chronic use, which wasted the child. "Some [surgeons] said they 'shrank up into little old men'; others that they 'wizened like a little monkey';" Hunter noted, "but none were willing to certify to any cause of death which would inculpate anybody, and each surgeon preferred the doubtful course of certifying the advanced symptoms as the cause of death."[48]

Medical men were also agreed that, however disastrous opium-taking might be for infants, it had almost no ill effects on the health of Fenland adults. Except for a tendency to constipation and a yellowish pallor, adult opium-eaters did not suffer any harmful effects after years of chronic use. Indeed, several doctors noted that there were numerous cases of octogenarian and nonagenarian opium-eaters, many of whom were in remarkably good health.[49]

Another observer, commenting on the moral effects of the drug, noted that while chronic opium eaters were "dirty, slovenly, lazy, lying, and sanctimonious," they were not nearly so violent as alcohol drinkers:

> There are none of the deeds of brutal violence that are inspired by beer, and none of the foul language. Where others say 'damn', they say 'bless'; and, in fact, you may almost know an opium-eater by his use of the word 'blessed'. 'Law, mum', said an old woman, 'what a beautiful dog of yourn, and what a blessed tail he've got!' 'Our Tom have been stealing, and deserve to be hanged, he dew, bless him!'[50]

Observers of the 1850s and 1860s believed that the rate of opium consumption was increasing in the Fens.[51] By the 1880s, however, the habit was waning. According to the author of a survey of the area in the mid-eighties, "the local chemists assure us that where they sold pounds and pounds [of opium] they now sell but a solitary ounce once and again."[52] And by the 1890s, there were "but few of these opium-eaters remaining."[53]

There were, finally, a very few places where opium was smoked in nineteenth-century Britain. The opium dens that existed in London's East End were discovered over and over again by enterprising journalists who set out to discover the nooks and crannies of mid-Victorian London. These social explorers, in uncovering the shocking and exotic underside of

urban life, made a visit to an opium den an obligatory part of
their itinerary. So conventionalized are the descriptions of the
dens that it is difficult to tell whether the authors actually made
the visit, or simply plagiarized from one another's accounts. One
such story, "East London Opium Smokers," published in *London
Society* in 1868, may stand for the whole corpus.

Recalling the "weird and fantastic interest" that is invested
in opium because of its reputation as a poetic inspiration and an
Oriental vice, the author sets out to find an "opium master" in
the "most vile and villainous part of the metropolis." His inquiries lead him to Bluegate Fields, a particularly sleazy corner
of the East End, "commonly known as Tiger Bay on account of
the number of ferocious she-creatures in petticoats that lurk and
lair there." In this dockland quarter, amidst the prostitutes and
hoodlums that prey on sailors, the author finds his sought-after
opium-master, one Chi Ki. Much to the author's disappoint-
ment, Chi Ki is not bedecked in "crimson silk" robes, but in dirty
and ill-fitting rags. The opium den itself—one shabby room in
Chi Ki's dark house—is inhabited by his English wife and a
single Chinese smoker. The author asks permission to examine
the opium pipe: "It was simply an eighteen-inch length of yellow
bamboo with the cup of dark-coloured baked clay . . . fitted into
a sort of spiggot hole near the end." Chi Ki's wife informs him
that this seasoned pipe, after fourteen years' use, is worth at least
£10. Chi Ki prepares opium the consistency of treacle, which he
dips a pin into. He extracts a drop of opium and grills it over the
lamp's flame until it bubbles and expands to the size of a pea.
Then Chi Ki holds it over the pinhole opening in the bowl of the
pipe while his Chinese customer sucks in the vapor hungrily:

> Gradually, as he sucked and swallowed, the veins of his forehead
> thickened, his cheeks flushed, and his half-closed eyes gleamed
> like those of a satisfied pig. Still he sucked, and the nostril wreaths
> became quicker and finer, and he grew more and more like an
> enraptured hog.

Inquiring about the price, the author discovers that opium-
smoking can be quite expensive. Chi Ki sells three different-

sized measures of prepared opium, "the smallest the size of a lady's thimble," ranging in price from four pence to a shilling. For the price, the customer also gets the loan of Chi Ki's valuable pipe and his expertise in "grilling" the opium. Most of Chi Ki's customers are Chinese or Lascar sailors passing through London. Business is often slack, his wife complains, except when a ship crewed by a large number of Oriental opium-smokers is in port, and "then we have a houseful." His wife continues:

> It is hot work I assure you when we are busy. As soon as one has smoked out, another is ready to snatch at it; . . . They are awful hungry after it sometimes when they've gone a long while without and got their pay. They'll smoke as much as a shilling's worth in half an hour, and there they'll lay like logs.

After joking a bit with the exasperated wife, the author thanks the opium master for his indulgence, and takes his leave.[54]

Throughout the later nineteenth century, a visit to the opium dens of East London was taken by many other journalists, and they all found more or less the same thing that had been there in 1868: a filthy "den" in a dockland slum, run by a Chinese and his English or Irish wife, patronized by transient Asian sailors who were usually described by a full range of bestial metaphors.[55]

However important these stories were as journalistic ventures into unknown London, the social reality which they documented was of little significance. Throughout most of the nineteenth century, the Chinese community in Britain numbered less than one hundred, and the number of opium dens catering to sailors could be counted on the fingers of one hand. Aside from the odd journalist and occasional spouse, there is no evidence that Britons were drawn to opium dens. The handful of dens continued to serve that trickle of Oriental seamen who passed through the port of London. Initially, there was little attempt to portray opium dens as social threats. Indeed, Britons regarded Chinese opium dens in London almost fondly, as evidence of the World City's magnetic power to draw fragments of a diverse humanity to its heart.

In the half-century following the publication of De Quincey's *Confessions,* opium became an integral part of Victorian society. It flowed from Anatolian poppy fields through Mincing Lane into the international drug traffic. It reached Victorians by way of doctors' surgeries, pharmacies, and even booksellers' and stationers' shops. It came in prescriptions, in penny packets of powder, in laudanum, and in patent medicines. De Quincey's panegyric to its intoxicating powers notwithstanding, opium's most important role in Victorian society was as a medicine. It was regularly used to alleviate life's petty aches and pains by most ordinary Englishmen. And it was occasionally used for darker purposes—as an infants' quietener or as an intoxicant. Yet despite De Quincey's warning, despite frequent opiate over-dose deaths, and despite occasional use of opium as an intoxicant, there was little public outcry about its dangers until the end of the 1860s. And then, suddenly, there was a marked change in public opinion, emanating from novelists, from medical men, and from public health reformers. Opium continued to have an important role in late Victorian and Edwardian society, but practices which had been previously condoned were now questioned or even condemned.

Notes

1. "The Unrestricted Trade in Patent Medicines," *C&D* May 15, 1879, 198.
2. "Report from a General Hospital near Nottingham," *Edinburgh Medical and Surgical Journal, 4* (1808), 271.
3. Margaret Hewitt, *Wives and Mothers in Victorian Industry* (London, 1958), p. 142.
4. "First Report of the Commissioners for Inquiring into the State of Large Towns and Populous District," *PP,* 1844, XVII, 94.
5. "Select Committee on the Protection of Infant Life," *PP,* 1871, VII, 695.
6. "Children's Employment Commission, Appendix to the Second Report of the Commissioners: Trades and Manufactures, Part I: Re-

ports and Evidence from Sub-Commissioners," *PP*, 1843, XIV, 629.

7. Elizabeth Lomax, "The Use and Abuse of Opiates in 19th Century England," *Bulletin of the History of Medicine, 47* (1973), 167–76; "Labour and the Poor: The Manufacturing Districts, Manchester," *Morning Chronicle*, November 15, 1849, 5; and "Select Committee on the Protection of Infant Life," 647, 690.

8. "Labour and the Poor," 5.

9. "Children's Employment Commission," 630.

10. "Opium in the Nursery," *C&D*, September 15, 1879, 398.

11. "Soothing Syrups and Mother's Friend," *C&D*, October 15, 1878, 469.

12. "Report from the Select Committee of the House of Lords on the Sale of Poisons Bill," *PP*, 1857, XII, pp. 609, 624.

13. "Soothing Syrups and Mother's Friend," 469.

14. "Select Committee on the Protection of Infant Life," 695.

15. "Children's Employment Commission," 630.

16. *C&D*, February 1, 1908, 175; June 1, 1907, 821; March 28, 1908, 471; July 5, 1902, 5; August 9, 1902, 227.

17. "The Drug Habit," *Pharm. J.*, September 12, 1903, 399; George Pernet, "The Opium Habit," *Pharm. J.* December 5, 1908, 755; and J. F. Brown, "The Opium Habit," *Pharm. J.*, December 12, 1908, 795.

18. "Report from the Select Committee on Inquiry into Drunkenness (Commons)," *PP*, 1834, VIII, 328.

19. "Labour and the Poor," 5.

20. "Poisons Committee Report," 593; "Minutes of Evidence taken at the Royal Commission on Opium," *PP*, 1895, LXI, 71.

21. "Children's Employment Commission," 629.

22. "Report on Kirkdale Gaol and House of Correction" *PP,* 1837, XXXII, 591.

23. "Opium-Eating," *BMJ*, November 9, 1867, 437.

24. "Laudanum Drinking Extraordinary," *Pharm. J.*, March 29, 1902, 266.

25. "Effects of Drug-taking," *Pharm. J.*, May 28, 1921, 416.

26. "Intelligence," *Pharm. J.*, April 2, 1904, 482.

27. Alexander Fleming, "Clinical Lecture on the Treatment of the Habit of Opium-Eating," *BMJ*, February 15, 1868, 137.

28. "Report on Kirkdale Gaol and House of Correction," *PP*, 1837, XXXII, p. 591; J. H. Howlett to Mr. Hooper, November 7, 1881, uncatalogued manuscript, Bedford County Record Office; A. Fleming, "Clinical Lecture on the Treatment of the Opium Habit," *BMJ*, February 15, 1868, 137–39; "Confessions of a Young Lady Laudanum-Drinker," *Journal of Mental Science, 34* (1899), 545–50; J. B. Harrison, "Opium-Eating," *Association of Medicine Journal*, October 11, 1856, 872–73; *Reece's Gazette of Health, 10* (1825), 270; "Oriental Pharmacy," *C&D*, November 14, 1868, 733; "The Consumption of Chlorodyne and Other Narcotics," *BMJ*, May 3, 1891, 817; J. D. Phillips, "Opium as an Aid to Surgery," *BMJ*, May 3, 1884, 885; "Extracts from Guildswomen's Letters . . .," *Life as We Have Known It . . .*, ed. M. L. Davis (New York: W. W. Norton, 1975), pp. 113–14; "St. Mary's Hospital," *Lancet*, 1853, ii, 280; E. A. Birch, "The Use of Indian Hemp . . .," *Lancet*, March 30, 1889, 625; "The Sale of Laudanum by Chemists," *Pharm. J., 9* (1849–50), 590–91; "An Extreme Dose of Landanum," *Pharm. J., 12* (1852–53), 254–55; "Laudanum-Drinking Extraordinary," *Pharm. J.* (1887–88), 864. "Laudanum-drinkers," *C&D*, April 18, 1896, 567; "Opium-Eating Extraordinary," *Pharm. J.* (1877–78), 801; "Laudanum Drinking," *Pharm. J.*, April 2, 1904, 482; "A Liking for Laudanum," *Pharm. J.*, March 28, 1908, 425; and "Laudanum," *Pharm. J.*, February 3, 1912, 141.

29. Walter White, *Eastern England, from the Thames to the Humber,* 2 vols. (London: Chapman & Hall, 1865), I, p. 265; Charles Whymper, "The English Peasantry at Home: I—The Fen People," *Good Words, 27* (1886), 45; L. Marion Springall, *Labouring Life in Norfolk Villages, 1834–1914* (London: Allen & Unwin, 1936), p. 59; C. F. Tebbutt, *Huntingdonshire Folklore* (privately published, 1952), p. 35.

30. "Notes on Madras as a Winter Residence," *Medical Times and Gazette,* July 19, 1873, 73; "Increased Consumption of Opium in England," *Medical Times and Gazette,* April 2, 1857, 426; and "A 'Laudanum District,'" *Lancet,* March 27, 1858, 330.

31. "Opium-Eating in Lincolnshire," *Public Health, 5,* (1892–3), 190.

32. "Sixth Report of the Medical Officer of the Privy Council: No. 14—Report by Dr. Henry Julian Hunter on the Excessive Mortality of Infants in Some Rural Districts of England," *PP*, 1864, XXVIII,

457–466; "Children's Employment Commission, Sixth Report of the Commissioners, Appendix: Report on the Agricultural Gangs in the Counties of Norfolk, Suffolk, Cambridgeshire, Northamptonshire, and Nottinghamshire, by Mr. J. E. White," *PP*, 1867, XVI, 93; "Royal Opium Commission Report," Question 24, 702; S. H. Miller and S. B. J. Skertchley, *The Fenland Past and Present* (London: Longmans, Green, 1878), p. 422; "Commission on the Employment of Children, Young Persons, and Women in Agriculture, First Report of the Commissioners," *PP*, 1867–68, XVII, 533.

33. "Letter to the Editor from William Murrell, M.D.," *BMJ*, July 2, 1885, 30.

34. "Opium in the Fens," *C&D*, December 3, 1904, 894.

35. "A 'Laudanum District,'" 330.

36. Hunter, p. 462.

37. "Opium Eating," *Pharm. J.*, February 1868, 396–397.

38. Charles Lucas, *The Fenman's World: Memories of a Fenland Physician* (Norwich: Jarrold & Sons, 1930), p. 52.

39. Hunter, p. 458.

40. "Notes on Madras," 73.

41. Charles Kingsley, *Alton Locke* (reprint of 1850 edition, London: Cassell's, 1967), pp. 124–125.

42. Hunter, p. 463.

43. Hunter, p. 463.

44. *Leeds and Yorkshire Mercury*, April 10, 1905.

45. "Letter to the Editor from William Murrell," 30.

46. Miller and Skertchley, p. 422.

47. Hunter, p. 464; "Commission on the Employment of Children, Young Persons, and Women in Agriculture," First Report of the Commissioners, *PP*, 1867–68, XVII, p. 533; "Children's Employment Commission," p. 93.

48. Hunter, p. 464.

49. "Longevity Among Opium Eaters," *Boston Medical and Surgical Journal*, February 1862, 95; "Letter to the Editor from William Murrell," 30; Miller and Skertchely, p. 422; "Royal Opium Commission," Questions 3522, 24,709.

50. "Notes on Madras," 73.

58 *The Great Victorian Drug Bazaar*

51. "Opium-Eating," *Pharm. J.*, February 1868, 396; "Increased Consumption of Opium in England," *Medical Times and Gazette*, April 25, 1857, 426.

52. Whymper, p. 45.

53. "Opium-Eating in Lincolnshire," *Public Health*, 5 (March 1893), 190.

54. "East End Opium Smokers," *London Society*, 14 (1868), 68–72.

55. "An Opium Den in Whitechapel," *C&D*, May 15, 1868, 275; "Opium-Smoking in Bluegate Fields," *C&D*, September 15, 1870, 259–261; "A Visit to an Opium House," *Eclectic Magazine*, n.s., 8 (November 1868), 1379–1385; G. Doré and W. B. Jerrold, *London* (1872), pp. 147–148; James Greenwood, "An Opium Smoke in Tiger Bay," *In Strange Company: Being Experiences of a Roving Correspondent* (London: Harry S. King, 1873), pp. 229–238; Richard Rowe, *Picked Up in the Streets, or Struggles for Life Amongst the London Poor* (London: W. H. Allen, 1880), pp. 38–43; Charles W. Wood, "In the Night-Watches," *The Argosy*, 65 (January–June, 1898), 191–223; Walter Besant, *East London* (London: Chatto & Windus, 1901), pp. 204–207; and "A Night in an Opium Den," *London Scene from the Strand*, Gareth Cotterell, ed. (London: Diploma Press, 1974), pp. 76–79.

PART TWO

The Perception of Danger, 1870–1910

CHAPTER FIVE

The Palace of Evil

The publication, in 1870, of Charles Dickens' unfinished novel, *The Mystery of Edwin Drood*, marked a new departure in the literary treatment of opium smoking. The filthy but harmless opium den described by Victorian reporters was superseded by the depiction of the opium den as a palace of evil. Gone was the image of the opium addict, set forth in De Quincey's *Confessions* and accepted by his contemporaries, as noble self-experimenter. In late Victorian literature, the opium addict was portrayed as a secret degenerate, she sought and found in the darkened opium den a refuge from the company of respectable men.

Edwin Drood begins inside the mind of John Jasper, whose opium-induced visions contain echoes of De Quincey's "Oriental dream." Jasper's glimpse of a bedpost calls forth fantasies of Oriental cruelty and excess, mixed with remembrances of the church spires of his home:

> An ancient English Cathedral tower? How can the ancient English Cathedral tower be there! The well-known massive grey square tower of its old Cathedral? How can that be here! There is no spike of rusty iron in the air between the eye and it from any point of the real prospect. What is the spike that intervenes, and who has set it up? Maybe it is set up by the Sultan's orders for the impaling of a horde of Turkish robbers, one by one. It is so, for cymbals clash and the Sultan goes by to his palace in long procession. Ten thousand scimitars flash in the sunlight, and thrice ten

thousand dancing-girls strew flowers. Then follow white
elephants caparisoned in countless gorgeous colours, and infinite
in number and attendants. Still the Cathedral Tower rises in the
background, where it cannot be, and still no writhing figure is on
the grim spike. Stay! Is the spike so low a thing as the rusty spike
on the top of a post of an old bedstead that has tumbled all awry?
Some vague period of drowsy laughter must be devoted to the
consideration of this possibility.[1]

   The double life of John Jasper, presaged in the dream, is
developed in the rest of the first chapter. Jasper awakens to find
himself in an opium den on London's waterfront. He expresses
disgust at his surroundings and companions. Of the old woman
who runs the establishment, he muses, "What visions can *she*
have?" And the sight of his fellow smokers, a Chinaman and a
Lascar, throws him into such a rage that he attacks them vio-
lently for no apparent reason. By the end of the chapter, we
learn that Jasper is not just another dockland drifter, but that he
is the choirmaster of Cloisterham Cathedral.
   In the juxtaposition between the two lives of John Jasper—
opium-smoker and choirmaster—Dickens has established the
theme that controls the development of the novel. In the opening scenes, Jasper presents himself as the respectable employee
of the Church, and the concerned uncle and guardian of young
Edwin Drood. Later in the book, after the disappearance and
presumed murder of his nephew, Jasper's secret passions and
secret life begin to be discovered. He declares his love to Rosa
Bud, the former fiancée of his missing nephew, thus establishing
a motive for committing Drood's murder. In the mumblings of
an opium dream, he reveals to the old lady who prepared his
pipe that he bears ill-will toward "Ned," the name that he calls
his nephew. He is seen in London by his Cloisterham acquaint-
ances under suspicious circumstances. And, most ominously, the
opium lady, who has fed his habit but does not know who he is,
tracks him to Cloisterham, and there learns his identity. Jasper's
secret life has begun to encroach upon his respectable life. The
novel is unfinished, but there can be little doubt that Jasper is
the murderer, and that his revelations to the opium lady are

essential to the unraveling of the mystery. Opium is the hall-mark of his degenerate life, and the source of his eventual undo-ing.

The double life of respectability and degeneracy is also the theme of one of Arthur Conan Doyle's best-known short stories, "The Man with the Twisted Lip" (1892). The scene is set by Dr. Watson's rescue of a friend, Isa Whitney. Whitney has become an opium addict as the result of self-experimentation, stimulated by his reading of De Quincey. When Dr. Watson finds him in an East End opium den, Whitney has sunk to a less than human state: He cannot remember the past two days; he twitches uncontrollably; and he breaks into tears. The descrip-tion of the den evokes a vision of hell: "Out of the black shadows there glimmered little red circles of light, now bright, now faint, as the burning poison waxed or waned in the bowls of the metal pipes."[2] But Isa Whitney is simply an overture; he does not figure in the rest of the story.

Once in the opium den, Watson meets Sherlock Holmes in disguise. The great detective has come to investigate the mysteri-ous disappearance of one Neville St. Clair, a respectable busi-nessman who lives in suburban Kent and works in the City. Several days earlier, Mrs. St. Clair, having business on the same street in East London where the opium den is located, hears a man yell from a window in the second story of a building. She looks up and sees her husband, who appears greatly distressed. However, he withdraws from the window before she can speak to him. Mrs. St. Clair tries to enter the building, but is repulsed by a Lascar, the proprietor of the opium den. When she returns with several policemen, she finds some of her husband's clothing and possessions, but no sign of the gentleman himself. In the room from which she saw her husband peer out, she finds only "the man with the twisted lip," a hideously deformed and filthy beggar, who exists on the charity of City businessmen, and lives in a room above the opium den. The beggar denies ever seeing Mr. St. Clair, despite the presence of the gentleman's apparel in his room. The beggar is carted off to jail, and Mrs. St. Clair calls in Sherlock Holmes to solve the mystery.

Holmes suspects that the beggar has overpowered St. Clair

and done away with him. The discovery of St. Clair's jacket in
the river, weighted down with hundreds of pennies, fuels his
suspicion. And the arrival at the St. Clair home of a note, in
Neville's hand, several days after his disappearance, begging his
wife not to despair, does not convince Holmes that the gentleman in question is still alive. After a sleepless night of cogitation,
Holmes announces that he has solved the mystery. He and Watson hurry to the police station to interview the beggar, who is
still in custody. Holmes vigorously washes the face of the sleeping beggar, who is suddenly revealed to be St. Clair himself!

Now unmasked, St. Clair tells his story. Once an actor and a
newspaperman, he discovered that he could make much more
money by making himself up in such a hideous fashion that even
hardened businessmen could not resist his pleas for a few cop-
pers. As a professional beggar, he was successful beyond his
wildest dreams. As he accumulated capital, he married, moved
to Kent, and sired two daughters, leading a life in the evenings
and on weekends at the eminently respectable Neville St. Clair.
During business days, however, he plied his trade as a beggar,
unbeknownst to his family. The only person to share the secret
of St. Clair's double life was the Lascar proprietor of the opium
den, from whom he rented a room where he slipped in and out
of disguise. The opium den was the vehicle of his transformation from one life to another. It catered to addicted gen-
tlemen, like Isa Whitney, as well as to filthy dockland beggars;
thus St. Clair's arrival either in or out of disguise was not particularly noteworthy. As in *Edwin Drood*, the protagonist's life
came unraveled when his secret could no longer be continued
within the opium den, but was revealed to respectable society.

In *The Picture of Dorian Gray* (1891), Oscar Wilde constructed a tale while turns on the two sets of double lives of the
title character. Dorian Gray is, throughout the story, what he
was at its beginning: a gay and witty *bon vivant* who moves in elite
society. But as the story progresses, his darker nature develops,
which the reader sees only in glimpses. Dorian Gray uses his
enormous charm and good looks to despoil young women and
to corrupt young men. Rumors of his unspeakable behavior
begin to haunt him, even as he moves easily in the fashionable

world of Pall Mall clubs and West End salons. The superficial disparity between Dorian Gray's two lives is a reflection of a much more troubling chasm in his psyche. In a bizarre fantasy which seems to reverse the relationship between the immutability of art and the changeability of life, Dorian perceives that the picture of him, painted by Basil Hallward in the blossom of his youth, is actually aging in a grotesque fashion, while his own face remains frozen in pristine youthful beauty, even after eighteen years of raucous living. For Dorian Gray, this mockery of art and life is unbearable. The two sets of double lives merge in Dorian Gray's murder of Basil Hallward. In killing the creator of the painting which troubles him so deeply, Dorian Gray has committed the action which places him, for all time, beyond the society of civilized men.

In a frantic attempt to forget this unforgivable act, Dorian Gray hurries to the East End in the dead of night: "There were opium-dens, where one could buy oblivion, dens of horror where the memory of old sins could be destroyed by the madness of sins that were new."[3] His physical craving for the drug is as depraved as his moral character: "The hideous hunger for opium began to gnaw at him. His throat burned, and his delicate hands twitched nervously together."[4] The opium den itself is a mixture of aliens and outcasts. Dorian Gray

> entered a long low room which looked as if it had once been a third-rate dancing-saloon. Shrill flaring gas-jets, dulled and distorted in the fly-blown mirrors that faced them, were ranged round the walls. Greasy reflectors of ribbed tin backed them, making quivering disks of light. The floor was covered with ochre-coloured sawdust, trampled here and there into mud, and stained with dark rings of spilt liquor. Some Malays were crouching by a little charcoal stove playing with bone counters, and showing their white teeth as they chattered. In one corner, with his head buried in his arms, a sailor sprawled over a table, and by the tawdrily-painted bar that ran across one complete side stood two haggard women mocking an old man who was brushing the sleeve of his coat with an expression of digust. 'He thinks he's got red ants on him,' laughed one of them, as Dorian Gray passed by. The man looked at her in terror and began to whimper.[5]

In the den, however, Dorian Gray does not find the oblivion that he seeks, but rather the objects of his corrupting influence. He meets Adrian Singleton, one of his former protégés. Now dishonored because of an unspecified but horrible action, Singleton lives only for the company of his fellow opium addicts. Dorian also encounters a consumptive prostitute, who calls him by the pet name, "Prince Charming," by which she had known him many years earlier, when he ruined her. And finally, he comes face to face with James Vane, brother of Sybil Vane, the beautiful young actress who committed suicide after Dorian first courted and then rejected her eighteen years before. Vane intends to shoot him, but is convinced that he has got the wrong man when he sees Dorian's face in the light—a face so youthful that it could scarcely belong to a man of nearly forty. Only because of this hideous trick of nature, by which he is perfectly preserved as his picture ages, is Dorian's life spared.

The scene in the opium den is critical to the novel's plot. The den is a sordid representation of Dorian Gray's dark nature. He seeks it out, expecting to find a refuge, but instead finds reminders of his past, which intensify his suffering, and nearly cost him his life. In the opium den, Dorian Gray learns that there will be no escape.

De Quincey's *Confessions* continued to be read, or at least remembered, into the late nineteenth century, as evidenced by the continued references to it. But the temper of the times had changed, and public opinion about opium had changed accordingly. Romantic exuberance, which had extolled the self and sought out the unconventional, gave way to high Victorian moralism. Self-experimenters, like Isa Whitney, who dabbled in opium, were not noble but depraved. Invariably, they were unable to control the drug's force, and inevitably, they succumbed to its debilitating effects. Opium dens became, in the writings of Dickens, Conan Doyle, and Wilde, moral slums which welcomed those whose actions had carried them beyond the pale of Victorian respectability.

Why did writers fasten on the opium den as such a potent symbol of depravity? Unlike the noisy, convivial British pub, the opium den was a place where each smoker was alone with his pipe and with his dream. In the perceptions of British commentators, when one went to a den, one did not escape *to* society—as Britons did when they went to a pub—but *from* society. Opium which was eaten (or drunk) was usually a medicine, even if De Quincey had found that it has other uses; opium which was smoked was always an intoxicant. The opium-smoker could not claim the morally ambiguous status of the opium-eater in the eyes of Victorian society. Finally, the opium den was an alien institution—where colored men dreamt strange dreams and spoke in unintelligible languages—in the heart of London. One need not be conversant with the new germ theory of disease to perceive in these foreign particles lodged in the body of British society an unsettling threat.

Notes

1. Charles Dickens, *The Mystery of Edwin Drood* (New York: New American Library, 1961), p. 7.

2. Arthur Conan Doyle, *The Adventures of Sherlock Holmes* (London: Pan Books, 1976), p. 139. Conan Doyle himself was reportedly a cocaine user. In any case, the cocaine addiction of Sherlock Holmes figures in several stories published in the late 1880s and early 1890s. For a witty and informative account of the famous detective's drug problems, see David Musto, "Sherlock Holmes and Sigmund Freud," in Robert Byck, ed., *Sigmund Freud's Cocaine Papers* (New York: New American Library, 1974), pp. 357–70.

3. Oscar Wilde, *The Picture of Dorian Gray* (London: Penguin Books, 1977), p. 204.

4. *Dorian Gray*, p. 205.

5. *Dorian Gray*, p. 207.

CHAPTER SIX

The Health Crusade: Opium as a Poison

Novelists were not the only Victorians to express alarm about opium. The drug, and other poisons, came under attack from public health crusaders in the 1860s. The public health movement waxed and waned in Victorian Britain: The 1840s were a period of advance; the 1850s were a period of retreat. Leadership of the movement passed from the abrasive Edwin Chadwick to the more politic Sir John Simon. In his role as Medical Officer to the Privy Council, Simon felt strong enough to open an offensive on a wide front of public health issues in the late 1860s, often basing his case for government intervention on the statistics assembled by Dr. William Farr, the Registrar-General. The legislative hallmarks of this campaign are the Public Health Acts of 1866, 1871, and 1875, which went a long way toward enacting "the sanitary idea" in Britain. The Poisons and Pharmacy Act of 1868, which first regulated opium and most other poisons, was one of the smaller triumphs of the larger campaign. It owed its introduction and passage through Parliament to the willingness of the representatives of the British people to set aside, at least temporarily, their distrust of government intervention and, as the *Times* once put it, "to be bullied into health."

In 1868, in response to reports on the incidence of poisonings and the vending of poisons by unqualified persons by Sir John Simon and Professor Alfred Taylor, the government brought in the Poisons and Pharmacy Bill. Both Simon and Taylor had argued that a substantial proportion of poisonings was due to the easy availability of highly toxic substances, especially strychnine, oxalic acid, prussic acid, and opiates, and the carelessness with which they were dispensed.[1] Poisons could be purchased from an oil dealer, a grocer, or even a draper or bookseller—by anyone, with no restrictions whatsoever. "So long as a person of any age has the command of a threepence," Professor Taylor wrote, "he can procure for this sum a sufficient quantity of one of the most deadly poisons to destroy the lives of two adults."[2] Moreover, there was no guarantee that the seller of the poison, even if he were a druggist, had any education or qualification to dispense and compound poisons.

Poisons were in wide demand for quite legitimate purposes. They were often used as cleaning agents, as pest-killers, and as medicines. The problem facing government was how to regulate their sale so as to minimize accidental (and suicidal) poisonings, while not interfering with their legitimate uses. The obvious answer seemed to be to restrict the vending of poisons to a certain class of sellers, and then to regulate the sellers. In this way, the 1868 Poisons and Pharmacy Act brought together the issues of the sale of poisons and the professionalization of pharmacists. There were precedents for government action in both areas.

In 1852, as a result of both public and professional concern about the high rate of accidental arsenic poisoning, Parliament had passed the Arsenic Act, which required a purchaser of the poison to register his name, the date, and the amount purchased with the seller. In the same year, Parliament passed the first Pharmacy Act, which empowered the eleven-year-old Pharmaceutical Society to designate those persons who passed the Society's rigorous examination as "pharmaceutical chemists." The Act gave the Society the right to exclusive use of this name, but it stopped short of handing to the Society the monopoly power over the sale of all drugs that it wanted. Thus drugs could still be sold by any person, just so long as he did not call himself a "pharmaceutical chemist."

In May 1857, in response to public outcry over several

highly publicized criminal poisonings, the government introduced a bill which would stringently regulate the sale of poisons. The Pharmaceutical Society, calling the bill's strict provisions "impracticable," opposed it. In November the ministry fell and the bill was withdrawn. The Pharmaceutical Society realized that legislation of some sort was inevitable. However, the attempt to present a unified professional front suffered a setback in the 1860s, when a rival organization, the United Society of Chemists and Druggists, was founded to represent the majority of chemists who did not belong to the older, elite body. The conflict between the two organizations effectively thwarted any further legislation in the early 1860s. By 1868, however, the feud had ended and the two groups united behind a single bill.[3]

The 1868 Poisons and Pharmacy Act was a typical mid-Victorian compromise. Certain substances were designated poisons, and the selling of these was restricted to registered pharmacists, chemists and druggists. The poisons schedule of the Act was split into two parts. The Act required that Part I substances, which included especially dangerous poisons such as strychnine and arsenic, be sold only to those persons whom the pharmacists knew personally, and that each sale be recorded in a poisons' register. Part II substances, however, which included opium, could be sold to anybody, in any amount, so long as the containers in which they were dispensed were labeled "poison."

British pharmacists rightly look back on the 1868 Act as a milestone in the establishment of their profession. It was a trade-off. For the first time, pharmacists secured a monopoly over the selling of certain substances. In return, they agreed that no one could sell poisons unless he had passed the Pharmaceutical Society's qualifying examination. Thus they subjected themselves—or, more accurately, their successors, since all pharmacists, druggists, and chemists in business in 1868 were automatically registered without having to sit the examination—to higher standards of professional knowledge. In addition, the Pharmaceutical Society promised to frame specific regulations under the Act which would make the storage and vending of poisons safer.[4]

The Bill whisked through Parliament, seemingly a piece of judicious legislation which would satisfy many constituencies. The pharmacists expected to receive a monopoly on the sale of certain important and profitable items; the government expected to have the assistance of a united profession which would help it frame regulations; and the public expected to benefit from the Act by a much-lowered rate of poisonings.

Pharmacists did not receive the monopoly that they had anticipated. In part, this was due to an enormous loophole in the Act, the significance of which was not fully appreciated at the time. Patent medicines, an important source of government revenue, were exempted from legislation altogether. This meant that anyone who paid the annual vendor's license fee, and the tax stamp required on each bottle of medicine, could continue to sell scheduled poisons quite legally. In the last third of the century, as the sales of patent medicines soared, the cost to pharmacists of this exemption became painfully apparent.

Other drug-sellers evaded or simply ignored the Act. Pharmacists complained bitterly that their "monopoly" was worthless:

> In the town where I reside (Sheffield) four, and I believe, five persons are selling poisons under a borrowed name [i.e., from a pharmacist]—for lending which the Pharmacy Act provides no penalty; five or six under the title patent medicine vendors and other similar disguises; two under 'uncompleted' executorships; while some scores of grocers are selling infants' mixtures with opium, and paregoric without, sweet nitre at 2d. per oz., and tincture of rhubarb ditto; and I have heard of one grocer who gets laudanum put up in 1-oz. bottles to supply known customers.[5]

The President of the Pharmaceutical Society, in 1883, claimed that drugs of all kinds were being sold by "barbers, booksellers, chandlers, confectioners, drapers, general dealers, grocers, hairdressers, herbalists, ironmongers, marine-store dealers, oilmen, printers, publicans, stationers, storekeepers, tailors, tobacconists, toydealers, [and] wine merchants."[6] It might be possible to dismiss a few of these complaints as self-serving exaggerations, but they are so numerous in the pharmaceutical press from the 1870s that they must be taken seriously.[7] The law was ignored because it was toothless. Any infringement of the 1868 Act had to be prosecuted at the expense of the Pharmaceutical Society. If a conviction were secured, the maximum fine that could be levied was £5. It quickly became obvious that, with violations so widespread, the Society lacked the resources to prosecute all but a few token cases. With the chances of being prosecuted so minimal, and the penalty for conviction being so paltry, many illegal drug sellers found that the Act could be ignored with impunity.

If the pharmacists were disappointed in their expectations, so was the government. As part of the compromise of 1868, the Council of the Pharmaceutical Society promised to draft regulations under the Act which would be submitted to the Privy Council. These would have mandated such measures as a separate cabinet for storing all poisons in every pharmacy, and specially marked bottles in which poisons alone would be dispensed. Once the Act was passed, however, and the Council of the Pharmaceutical Society began to debate specific regulations, it was greeted with a furious outcry from the Society's members. They claimed that a separate poison cabinet and poison dispensing bottles would be unwieldy and expensive burdens. Moreover, they would probably be of negligible significance in preventing accidental poisonings. Put simply, the majority of Britain's pharmacists, once they had got the 1868 Act passed, did not want to be further inconvenienced by regulations which might disrupt their everyday shop procedures. In the face of the Pharmaceutical Society's reluctance to cooperate, the Privy Council decided to draft its own regulations. However, a change of government forestalled their implementation, and the task was never completed. The legacy of the failure of the 1868 Act was to leave both government and pharmacists resentful. Despite the Act's acknowledged inadequacies, it was not successfully changed for another forty years.

In 1908, a second Poisons and Pharmacy Act was passed. Although it extended the provisions of the first Act, it still did not secure the monopoly on the vending of drugs for pharmacists. Patent medicines still escaped significant regulation. However, a number of substances, including opium and its derivatives, were moved from Part II to Part I of the poisons schedule. This meant that the purchaser of an opiate had to be known to the pharmacist (or introduced by a mutual acquaintance), and sign for his purchase in the poisons register.

What of the expectation that the legislation would drastically reduce the number of poisonings? Was this fulfilled by the 1868 and the 1908 Poisons and Pharmacy Acts? It is possible to address this question by analyzing the Registrar-General's statistics on poisonings, which were kept sporadically before 1863, and systematically thereafter. However, a word of caution is necessary. The statistics, which are drawn from death certificates, are not entirely accurate. Until 1874, for example, it was optional for medical practitioners to furnish a certificate for the cause of death.[8] As William Farr complained in 1870, "numerous cases are returned simply as murders, suicides, or injuries, without any information as to whether poison or any other instrument was employed in the deed."[9] Furthermore, poisonings were often difficult to detect. Opiate poisoning in particular resembled death from natural causes, and thus was probably consistently understated in the statistics throughout the period. Given these limitations, how ought one to proceed? Above all, it is necessary to be aware of the lack of precision of the statistics when drawing conclusions from them. One must ignore annual variations, especially of small magnitude, and instead look for secular, gross trends.[10] At this level of analysis it is possible to wring some interesting information out of the poisoning statistics.

Was the agitation in the early 1860s a response to an actual increase in poisonings? Although earlier figures are scanty, they clearly indicate that the number of suicidal and accidental poisonings did not increase dramatically in the early 1860s, certainly in comparison with the previous decade (see Tables 5 and 6 in the Appendix). In the five-year period from 1852 through 1856, there was an average of 111 suicidal and 378 accidental poisonings per annum. A decade later, between 1863 and 1867, the figures were very similar: suicides rose slightly to an average of 134, and accidents fell slightly to an average of 362 per annum. There is an irony here. Although the statistics showed that the rate of poisoning was not increasing in the 1860s, the very act of keeping statistics drew attention to certain causes of death—such as accidental poisoning—which could seemingly be altered by government action. The poisons' agitation of 1860s, then, was not a response to a specific increase in poisonings, but rather an outgrowth of a more general public health concern of which mortality statistics were both cause and effect.

What were the effects of the two Acts? Did they succeed in reducing accidental poisonings as was intended? Annual variations aside, there are several secular trends in the statistics (see Table 5, column1). Between 1863 and 1873, accidental poisonings averaged 354 per annum. From 1874 through 1880, the figure rose sharply to 444. From 1881 through 1893, it fell to 256. From 1894 through 1901, it rose again to 313, and then fell sharply to 250 until World War I. Beginning in 1915, it fell again to 129. (The long-range decline in accidental poisonings is even more dramatic than these figures indicate, since the population approximately doubled during this period.) The changes in the rate of accidental poisonings do not obviously correlate with either of the two Poisons Acts. Indeed, six years after the passage of the 1868 Act, there was a 25 percent *increase* in accidental poisonings, followed, eight years later, by a 42 percent decrease. In 1908, when the second Act was passed, there was some change in the rate of accidental poisoning, from an average of 268 per annum between 1904 and 1908, to 235 per annum between 1909 and 1913, a decline of 12 percent. This is not such a dramatic change, however, that we may assume with certainty that it was the result of the 1908 Act. Thus the 1868 Act had no demonstrable effect on the rate of accidental poisoning, while the 1908 Act may have had some slight effect.

For accidental poisonings caused by opiates, the rates of change were somewhat different (see Table 5, columns 2 and 3). From the 1850s until World War I, more accidental poisoning deaths were attributable to opium than to any other agent, an indication of its easy availability and its widespread use. In any given year, between 21 and 43 percent of all accidental poisonings were caused by opium. Did the Poisons Acts have any effect on opiate poisonings? In the five years before the 1868 Act, accidental opiate poisonings averaged 133 per year. In the next five years, the average fell to 99, a decline of 26 percent, where it remained until the end of the century. In the five years preceding the 1908 Act, the average was 70 per annum. In the next five years, the average was 56, a decline of 20 percent. Thus the two Poisons Acts had a much more demonstrable effect on accidental opiate poisonings than on accidental poisonings in general. This disparity is due to the fact that new poisons, such as carbolic acid, were continually being developed and used before they were put on the poisons' schedule, and some poisons, such as those available in patent medicines, were not placed on the poisons' schedule at all. Since the mortality figures for accidental poisoning reflect deaths from these unscheduled poisons, they do not accurately measure the success of the Poisons Acts. The substantial drop in accidental opiate poisoning after 1868 and 1908 is a much truer indication of the Acts' effects. Even the minimal safeguard of labeling each opiate dispensed as a poison was sufficient to produce a 26 percent decline in the mortality rate. The more substantial regulation of opiates after 1908 brought about a further decline of 20 percent.

Finally, it is important to note the gradual decline, throughout the entire period, of accidental opiate poisonings of children under five (see Table 5, column 4). It is impossible to know the exact effect the 1868 Act had on this category of poisonings, since figures are not available before that date. The steady decline after 1868 was probably the result of increasing public awareness of the dangers of drugging infants. The practice of quietening infants with opiates had received more publicity than any other opium-related issue, especially in the early 1860s. By the 1890s, the results can be seen in popular medical pamphlets and periodicals warning parents against using opiates on children, and also on the advertisements for many patent medicines for coughs and children's ailments, which often carried the words, "contains no opium."

In contrast to accidental poisonings, suicidal poisonings

were rising throughout the entire period until World War I at a higher rate than that of population growth (see Table 6, column 1). The explanation for this general rise in suicides is beyond the scope of this book. Nevertheless, it is noteworthy that opiates remained one of the most preferred forms of poison for suicides (see Table 6, columns 2 and 3). Opium had certain advantages: it was cheap, accessible, and relatively painless. Other poisons came and went in popularity: strychnine and oxalic acide through the 1870s; carbolic acid from the 1880s through the First World War; and Lysol in the 1920s. In the 1850s, opiates accounted for 26 percent of all poisoning suicides. They declined dramatically in the 1860s to 17 percent, and remained at about that level until the mid 1890s, when they declined to 13 percent until 1908, and to 8.5 percent until the war. It is likely that the 1908 Act was responsible for this latter decline since, after its passage, the increased difficulty of obtaining opiates induced some potential suicides to turn to other poisons. The 1868 Act, however, had no effect on the opiate suicide rate.

In fact, neither the 1868 nor the 1908 Poisons and Pharmacy Acts greatly reduced accidental poisoning deaths as their sponsors had intended. It is possible that the first Act would have had a greater effect had it not been for the patent medicine loophole, which virtually emasculated it. Even so, the rate of accidental opiate poisoning fell significantly. The long-term decline in accidental poisoning, and accidental poisoning in general, must be explained by a combination of factors, of which the Acts are only one part. A higher literacy rate, which allowed people to read labels; the gradual spread of a more enlightened health consciousness among the public; the safeguards of the poison schedules and higher professional standards among pharmacists, which removed the ignorant clerk from behind the dispensing counter all contributed to a reduction in accidental poisonings during the period.

The 1868 Poisons and Pharmacy Act (and its 1908 extension), if evaluated by the expectations that accompanied it, must be judged only a partial success. The pharmacists' monopoly on the sale of poisonous substances did not immediately materialize; the government and the pharmaceutical profession remained at loggerheads; and, although the rate of poisoning with opiates and most other scheduled substances declined, the accidental poisoning rate as a whole did not decline precipitously. But from a longer perspective, these expectations must be understood as part of the overly sanguine hopes and fulsome rhetoric that accompanied "improving" legislation in mid-Victorian Britain. The public health legislation that was passed in the 1860s and 1870s did not usher in the new social paradise that its sponsors had occasionally predicted. But it did lead to the slow and steady amelioration of some of the most offensive conditions of life in nineteenth-century Britain. In this context, the Poisons Acts qualify as limited successes. Pharmacists were professionally upgraded by compulsory registration and the educational requirement that underlay it. The principle of government regulation of medicines was established, however timidly. And the rate of poisoning by opiates and other dangerous substances began a long and slow decline to which the Acts contributed significantly.

Notes

1. Sir John Simon, "The Practice of Pharmacy in Great Britain; Accidental and Criminal Poisoning; From the Sixth Report to the Privy Council, 1863," *Public Health Reports*, I (London, 1887), pp. 541–550; "Professor Alfred S. Taylor's Report on Poisoning, and the Dispensing, Vending, and Keeping of Poisons," *Pharm. J.*, (1864–65), 172–184.

2. Taylor, 180.

3. There are a number of histories of nineteenth-century British pharmacy, including Theophilus Redwood and Jacob Bell, *Historical Sketch of the Progress of Pharmacy in Great Britain* (London, 1880); Leslie G. Matthews, *History of Pharmacy in Britain* (Edinburgh: Livingstone, 1962); George E. Trease, *Pharmacy in History* (London: Ballière, Tindall & Cox, 1964); F. N. L. Pynter, Ed., *The Evolution of Pharmacy in Britain* (London: Pitman, 1965); Joseph Ince, "The Old 'Pharmaceutical Journal': A Reminiscence," *C&D*, October 15, 1880, 434–436; Joseph Ince, "The Rise of English Pharmacy," *C&D*, November 14, 1868, 706–707; J. P. Gilmour, "British Phar-

macy as a Profession," reprinted from *International Clinics, 3,* series 39 (1929); "The Pharmaceutical Society of Great Britain: The Story of its Origin and Progress in Nine Parts," *The Indian and Eastern Chemist,* August 1920–April 1921; and R. W. Giles, "Pharmaceutical Politics," *Pharm. J.,* April 14, 1883, 851–855, and April 21, 1883, 871–874.

4. There is a complete copy of the 1868 Act in the *Chemist and Druggist,* August 15, 1868, 478–482. See also "The Amended Pharmacy Bill and the Press," *C&D,* June 15, 1868, 337–338.

5. "A Dissatisfied One," *C&D,* February 15, 1877, 74.

6. "The Presidential Address," *C&D,* October 15, 1883, 491.

7. A representative selection of complaints includes "An Old Druggist," "The Pharmacy Act and its Results," *C&D,* March 15, 1871, 99; "A Registered Chemist," "The Pharmacy Act, 1868," *C&D,* May 15, 1873, 165; J. C. Thresh, "On the Condition of Chemists and Druggists under the Pharmacy Act," *C&D,* July 15, 1876, 240–242; "Anti-Traitor," "Chemists Aiding and Abetting Persons to Break the Pharmacy Act," *Pharm. J.,* December 17, 1881, 516; "The Neglect of the Pharmacy Act," *C&D,* January 7, 1893, 16–17; and "The Sale of Laudanum," *C&D,* March 26, 1898, 505.

8. William Farr, *Forty-Second Annual Report of the Registrar General* (1882 Blue Book), p. xxxii.

9. William Farr, *Thirty-First Annual Report of the Registrar-General* (1870 Blue Book), p. 201.

10. I have not included criminal opiate poisonings (manslaughter and murder) because they occurred so infrequently and irregularly that the statistics defy meaningful analysis. In addition, because opiate poisoning was a common cause of accidental and suicidal death, criminal opiate poisoning was probably not often recognized for what it was. In short, I think it likely that there were many more murders with opiates than were detected. There is an interesting account of the opium murder of Mary Kirkbride of the village of Benniddenck, Cumbria, in 1827, in the Lowther Manuscripts, Cumbria County Record Office (letter from William Conlohass to the Earl of Lansdale, 1828).

CHAPTER SEVEN

Morphia and the
Morbid Craving

Novelists and public health reformers, in their late-nineteenth-century attacks on opium, perceived a new danger in an old product. Medical men were, for the most part, uninterested in the threat to public morals presented by opium-smokers, and even in the threat to public health presented by occasional careless dispensing of opium. They were, however, intensely interested in a new therapy made possible by advancing medical technology: subcutaneous injection of morphia, the alkaloid of opium. At first they welcomed it as the new panacea which would relieve pain quickly and easily with no deleterious side effects. Then medical men began seeing patients who had become so dependent upon this new therapy that they seemed to be in the throes of a disease far worse than the medical condition for which the therapy had been prescribed. Between 1870, when the first warning was sounded, and 1910, the British medical community did a complete turnabout on morphia. Within four decades, the promising new therapy came to be seen as a deadly pathogen.

Morphia was isolated from opium by Friedrich Sertürner in 1806, and it was commercially available in Britain from the 1820s. But as long as it had to be taken orally, there was little to recommend it over opium. Morphia did not come into widespread use until the 1860s, a few years after Dr. Alexander

Wood perfected the hypodermic syringe, which made possible
an entirely new mode of administering medication. Wood and
Dr. Charles Hunter publicized the use of hypodermic injections
of morphia for the relief of neuralgia. Wood's paper of 1858,
delivered before the British Medical Association and then published in the *British Medical Journal,* was particularly important in
making ordinary practitioners aware of the new therapy.[1]
Within a few years it was being applied to a variety of problems,
including inflammations of the eye, acute rheumatism, uterine
pain, and delirium tremens.[2] This early literature on subcutaneous injection of morphia was unreservedly euphoric about its
uses. Injected morphia was lauded as being more effective than
ingested opium and free from opium's most unpleasant side
effects, such as constipation and stupor. In 1869, Dr. Edward
Wilson began an article on subcutaneous injection of morphia by
stating that

> few really important discoveries have glided so silently into every-
> day use as the subcutaneous injection of remedial agents. Slowly
> and surely this new method has won its way and established itself
> in the profession until there are probably few medical men now to
> be found who cannot bear testimony, from their own experience,
> to the marvellous power of narcotics introduced beneath the
> skin.[3]

Wilson reviewed the possible uses of injected morphia, and concluded by calling it "the greatest boon given to medicine since
the discovery of chloroform.[4] In the same year, Dr. Arthur
Evershed chided his "professional brethren" whose misplaced
caution about injected morphia kept them from using this
"means of relief so satisfactory to their patients and to themselves."[5] The only note of caution in the papers of the 1850s and
1860s concerned the dangers of poisoning through an overdose:
the line between a therapeutic and a toxic dose could be very
thin indeed.

Initially, patients who became regular users of morphia
shared their doctors' sanguine appraisal of the drug's benefits.
Even after the 1870s, when medical opinion about morphia be-

gan to change, many morphia-addicted patients found little to complain about. They took their injections regularly and carried on with their daily routines. Consider, for example, this letter, written by a chemist's wife, and published in a trade journal in 1888:[6]

> I have myself been in the habit of taking morphia for thirty years. I began by taking chlorodyne for a spasmodic complaint, as ordered by two eminent medical men. It was changed by my husband for morphia, with the result that by constantly increasing the dose it came at last to 4 scruples per week, which has been the regular quantity taken now for very many years.
>
> This medicine—so deleterious in most instances—has by no means impaired the vitality of my system, or tended in any degree to reduce my activity, which is equal to that of many young women, although I am now 67 years of age.
>
> My enjoyment of life is perfect, and I have none of the haggard, emaciated look borne by most persons who adopt this treatment. My eyes are black and bright, the sight being no worse than that of most persons my age.
>
> The only evil which appears to arise from the use of this medicine is a considerable increase of fat, and I should be considerably obliged if any of your contributors will kindly inform me if this increase of adipose tissue is a natural result of the morphia.
>
> I am, sir, yours faithfully,
>
> E.L.P.B.

The letter is interesting, both because of what it says directly about one woman's drug habit, and also because of what it says indirectly about the social perception of morphia habituation. A respectable, elderly lady has a morphia habit of long duration. She has no hesitation about admitting it in print, and her only regret is that she fears the morphia is making her fat. Yet she is sufficiently aware of the contemporary professional literature on morphia-takers to consider herself something of an exception. Most habitual morphia-takers, she believes, suffer from deleterious side effects which, for some reason, do not seem to trouble her. But what is most striking about the letter is the lack of moralizing about her circumstances. She obviously does not regard herself as a social parish, enslaved to an immoral vice, nor does the tone of the letter suggest that she is challenging such a stereotype. She is not a dope fiend, but a gentlewoman who has slipped into a relatively harmless habit in the course of medical treatment. Her self-image, which was presumably shared by her readers, reflected the dominant perception of drug habituation in mid-Victorian Britain. But in 1888, when the letter was published, a change was already under way, a change which we see presaged, perhaps, in the edgy, slightly defensive tone of the lady's self-description.

Cases began to be reported in the medical press of morphia users who, unlike the elderly chemist's wife, had suffered a severe deterioration of their health after prolonged use of the drug. The most common symptoms of morphia addicts included emaciation, loss of sexual appetite, a "haggard" appearance, and constipation. Most alarmingly, they discovered that attempts to discontinue the drug's use brought on severe flu-like symptoms. It seemed nearly impossible to shake off the "craving" for morphia which regular users developed.

One of these addicts detailed his life-long struggle with morphia in his anonymous autobiographical memoir, *Experiences of a Medical Morphinist.* One should not think, says the author, that the joys of morphia are prolonged. After taking the drug for several months

> the habitué begins to find that tolerable comfort is now the best that he can look for; and even that negative effect cannot be won except by increasing both the amount and frequency of his dose. Until he has saturated his system he does not even get peace.[7]

He was introduced to morphia in 1896, when he was 22, in Winnipeg, while on his way to the Yukon gold fields. A local doctor gave it to him for acute rheumatic iritis, a condition which periodically troubled him for the rest of his life. He returned to England and entered medical school. Whenever troubled by eye problems he would resort to morphia. But it was not until he settled into regular practice in north London, in 1907, and his eye pain worsened, that he became a regular morphia user: "At first half a grain, taken night and morning, was sufficient. But gradually the dose was increased, and when I discovered that alcohol in my case reinforced the effects of the morphia, I became a heavy drinker as well."[8] At first, the drug revitalized him: "An injection made me feel that, Atlas-like, I could obliterate fatigue; I was able, or seemed to be able, to score over any opponent, and to face any crisis."[9]

Gradually the author found his sexual appetite diminished, and then obliterated. His dose grew to six grains per day, and morphia became the only focus of his life. After a few years of increasing doses and increasing misery, he resolved to break the habit. He tried three different cures, ranging from the "knockout" cure of total and sudden withdrawal (which nearly killed him), to the famous Dr. Oscar Jennings' system of "voluntary withdrawal." This latter was apparently so successful that, for a time, he became associated with Dr. Jennings in practice. But after each cure, some minor physical or psychological setback would bring back the old craving for morphia, and he would resume the injections. "After this I gave up all hope of cure, and settled down to the dull miseries which are the lot of the incurable."[10] Finally, he restored to the "Lambert treatment," which combined large doses of belladonna with gradual reduction of the morphia "on a more or less fixed and arithmetical plan, almost without reference to the needs of the patient."[11] After a month in a nursing home, during which the treatment was effected, he was successfully withdrawn from morphia with relatively little pain. The author is aware enough of his past failings "not [to] be led into any rash assertion as to the permanence of my recovery." But, as of October 1919, after over twenty years' addiction to morphia, he "will say no more than that I hope and believe that I am cured."[12]

As a middle-aged medical man with a morphia addiction of long duration, the author is typical of 51 cases which were reported in the medical press between the 1870s and the 1920s. The average age of the 32 male addicts was 44. Of the 29 whose occupations were reported, 19—or 66 percent—were medical men. The duration of their habits ranged from one to 30 years, the average being nine. Their doses varied from one to 60 grains of morphia per day, the average being 13. The 19 women whose cases were reported were only slightly younger, with an average age of 40. Only three were reported to have occupations—two nurses and one dentist—although a few were married to medical men. The average duration of the female addicts' habits was 11 years, slightly longer than that of the males. The average dose among the women was 10 grains per day, three less than the men's. Interestingly, four of the women, but only one of the men, were addicted to heroin.

What is strikingly common to almost all of the cases, men and women, is that the addiction was therapeutically induced. In only two cases did the addict begin using morphia for a nonmedical reason. In all of the others, the addict began taking morphia for a medical problem, usually relief of pain for some chronic condition, or after a traumatic and painful event, like childbirth or an operation.[13]

Of course, these cases are not perfectly representative of the morphia-addicted population of Britain from 1870 through the 1920s. Since the cases are those who sought treatment for their condition, the sample is biased in favor of those persons—such as working professionals and businessmen—who had the most to lose by continuing their addiction. Likewise, medical men are somewhat overrepresented, since they would presumably be more informed about and receptive to therapy than the general population. Nevertheless, there are a few trends which are so strong that they justify several conclusions about British morphia addicts. For the most part, they were well-to-do, middle-aged professionals (especially in health-related fields where they had easy access to morphia) and businessmen who had become addicted in the course of medical treatment. Their addiction did not immediately lead to the ruin of their businesses or practices, or their family lives. Indeed, several long-term addicts managed to conceal their conditions even from their spouses. (This was possible, perhaps, only in Victorian Britain, where the exaggerated prudishness of the age condoned husbands and wives

who never saw one another's nude bodies.) But in the long run,
morphia addiction proved to be physically and psychologically
debilitating to most persons, and many of the victims sought
treatment for it.

It was the first appearance of substantial numbers of patients who complained of similar symptoms after regular morphia use that led some doctors to raise warning flags about the
drug. The first of these was an article published by Dr. Thomas
Clifford Allbutt in 1870:

> Does morphia tend to encourage the very pains it pretends to
> relieve; or if not, does it at any rate induce in those who use it
> constantly, an artificial state which makes its further use a neces-
> sity? Are the subjects of morphia injection, that is, liable to be-
> come depressed, relaxed, irritable and dependent on a new habit
> of constant intoxication? If this be so, we are incurring a grave
> risk in bidding people to inject whenever they need it, and in
> telling them that morphia can have no ill effects upon them so
> long as it brings with it tranquility and wellbeing.[11]

In retrospect, this appears extremely tentative, although in
contrast to the enthusiasm of his colleagues in the previous decades, Allbutt must have seemed unduly pessimistic. The paper
touched off a small debate in *The Practitioner,* in which Drs.
Oliver and Anstie, while not denying that morphia injections
could create patient dependence, argued that this occurred relatively infrequently and could be easily avoided.[15]

There was a substantial medical literature on opium in
Latin, and later, in English, that went back to the writings of the
famous seventeenth-century physician Thomas Sydenham,
whose enthusiasm for the drug had earned him the sobriquet
"Opiophilos."[16] Opium had been the subject of books and
papers by both clinicians and toxicologists in the eighteenth and
early nineteenth centuries.[17] Throughout these writings there
was a recognition of such phenomena as patient dependence,
physiological tolerance, and withdrawal pains.[18] Yet there was
little tendency by medical men to take these warnings seriously,
and certainly no attempt to define addiction as a disease. That

did not occur in Britain until the late 1870s, in the wake of concern over the growing number of morphia-dependent patients.

Unquestionably the most important contribution to the addiction literature of the late nineteenth century was Edward Levinstein's *Die Morphiumsucht,* translated into English in 1878 as *The Morbid Craving for Morphia.* The most significant feature of this book is the form in which it was cast, with sections on symptomatology, etiology, prognosis, and prophylaxis. Levinstein was not simply warning his colleagues about unpleasant side effects of a new drug therapy; he was describing a new disease: "the uncontrollable desire of a person to use morphia as a stimulant and a tonic, and the diseased state of the system caused by the injudicious use of the said remedy."[19]

Of utmost importance in Levinstein's case is his argument that the morbid craving for morphia is *not* a form of mental alienation. In contrast to fellow German psychiatrists Lähr and Fiedler, Levinstein stressed that "the desire for morphia injections . . . results from [a person's] natural constitution and not from a certain predisposition to its use."[20] Levinstein was insistent upon the somatic origins of drug addiction because only by doing so could he convince his medical colleagues to take it seriously as a disease. A mechanical model of disease, which virtually ruled out nonsomatic causation, was at the height of its influence in the third quarter of the nineteenth century. While later developments would make psychic diseases medically respectable, a different wind prevailed in the 1870s, and Levinstein trimmed his sails accordingly.

Levinstein dealt with morbid craving for morphia like any other disease. The treatment that he prescribed is what is known, in American drug slang, as "cold turkey." The patient is to be locked in a set of rooms for "a period of eight to fourteen days, all opportunities for attempting suicide having been removed," attended by nurses and overseen by a physician.[21] In order to see him over the more difficult periods of withdrawal pain, the patient is allowed recourse to warm baths, bicarbonate of soda, chloral hydrate, and, interestingly enough, unlimited amounts of champagne and brandy. Only in the case of a patient's complete collapse, with the threatened loss of life, should the physician resort to a one-half grain injection of morphia. After four weeks, at the most, patients can be returned to society. Levinstein was unconcerned about relapse: Once a patient was restored to physical health, Levinstein considered him cured. He was similarly sanguine in his description of "prophylaxis":

> We shall not be wrong in saying that morbid craving for morphia, after the lapse of several years, will be of rare occurrence in Germany, as soon as the governmental decrees, already issued by some of the states, are obeyed; the doctors in future not allowing the morphia injections to be practised by anyone but themselves.[22]

From our present perspective, Levinstein's formulation seems particularly antiquated, both in its rigidity and in its naiveté. But we should not underestimate its appeal in the 1870s. It was a forceful statement of a problem about which medical men were anxious, in a form which they recognized as appropriate.

The most important British spokesman on the question of addiction in the late nineteenth century was Dr. Norman Kerr, the founder and first president of the Society for the Study and Cure of Inebriety, abbreviated as SSI. The SSI was founded, in 1884, as an association of eminent medical men, "to investigate the various causes of inebriety, and to educate the professional and public mind to a recognition of intemperance."[23]

The central message of Kerr and his SSI associates, which recurs like an incantation throughout their publications, is that "inebriety is a disease." Kerr claimed that inebriety "is for the most part the issue of certain physical conditions . . . the natural product of a depraved, debilitated, or defective nervous organization, . . . as unmistakably a disease as is gout, or epilepsy, or insanity."[24] In his book, *Inebriety or Narcomania,* Kerr accepted the "narrow" definition of disease as the result of a structural alteration which can be pathologically verified, and then attempted to demonstrate how alcoholic inebriety clearly conforms to it.[25]

What was at stake for Kerr and his associates was far more than a mere question of medical classification. Up until the present time, they claimed, society has condemned the inebriate as a sinner, or punished him as a criminal, but it has not seen him for what he really is—a sick man. If inebriety, like gout or epilepsy, is the result of a physical defect over which the sick person has no control—that is, if inebriety is not a willful act—then the inebriate should not be jailed, but hospitalized. This is the essence of the case made by Kerr and his associates in the late nineteenth century in their attempt to secure legislation which would create publicly funded retreats for the treatment of inebriates. They were not very successful. The Habitual Drunkards' Act of 1879 and the Inebriates' Act of 1898 did license a few retreats, but they were private and received only minimal public support. Above all, the Acts did not allow for the confinement of noncriminal inebriates against their will, as the Lunacy Acts had done for the mentally ill. Late Victorian legislators, moved equally by a stinginess with public funds and a greater regard for the liberty of the citizen than the necessity of therapeutic confinement, ultimately frustrated Kerr and his colleagues.[26]

Nevertheless, in their efforts to build a case for compulsory confinement, the SSI produced a very considerable number of scientific publications which were crucial in shaping the idea of drug addiction in Britain. Kerr and his colleagues were most concerned about alcoholism, which they rightly regarded as the most significant form of inebriety in Britain. But they also wrote about other "narcotizing agents," including opium, chloral hydrate, chlorodyne, and cocaine. Kerr claimed that "the opium habit" is a "true inebriety," although it is a "functional neurosis," in which "organic lesions are comparatively rare."[27] Altogether, in contrast to alcoholism, the opium habit is much less dangerous, both as a social and as a physical disease:

> The opium inebriate does not destroy his furniture, beat his wife, dash his child's head against the wall, or use his narcotic career dealing with his hand death and desolation all around. Nor does he, as the tippler of alcohol, so degenerate his tissues, injure the structure of his vital organs, or originate organic disease, by the

direct poisoning action of the stupefying agent which consigns him to an early grave.[28]

Yet, Kerr claimed, "opium transcends alcohol in the generation of a more irreclaimable and incurable diseased condition. Cured alcohol inebriates are not uncommon [but] . . . cured opium inebriates are comparatively few in number."[29] Although he regarded opium-smoking and opium-eating as harmful, Kerr believed that "the hypodermic injection of morphia is, however, the most swift and the most potent of all the methods of administration."[30]

Finally, Kerr addressed the objection that some persons can use moderate amounts of intoxicants, even opium, without damaging themselves. This argument, which was made frequently in Britain in the 1890s, naturally tended to undercut the idea that opium-taking, in whatever form, was a disease. Kerr's reply to this is a classic example of the way in which moral judgments were intertwined with scientific facts in his writings: "Opium is a poison which excites, intoxicates, and enervates the whole man; by repeated indulgence inducing bodily and mental prostration and moral perversion."[31] Kerr personally, and the SSI as a whole, publicized in British medical circles the idea that inebriety, including drug addiction, was a disease whose treatment was properly the responsibility of the physician. In addition, Kerr modified Levinstein's conception of the disease of addiction by stressing that it had a psychological etiology and by emphasizing the difficulty of reversing a patient's opium habit once it was fully established. Both of these themes became prominent in the twentieth-century literature on addiction.

While Kerr and his colleagues labored to establish the disease model of addiction in the 1880s and 1890s, quite a different evaluation of the effects of opium was being put forward by a group of medical men and politicians writing in defense of the opium trade between British India and China. Their publications were provoked by the anti-opium publicity generated by the Society for the Suppression of the Opium Trade, a Quaker-based organization founded in 1874. The SSOT was dedicated to forcing the Indian government out of the lucrative business

of supplying Chinese smokers with opium grown on a government monopoly. The Society argued that Britain was morally
compromised by selling opium—"a poison"—to the Chinese,
and demanded that the trade cease at once.[32]

The opium apologists met this argument on several different levels. There was, to begin with, the economic issue. Sir
Rutherford Alcock and Sir George Campbell argued that, despite its hypocritical denunciations of Indian opium, the Chinese
government allowed opium to be grown within its own borders.
Given the constant demand for opium by Chinese smokers, the
only effect of a ban on Indian opium imports would be an increase of tax revenue for the Chinese government, while the
government of India suffered accordingly.[33]

A somewhat different, although complementary line was
argued by several eminent medical men who had served in the
opium-eating regions of India and the opium-smoking regions
of China. Sir George Birdwood wrote two letters on the subject
which were published in the *Times* in 1881 and 1882: "As regards opium-smoking," he claimed, "I can from experience tes-
tify that it is, of itself, absolutely harmless."[34] And of opium-
eating he declared that

> sound, hale people, in comfortable circumstances who lead
> healthy lives, seldom or never suffer from the habitual use of
> opium, even in quantities that seem to be excessive. There are few
> finer people in the world than those of Goojerat, Kattywar,
> Cutch, and Central India, and they are all addicted to the habitual
> use of opium.[35]

Surgeon-General Sir William Moore stated flatly that "opium is
not the destructive agent which anti-opiumists have declared it
to be."[36] To those who claimed that the prolonged use of opium
is deleterious to health, Moore replied that

> there is no organic disease traceable to the use of opium. Func-
> tional disorders, more or less, may be induced by the excessive
> use of opium. But the same may be said of other causes of de-
> ranged health—gluttony, tea, tobacco, bad air, mental anxiety,
> etc.[37]

In fact, Moore asserted, those Indians who use opium regularly and moderately are in better health than those who do not. Finally, both Moore and F. J. Mouat, formerly a government medical inspector in India, declared that opium-eating was a much less serious social problem than alcohol-drinking.[38] "Has an opium-eater ever been found to have knocked out his wife's brains?" Mouat asked, "Is that civilised proceeding altogether unknown to the alcoholic drunkard at home?"[39] If opium were banned in India and China, they argued, the result would be to drive opium users to more harmful stimulants like alcohol or ganja.

The capstone to the opium apologists' argument came in the unlikely form of a parliamentary blue book. In 1893, in response to the successful agitation by anti-opiumists, Gladstone and the Liberal government of the day created a Royal Commission to investigate opium-growing and opium-eating in India and to make recommendations on policy changes. In 1895, after two years of interviews with experts in both London and India, the Commission published its final Report. Much to the dismay of the anti-opiumists, the Report was a complete endorsement of the views of the opium apologists. The Commissioners found little evidence that opium-eating led to the physical or moral decay of users. To the contrary, they found that opium was used intelligently as a medicine and in moderation as a stimulant, and that to deprive the natives of the drug would cause great suffering.[40]

The Report was widely publicized in the medical press and caused consternation among those who argued that opiate addiction was a disease. How could a substance which had been found to be harmless, and even beneficial, in India, be so pernicious in England? The Opium Commission Report put the disease theorists on the defensive. Virtually every discussion of the problem in the 15 years after 1895 made mention of it. The only paper published by the SSI in an attempt to reassert the disease theory of addiction in the face of the Report's evidence was rambling and unconvincing.[41] Yet in spite of its influence, the Opium Commission Report did not refute the disease theory of addiction. The Report delayed its triumph by making its proponents somewhat more cautious and its audience somewhat more skeptical. But in the end, the Report was only a rearguard action.

From the 1890s until 1916, a number of books and articles were published which addressed the issue of drug addiction. In addition, the leading medical textbooks began to include a chapter on the topic. The fundamental disputes of the nineteenth century had either been resolved or brushed aside, and a wide consensus emerged on most of the important aspects of a theory of drug addiction.

1. *Drug addiction is a disease like alcoholism; but narcotic drugs, while less damaging in their social effects, are more ruinous for the individual user.* Although all were in agreement with this central tenet, there was still considerable room for maneuver. J. B. Mattison adhered to a "physicalist" definition of drug addiction:

> Tersely stated, it may be said that this disease involves the cerebro-spinal and sympathetic systems, well attested clinical fact proving that they bear the brunt of opium excess, which induces changes that give rise to great nervous derangement when the opiate is withdrawn, and which, in gradual withdrawal, is seldom entirely avoided.[12]

Harrington Sainsbury, however, claimed that addiction is "a form of Moral Insanity,"[43] and Sir William Collins called it "a disease of the will."[44] In fact, these definitions did not reflect fundamental disagreements among the authors, but rather differing emphases on parts of the same problem. If one considered the disease of addiction simply in terms of the morbid effects of opiates on the central nervous system, then the physicalist definition was quite adequate. But Sainsbury and Collins, by borrowing contemporary psychiatric terminology, were really trying to answer the question of why a person voluntarily habituates himself to morphia. Allbutt and Dixon, in addressing the same question, slipped into an older vocabulary, derived from a traditional morality, as Kerr had occasionally done in the previous decade.[45] Essentially the problem was how to describe a disease in which some persons willfully adopted a course of self-destruction, with full knowledge of its probable consequences.

T. D. Crothers made the most ambitious attempt to resolve this problem by distinguishing between "morphinism" and "morphinomania." The former "describes a condition following the prolonged use of morphin," while the latter designates "the condition of persons in whom the impulse to use morphin is of the nature of a mania, possessing the mind and dominating every thought, leaving but one supreme desire—to procure morphin and experience the pleasure it gives."[46] The morphinist, although he had contracted the physical habit, retains his moral sensibilities and sanity, whereas the morphinomaniac has lost both. Yet even Crothers admits that this theoretical distinction, which separates out the two elements of addiction, is of limited utility in identifying patients: "The morphinist not infrequently becomes a morphinomaniac . . . These two classes are not always marked. They frequently merge into each other, making it difficult to distinguish between them."[47] Although Crothers' solution was inadequate, he clearly recognized and addressed a problem which continues to plague drug researchers today: How does one satisfactorily describe a disease which has both physiological and psychological elements?[48]

2. *Some persons have a psychological predisposition to the use of stimulants generally, and these people will often switch from one drug to another, or use them in combination.* Many persons change to alcohol in an attempt to break the morphia habit, or vice-versa, and remain addicted to both. Lawton, Jennings, and Crothers all agreed that those most disposed to become drug addicts were "neurotics"—that is, those persons who had inherited a defective nervous system.[49] Allbutt and Dixon defined neurotics as persons "who scent intoxicants from afar with a retriever-like instinct, and, curious in their sensations, play in and out with all kinds of them."[50] Jennings stressed the futility of distinguishing among different kinds of addiction because narcotics were used so interchangeably by addicts:

> It may be objected that cocainism is not morphinism, but this would be an error, for it is exceptional for a cocaine addict not to take morphia as well. Heroin-taking is also on the increase, and this synthetic alkaloid being a derivative of morphia, heroin ad-

diction is, to all intents and purposes, identical with morphinism.[51]

3. *Most drug habits are therapeutically induced.* A patient is
given morphia and perhaps instructed in the use of a syringe by
his doctor. After using morphia regularly for a period of weeks
or months, he finds that he is unable to do without it. Allbutt and
Dixon noted that addiction is particularly easy for those who
begin to use morphia for "pain which is wearisome rather than
acute."[52] Sainsbury claimed that most persons "fly to drugs . . . to
escape a distress of mind or body."[53] Crothers confessed that
given its therapeutic importance, "actually no known dividing-
line exists between the use and abuse of morphin."[54]

4. *Morphia addiction is a disease of modern civilization, which
particularly afflicts those who feel its pressures most acutely.* As early as
1876, Benjamin Ward Richardson had devoted a chapter to
drug addiction in his *Diseases of Modern Life.* T. D. Crothers
echoed the same theme 25 years later when he said that morphinism is due "in large measure to modern civilisation, associated with the rapid exhaustion following changes in life and
living." He claimed that morphia was the popular antidote to
those newly emergent nervous diseases, "neurasthenia and cerebrasthenia."[55] Morphinism is particularly prevalent among "active brain-workers, professional and businessmen, teachers and
persons having large cares and responsibilities."[56] Lawton noted
that in addition to neurotics, persons of "artistic temperament,"
including "geniuses," often succumb to addiction.[57] Osler
claimed that "the habit is particularly prevalent among women
and physicians." Mattison agreed that "medical men . . . com-
pose the better class of habitués,"[58] and Jennings was so im-
pressed by the percentage of medical men among his patients
that he ventured the estimate that one out of every four medical
men was addicted to narcotic drugs.[59]

5. *While it is true that a few addicts can carry on a completely
normal life so long as they are not deprived of the drug, most will begin to
show symptoms of physical, psychological, and moral decline after prolonged use.* Allbutt and Dixon gave a typical description of the
process of degeneration.

But if the habit be continued and the doses increased, as will be
assuredly the case and that quickly, symptoms of bodily disease
will appear; say in six or eight months at farthest. The flesh begins to fall; the face loses colour and takes on a sallow, lustreless
hue and an aged expression; the teeth are loosened, and gradually even a young person becomes wizened, emaciated, and haggard. To this rule there are some exceptions; a few patients keep
their flesh, or even grow fat and puffy: such persons are good
feeders, take wine freely, and probably escape the catarrh of the
stomach which attacks the greater number of their fellows. Constipation is always present, often in most obstinate degrees; the
mouth is parched, and other secretions as a rule are arrested;
though some morphinists sweat profusely. Still, for many years
life goes on, and the constitution does not break up: morphinists
do not, however, live to full age; and, if the habit be contracted in
old age, the patient fades away in no long time. In younger subjects, the social affections grow cold; waywardness and caprice
deepen into selfishness and physical and moral degradation; the
fitful charms of character or the powers of mind, if any such there
were, are blotted and spent; memory fails; amenorrhoea and
sterility overtake the woman, and impotence the man; irregular
febrile attacks appear; albumin may be found in the urine; even
sleep is heavy, or is exhausting and disturbed by hallucinations;
abscesses arise at the punctures of the unclean needle, and heal
badly; the mouth is dry; the teeth decay; gastric catarrh increases,
with symptoms of nausea, retching and flatulence, and of an
epigastric or sub-sternal pain which is rather too characteristic of
morphinism to be put down merely to catarrh; the thread of life
grows frailer; all capacity for fitful work disappears; the inter-
current miseries of the habit are intensified, the moments of ex-
citement briefer and less effectual, until the patient curses the day
he was born: in later middle life at farthest he dies, usually cut off
quickly by some chance malady.[60]

6. *Gradual withdrawal over a period of several days or two or three
weeks is preferable to either sudden withdrawal or drug substitution.*
Allbutt and Dixon, writing in 1906, noted that "the chief and
most grievous symptom is the dangerous collapse which may
follow withdrawal, and if the withdrawal be sudden it may reach
an alarming and even fatal degree." But they added that "as the

sudden withdrawal of morphine is no longer practised this collapse may pass out of observation."[61] The writers who touched
on the subject agreed on the superiority of gradual withdrawal,
although a few added modifications. Jennings stressed the importance of modifying the speed of the withdrawal to the ability
of the patient to sustain it;[62] Hare advocated sudden withdrawal
for those recent addicts who had built up little tolerance for the
drug;[63] and Crothers suggested that "a certain number of persons whose addiction has continued for many years, and who
have passed middle life and are very much debilitated physically
and mentally" might be maintained on morphia under a physician's care.[64]

7. *The prognosis for the cured patient depends upon many factors.*
Osler voiced the widespread opinion that "after an apparent
cure the [addict] patients are only too apt to lapse into the
habit."[65] Perhaps understandably, his pessimism was not shared
by those physicians who specialized in curing addicts. Allbutt
and Dixon cited the high rate of failure for others, but claimed
that "on the whole, our own cases have shown no inevitable
tendency to relapse."[66] Jennings, who admitted that he took
only those patients who showed a strong desire to be cured,
claimed an astounding success rate of 90 percent.[67] Lawton
wrote that "morphinism is very curable," although he regarded
those addicted to cocaine as beyond hope.[68] The most careful
consideration of the question of relapse was written by T. D.
Crothers: "The prognosis in morphinism will vary very widely
according to the condition of the patient, the length of time of
the addiction, and the influence of heredity."[69] The possibility
of a cure, he believed, is especially doubtful in cases in which the
patient has a long-standing addiction, a chronic disease, a
neurotic temperament, or a second addictive drug habit. All
such patients invariably relapse.[70]

Even on the question of treatment, about which many
heated words were exchanged, the writers were in agreement on
the major issues: Patients must be isolated in an asylum or other
institution; and substitution of such drugs as cocaine, cannabis
indica, or even heroin—which had been variously recommended in the last three decades of the nineteenth century—

was a terrible mistake. They disagreed only on the technical questions of how to alleviate withdrawal pains. Mattison recommended regular doses of sodium bromide to subdue the "aches, pains, yawning, sneezing, shivering, nausea, vomiting, diarrhoea, restlessness, delirium, convulsions, exhaustion, [and] collapse" which are "incident to sudden opiate quitting."[71] Crothers noted that many patients are dependent upon the needle and that injections must be continued during withdrawal, even if they contain only minute traces of the drug.[72] Jennings proselytized for his "therapeutic triad" of heart tonics, bicarbonate of soda to neutralize hyperacidity, and Turkish or hot-air baths as a sedative.[73] Allbutt and Dixon disagreed with Jennings' advocacy of heart tonics, and preferred hot water enemas to bicarbonate of soda for diarrhea. But, they claimed,

> whatever the value of auxiliary drugs, the importance of nourishment is much greater. . . . When the nausea or vomiting are troublesome, cold-meat jellies, iced coffee with or without cream, iced champagne, and the like, must be tried by the mouth, and supplemented by nutritive enemas. As the stomach becomes more capable of work, turtle and other strong soups, and like generous restorative foods, must be pressed on the patient; and gentle massage used to promote absorption and blood formation.[74]

These heated exchanges over the relative values of Turkish baths, champagne, and turtle soup may have absorbed their authors, but in fact they represent little real divergence of opinion. On the important issue, British physicians agreed about how to cure drug addiction.

By 1910, the disease model of drug addiction was mature. Although it had originally been developed in the professional medical literature, it eventually filtered into popular fiction and journalism.[75] Particularly in the decade after 1908, there was an outburst of popular writing on the subject. One can see, through the raging emotions of these tales, the clear outline of the disease model of drug addiction that had been developed in the previous decades. Consider, for example, this fairly typical piece of pulp fiction: "The Grey Land of Drugs, Arranged from the

Confessions of a Sojourner, by Kate Jordon," published in *Pearson's Magazine* in 1916. The heroine is a young widow who becomes a drug addict to assuage the physical and psychic pain she feels immediately after the death of her husband. She begins taking orally the morphia that has been prescribed for her by her physician. Her habit grows from a half grain to six grains per day by the end of the year. Her behavior changes from eccentricity to mania. When an old friend guesses that she is a morphia-taker, the heroine denies it, and breaks off their friendship. She moves to London, but continues to deteriorate, both physically and morally, becoming a recluse and a shoplifter. Eventually she meets a fellow drug addict from whom she learns how to inject morphia hypodermically.

> It is true a twinge of my native fastidiousness made me shudder when I first saw the secret parts of her body lacerated and green from a thousand needle pricks, with scattered inflammations and small ulcers; but this oozed away, as did all normal sensations, to become a part of the haze in the grey land where I was a psychic cripple, drifting to complete demoralisation.[76]

In the company of her fellow addict, the heroine squanders all of her capital and reaches the depths of human existence:

> The last stages of my debilitation had set in. In my old clothes I only went out at night. My drugged days were spent reading trashy, exciting romances picked up by the armful at second-hand book-shops, and talking gibberish to animals. . . . I had been growing steadily unclean. Soon I dispensed with my maid, and the home grew into a well of disorder. I ceased changing my clothing or my undergarments. I ceased taking baths; even the thought of freshening water on my flesh would put an edge on my teeth. From tolerating dirt I came to find warmth, even comfort, in bodily staleness. . . . Though my dose of poison was now very heavy, its effects were failing. No longer that first feeling of *bien-être!* No more hazy beatitudes! . . . As this could not be endured without a palliative of some sort I began to drink whiskey. My calloused senses to be affected required large quantities of it, and I took it raw. All this before I was thirty.[77]

Suffice it to say that our heroine is finally rescued by her rejected but faithful friend who brings her to her senses. She undergoes a gradual detoxification program and is restored—almost—to her former self.

> Yet it would be futile to suppose that anyone could have lived so long debased and come so close to death, and bear no marks. My health will never fully return. I must always hide my needle-corroded arms. But this is a small price, after all, for sanity and fearless eyes to meet the clean sweet sun![78]

Thus the disease theory of drug addiction, in virtually every specific, was translated into popular literature, and the image of the drug user was transformed accordingly.[79]

If medical men had been aware that opium produced patient dependence, tolerance, and withdrawal as early as the eighteenth century, why was it not until the 1870s and 1880s that they began to consider opium addiction a disease? The answer to this question is multilayered.

First, and most important, subcutaneous injection made it possible for the patient to take a much larger dose of morphia than was usually taken in laudanum. An ounce of laudanum contained about a grain of morphia. Although some morphia addicts kept their daily dosage at six grains or less, 10 to 13 grains was the average, and 30 or 40 grains per day was not unknown. While there were a few laudanum addicts—most notably De Quincey—whose dosage was a pint or more of laudanum per day, these were very unusual. The more typical dose for a laudanum addict was one or two ounces, far below the usual quantity taken by a morphia addict.[80] Because morphia was injected rather than ingested, less was lost in the process of absorption, and a higher proportion of the drug reached the central nervous system. Thus medical men were seeing, in morphia addicts, patients who were absorbing a much greater quantity of the drug than were opium addicts, and whose physiological complaints were therefore intensified.

Second, the concept of drug addiction—especially in this more rigid and moralistic formulation—was in part a reaction to the sanguine predictions about morphia in the 1850s and 1860s. A theme that runs through the drug addiction literature is that physicians were, and are, guilty of creating drug dependence in their patients because of their incautious administration of morphia. One way to counter this trend is to warn physicians that, by using morphia, they risk creating a new disease even more dangerous than the disease they are trying to treat with it.

Third, physicians were appalled that they had lost control of this new therapy. Initially, hypodermic injections were administered only by physicians, often in a hospital or other institution. But syringes passed eventually into the hands of patients, their servants and relatives, since it was often not possible for a medical man to administer every injection personally. Furthermore, there was no significant legal restriction on the sale of morphia until 1920. Medical prescriptions belonged to the patient and could be refilled indefinitely. From the 1890s, medical men lobbied for legislation to make prescriptions for narcotic drugs nonrepeatable. It is possible to interpret this as a self-serving attempt by medical men to enhance their fees by making patients more dependent upon them. In part, it probably was. But from a different perspective, the same demand can be seen as a call for a preventative public health measure. If addiction is a disease, then it is essential to keep the infectious agent away from the potential victim to the greatest extent possible.

Fourth, the concept of addiction was shaped in part by the class of patients that physicians were seeing. Opium—in powder, pills, laudanum, or in patent or proprietary medicines—could be purchased over the counter at chemists' and other shops. In an age when the fees of medical men often placed their services out of reach of poor people, opium was a cheap and effective form of self-medication. Many persons became opium habitués without ever seeing a physician, and without accepting that they were "sick." Morphia addiction, however, as a therapeutically induced disease, was usually limited to the well-to-do because they were most likely to consult a physician when they were ill, and to be able to afford the cost of morphia and syringes. Finally, the cost of treatment for addiction could be very high. Dr.

Oscar Jennings, for example, charged 200 guineas, payable in advance, for treatment in his retreat outside of Paris.[81] Not surprisingly, medical writers defined drug addiction as a disease of "brain workers" or "the upper classes." Quite simply, those were the patients whom they saw.

So far the explanation for the medical definition of drug addiction as a disease has been limited to factors arising from the doctor's interaction with his patient. But there is another, less immediate level of causation, rooted in the changing role and status of medical men in Victorian society. It is by now a commonplace among social historians that nineteenth-century physicians were appropriating certain functions previously exercised by priests. As the new guardians of morality, they simply substituted new names for ancient evils: madness became mental illness; drunkenness became alcoholism; and the sin of Onan became masturbation. The old sins to be confronted and overcome were, by the late nineteenth century, diseases to be cured.

As late as the early nineteenth century, the very concept of disease was still ill-formed. Nineteenth-century medical men managed symptoms, not just because they could not cure diseases, but often because they had difficulty identifying them. While some diseases, especially acute, epidemic diseases like smallpox, had been identified and even treated effectively, others, especially endemic and chronic diseases, were often confused with the symptoms they produced. The old humoral theory of disease had been discredited in the eighteenth century. While other comprehensive theories, such as Brunonianism and iatrophysics, had arisen and enjoyed a degree of popularity, none was universally accepted.[82]

Adding to the discomforts of medical men in the early nineteenth century was their organizational disarray. The tidy distinction among physicians, surgeons, and apothecaries was breaking down. The elitist medical establishment, centered in the Royal Colleges, was under severe attack from reformers like Thomas Wakley and his journal, *Lancet,* and organizations of dissatisfied general practitioners, like the Provincial Medical and Surgical Association (later to become the British Medical Association).[83] Thus on both theoretical and organizational levels, the medical profession in the early nineteenth century was weak and on the defensive.

By the late nineteenth century, however, the situation had changed considerably. From pioneering studies at the Paris Hospital and the work of Schwann and Virchow came the basis of a scientific, cellular pathology. The work of bacteriologists, most notably Koch and Pasteur, eventually gave medical men the germ theory of disease.[84] While these accomplishments did not immediately lead to dramatic advances in therapeutics, they did give medical men a confidence that they could identify diseases and their causes with a precision previously unknown. The work of the reformers eventually produced the Medical Act of 1858, which laid the foundation for the legal structure of the modern medical profession in Britain. Moreover, as M. Jeanne Peterson has recently shown, medical men began to carve out a new autonomy for themselves by the power they wielded first in medical schools and later in the major teaching hospitals.[85] Finally, the public health movement achieved considerable legislative success in the 1860s and 1870s, which vindicated an interventionist stance and encouraged British medical men to extend the scope of public health concerns.[86] By the 1880s, medical men were considerably more confident and aggressive than they had been just thirty years before. They believed that they could define disease with accuracy, and they were willing to push for legislation which they believed was necessary to control it.

The attempt to define drug addiction as a disease was a part of this aggressive thrust, but it was derived from, and secondary to, the more important attempt to define alcoholism as a disease. Unlike some German and American physicians who saw drug addiction as a unique problem to be discussed singularly, British physicians tended to see it as part of the much wider problem of "inebriety" or "narcomania." Indeed, drug addiction was often called "drug inebriety." It was regularly subsumed in broader discussions, such as Richardson's *Diseases of Modern Life* or Kerr's *Inebriety or Narcomania,* and it occupied a decidedly secondary position in the concerns of the SSI. Even many of the most important subissues—inheritability, psychic as opposed to physiological causal factors, or compulsory confinement of addicts—were derived from the contemporary discussion on alcoholism.[87] Not until the end of the first decade of the twentieth century did drug addiction clearly emerge in Britain as an entirely separate issue in both professional and popular literature. At this level of analysis, then, the definition of drug addiction as a disease was simply one of the smaller conquests made by the advancing medical army in the late nineteenth century.

Between 1870 and 1910, public and professional opinion about narcotic drugs turned around. Opiates, and later cocaine, came under attack from novelists, public health reformers, and medical men for being morally corrupting, poisonous, and pathogenic. Furthermore, the attack on narcotic drugs coincided with the development of new drugs which often fulfilled the same function with considerably less risk. The real wonder drug of the twentieth century, acetylsalicylic acid ("aspirin"), was first marketed by the Bayer Company in 1899. It filled the role of a cheap analgesic for relief of such chronic conditions as rheumatism, as well as periodic problems such as headaches or menstrual cramps, for which laudanum or even morphia had previously been taken. The first barbiturate, veronal, was developed in 1906, and was quickly followed by others. While barbiturates are far from harmless—as British medical men realized almost immediately—they were relatively safer than opiates when used as sedatives. Finally, the development of procaine ("novocaine") in the first decade of the twentieth century meant that cocaine was no longer essential as a local anesthetic in dental surgery. Thus the therapeutic range of narcotic drugs began to shrink in the early twentieth century, and continued to do so in the 1920s with the refinement of substitute drugs.

Bombarded with warnings about the dangers of narcotic drugs, both professional medical men and the public restricted their use. Persons who used narcotic drugs increasingly stood out from the mass of the population who did not. What was the effect of this changed perception on actual narcotic drug use?

Unfortunately, there is no way of discovering exactly when narcotic drug use in Britain began to decline and by how much. In fact, 1859 was the last full year in which the amount of opium which entered Britain for home consumption was recorded in the customs records. Nor is there any survey data, comparable to nineteenth-century American surveys of pharmacists and medical men, from which one could estimate the extent of drug use. While the amount of opium imported into Britain remained very high until 1920, that does not mean that all of it was consumed in Britain. To the contrary, some of it was made into patent medicines, which were then exported. But most of the opium imported into Britain from the 1890s onward was converted into morphia and then exported (see Chapter 10).

In his book, *Dark Paradise: Opiate Addiction in America before 1940*, David Courtwright establishes, on the basis of extensive survey data, that American narcotic drug use peaked in the early 1890s and declined rapidly thereafter. Therapeutic drug users who had become addicted in the 1860s and 1870s had begun to die off. Because narcotic drugs were somewhat harder to procure, and much more cautiously administered by physicians who had become convinced of their dangers, there were many fewer persons addicted after the 1890s. Because the developments in medicine, and even in narcotic drug regulation, were similar in both countries, there is every reason to believe that the general pattern of medical drug use in Britain corresponded to that in America. In other words, it is likely that narcotic drug use peaked in Britain in the period between 1885 and 1895, and declined thereafter.

If drug use was declining in Britain during the early twentieth century, then how does one account for the fact that it came to be seen as a significant social menace in the period 1910 to 1930? Broadly speaking, it was because the *types* of persons who were using drugs changed. Opium addiction in the nineteenth century was largely invisible because so many persons used the drug for everyday medical purposes. Insofar as morphia addiction *was* visible, it was largely confined to therapeutically addicted, middle-class, middle-aged persons. While later Victorians may have felt sorry for these poor souls, or may even have felt mild disapproval for their lack of will power, they did not see them as a social threat. But in the early twentieth century, many more "recreational" drug users began to appear: Chinese smokers in Limehouse, Soho drug hustlers, and cocaine-sniffing young bohemians in West End night clubs. Even the pharmaceutical industry, through its involvement in the morphia traffic to China, was implicated in this new pattern of drug use. People no longer took narcotic drugs, it seemed, because they were sick, but because they were seeking kicks. In short, the paradigmatic drug user shifted from the harmless habitué of the nineteenth century to the street-wise dope fiend of the twentieth. That was cause for concern.

Notes

1. Alexander Wood, "Treatment of Neuralgic Pains by Narcotic Injections," *BMJ*, August 28, 1858, 721–723. Wood had an earlier article which did not attract much attention: "A New Method of Treating Neuralgia by the Direct Application of Opiates to the Painful Points," *Edinburgh Medical and Surgical Journal, 82,* (1855), 265–281. See also Charles Hunter, "On Narcotic Injections in Neuralgia," *Medical Times and Gazette,* October 16, 1858, 408–409; "On Narcotic Injections in Neuralgia," *Medical Times and Gazette,* October 30, 1858, 457–458; "A Series of Narcotic Injections into the Cellular Tissue in Neuralgia and Other Diseases," *BMJ,* January 8, 1859, 19–20; "Practical Remarks on the Hypodermic Treatment of Disease," *Lancet,* October 17, 1863, II, 444–445, 675–676; *On the Speedy Relief of Pain and Other Nervous Affections by Means of Hypodermic Method,* (London, 1865); and "Hypodermic Administration of Certain Medicines," *Medical Times and Gazette,* June 3, 1865, 584–587.

2. Zachariah Laurence, "The Antiphlogistic Powers of Morphia Illustrated by Its Use in the Treatment of Acute Inflammations of the Sclerotic and Iris," *Medical Times and Gazette,* December 31, 1859, 651–652; John K. Spender, "The Hypodermic Action of Morphia," *BMJ,* June 9, 1860, 436–437; J. Henry Bennet, "On the Hypodermic Treatment of Uterine Pain," *Lancet,* March 12, 1864, *I,* 296–297; and W. Ogle, "Injection of Acetate of Morphia into the Cellular Tissue of the Arm, in Delirium Treatments," *Medical Times and Gazette,* July 21, 1869, 54–55. For a detailed study of the development of hypodermic medication, see Norman Howard-Jones, "A Critical Study of the Origins and Early Development of Hy-

podermic Medication," *Journal of the History of Medicine, 2* (Spring 1947), 201–247.

3. Edward T. Wilson, "Notes on the Subcutaneous Injection of Morphia," *St. George's Hospital Report, 4* (1869), 19.

4. Wilson, p. 30.

5. Arthur Evershed, "On the Hypodermic Injection of Morphia," *Medical Times and Gazette,* May 1, 1869, 463.

6. *C&D,* March 3, 1888, 297–298.

7. G. Laughton Scott, *The Morphia Habit and its Painless Treatment* (London, 1930), p. 71.

8. Scott, p. 75.

9. Scott, p. 75.

10. Scott, p. 90.

11. Scott, p. 91.

12. Scott, p. 93.

13. I do not claim that these 51 cases are all that were reported in the medical literature; they are simply the cases that I found in the course of my research. Several books and a few articles detailed more than one case: "Morphia Tolerance," *C&D,* September 14, 1878, 395; "The Sudden Discontinuance of Hypodermic Injections of Morphia after Protracted . . . Use," *Lancet,* January 11, 1879, 70; "Cure of Morphine Habit by Sodium . . . Bromide," *BMJ,* April 15, 1899, 897; "An Extraordinary Morphia Case," *Lancet,* March 4, 1882, 343; "Morphine Habit . . . of Long Standing Cured by Bromide Poisoning," *BMJ,* July 10, 1897, 76; "A Remarkable Case of Morphia Addiction," *BMJ,* May 11, 1889, 1051; Robert Jones, "Notes on Some Cases of Morphinomania," *Journal of Mental Science,* July, 1902, 479–94; W. S. Playfair, "On the Cure of the Morphia and Alcoholic . . . Habit," *Journal of Mental Science,* July, 1889, 179–84; G. Laughton Scott, *The Morphine Habit and its Painless Treatment* (London, 1930); S. Sharkey, "The Treatment of Morphia Habitués by Suddenly Discontinuing the . . . Drug," *Lancet,* December 29, 1883, 1120; O. Jennings, *The Morphia Habit . . . and its Voluntary Renunciation* (London, 1909); A. H. Prichard, "An Aspect of the Morphia-Habit in an Early Stage," *Clinical Journal,* August 5, 1903, 255–56; W. O. Jennings, "On the Physiological Cure of the Morphia Habit . . .," *Lancet,* August 10, 1901, 360–68; and F. E. Anstie, "On the Effects of the Prolonged Use of Morphia by Sub-

cutaneous Injection," *The Practitioner, 6* (1871), 148–57; B. W. Richardson, "Practical Notes on the Morphine Habit," *Asclepiad, 5* (1888), 301–15.

14. Thomas Clifford Allbutt, "On the Abuse of Hypodermic Injections of Morphia," *The Practitioner, 5* (1870), 329–330.

15. George Oliver, "On Hypodermic Injections of Morphia," *The Practitioner, 6* (1871), 75–80; and F. E. Anstie, "On the Effects of the Prolonged Use of Morphia by Subcutaneous Injection," *The Practitioner, 6* (1871), 148–157. See also J. Pennock Sleightholme, "Hypodermic Morphia in a General Hospital," *The Practitioner, 7* (1872), 23–28.

16. Joseph F. Payne, *Thomas Sydenham* (London: T. Fisher Unwin, 1900), p. 182.

17. Melvin P. Earles, "Studies in the Development of Experimental Pharmacology in the 18th and Early 19th Centuries," unpublished Ph.D. thesis, University of London, 1961.

18. See John Jones, *The Mysteries of Opium Reveal'd* (London, 1701), pp. 27–28; Samuel Crumpe, *An Inquiry into the Nature and Properties of Opium* (London, 1793), p. 178; and Sir Astley Cooper, "On Vegetable and Mineral Poisons," *Lancet,* 1824, III, 171.

19. Edward Levinstein, *Morbid Craving for Morphia* (London: Smith, Elder, 1878), p. 3. Another German whose papers were occasionally published in English was Dr. H. Obersteiner, "Chronic Morphinism," *Brain, 2* (1879–1880), 449–465, and "Further Observations on Chronic Morphinism," *Brain, 5* (1882–1883), 324–331.

20. Levinstein, p. 7.

21. Levinstein, p. 113.

22. Levinstein, p. 126.

23. *Proceedings of the SSI,* No. 1 (July 1884), 1. The SSI grew out of an older organization, The Society for Promoting Legislation for the Control and Cure of Habitual Drunkards, which had been founded in 1876.

24. *Proceedings,* p. 3.

25. Norman Kerr, *Inebriety or Narcomania: Its Etiology, Pathology, Treatment and Jurisprudence* (London: H. K. Lewis, 3rd ed., 1894), pp. 10–11.

26. Roy M. Macleod, "The Edge of Hope: Social Policy and Chronic

Alcoholism, 1870–1900," *Journal of the History of Medicine, 22* (July 1967), 215–245.

27. Kerr, pp. 100–101.

28. Kerr, pp. 102–103.

29. Kerr, pp. 105–106.

30. Kerr, p. 109.

31. Kerr, p. 117.

32. Bruce D. Johnson, "Righteousness Before Revenue: The Forgotten Moral Crusade Against the Indo-Chinese Opium Trade," *Journal of Drug Issues, 5* (Fall 1975), 304–326.

33. See Rutherford Alcock, "Opium and Common Sense," *Nineteenth Century, 10* (December 1881), 854–868; "The Opium Trade," *Journal of Society and the Arts,* January 20, 1882, reprinted in Hartmann Henry Sultzberger, ed., *All About Opium* (London, 1884), pp. 27–66; and "Sir George Cambell's letter to the 'Times'," in Sultzberger, pp. 191–193.

34. "Sir George Birdwood's first letter to 'The Times'," in Sultzberger, p. 22.

35. Sultzberger, p. 24.

36. William J. Moore, "Opium: its Use and Abuse," *Medical Reporter, 1* (December 1, 1892), 224.

37. Moore, p. 225.

38. Moore, "The Opium Question," *Indian Medical Gazette,* September 1 and October 1, 1880, 225–230, 257–264; and F. J. Mouat, "The Ethics of Opium and Alcohol," *Lancet,* November 12 and 19, 1892, 1090–1092, 1152–1154.

39. Mouat, p. 1092.

40. "Report of the Royal Commission on Opium," *PP,* 1895, *XLII,* p. 31ff.

41. William Huntly, "Opium Addiction: Is It a Disease?" *Proceedings of the SSI,* No. 50 (November 1896), 1–12.

42. J. B. Mattison, "The Treatment of the Morphine Disease," *Proceedings of the SSI,* No. 33 (August 1892), 1. Mattison and T. D. Crothers, although Americans, were highly regarded in Britain. Their work was well-known, and Mattison was an honorary member of the SSI. Another American physician, H. H. Kane, whose books on drug addiction were published in the 1880s, was not influential in Britain.

43. Harrington Sainsbury, *Drugs and the Drug Habit* (London: Methuen, 1909), p. 223.

44. Sir William Collins, "The Ethics and Law of Drug and Alcohol Addiction," *British Journal of Inebriety, 13* (January 1916), 141.

45. T. Clifford Allbutt and W. E. Dixon, "Opium Poisoning, and other Intoxications," in Thomas Clifford Allbutt and Humphry Davy Rolleston, eds., *A System of Medicine by Many Writers* (London: Macmillan, 1906), II, p. 949.

46. T. D. Crothers, *Morphinism and Narcomanias from Other Drugs* (Philadelphia: W. B. Saunders, 1902), p. 42.

47. Crothers, pp. 43, 44–45, 56.

48. See also Francis Hare, "The Withdrawal of Narcotics from Habitués," *British Journal of Inebriety, 8* (October 1910); Oscar Jennings, *The Morphia Habit and its Voluntary Renunciation* (London: Ballière, Tindall & Cox, 1909), pp. 2, 29, 44–45; Walter Lawton, "Stimulants and Narcotics and their Users and Abusers," *Pharm. J.*, February 1908, 268; Huntly, pp. 4–5; and William Osler, *The Principles and Practice of Medicine* (London: Y. J. Pentland, 1894), p. 1005.

49. Lawton, p. 269; Jennings, "On the Physiological Cure of the Morphia Habit," *Lancet*, August 10, 1901, 361; and Crothers, pp. 57, 134.

50. Allbutt and Dixon, p. 951.

51. Jennings, 1901, 193–194.

52. Allbutt and Dixon, p. 951.

53. Sainsbury, p. 227.

54. Crothers, p. 46.

55. Crothers, pp. 32–33.

56. *Ibid.* Robert Armstrong-Jones used almost exactly the same language in "Drug Addiction in Relation to Mental Disorder," *British Journal of Inebriety, 12* (January 1915), 129.

57. Lawton, p. 269.

58. Osler, p. 1005.

59. Jennings, 1909, Preface; and Jennings, "The Frequency of Morphinism," *British Journal of Inebriety, 8* (July 1910), 193–196.

60. Allbutt and Dixon, pp. 954–955. See also Osler, p. 1006; Lawton, 545; Jennings, 1909, pp. 14–18; Jennings, 1910, 194; A. H. Prichard, "An Aspect of the Morphia Habit in an Early Stage,"

110 The Perception of Danger

Clinical Journal, August 5, 1903, 256; Sainsbury, pp. 219–223; Huntly, p. 9; and Crothers, 45–53, 106–115.

61. Allbutt and Dixon, p. 958. This had not always been the case; see S. J. Sharkey, "The Treatment of Morphia Habitués by Suddenly Discontinuing the Drug," *Lancet,* December 29, 1883, II, 1120–1121.

62. Jennings, 1901, 361.

63. Hare, 87.

64. Crothers, p. 141.

65. Osler, p. 1007.

66. Allbutt and Dixon, p. 962.

67. Jennings, 1909, p. 9.

68. Lawton, 570.

69. Crothers, p. 139.

70. Crothers, pp. 139–141.

71. Mattison, p. 1.

72. Crothers, p. 173.

73. Jennings, 1901, and 1909, 6–7.

74. Allbutt and Dixon, p. 256; and Hare, pp. 89–90.

75. The popularization had begun as early as the 1880s, most notably with Seymour Sharkey's "Morphinomania" (*Nineteenth Century,* 22, September 1887, 335–342).

76. Kate Jordan, "The Grey Land of Drugs, Arranged from the Confession of a Sojourner," *Pearson's Magazine,* 1916, 306.

77. Jordan, 307.

78. Jordan, 308.

79. Other contemporary fiction embodying the disease theory of drug addiction includes Maud Diver, *The Great Amulet* (1908), and Mary Lake, *The Drug Slave* (1913).

80. The data for these generalizations are drawn from the cases cited in Chapter 4 (note 28) and Chapter 7 (note 13).

81. G. Laughton Scott, *The Morphine Habit and its Painless Treatment* (London: H. K. Lewis, 1930), p. 87.

82. See Erwin Ackerknecht, *Therapeutics from the Primitives to the 20th Century* (New York: Hafner, 1973); Lester S. King, *The Medical World of the Eighteenth Century,* (Huntington, N.Y.: R. E. Krieger,

1971); "Medical Philosophy, 1836–1844," in Lloyd G. Stevenson and Robert P. Multhauf, eds., *Medicine, Science, and Culture* (Baltimore: Johns Hopkins University Press, 1968), pp. 143–159; and Gerald Geison, "Social and Institutional Factors in the Stagnancy of English Physiology, 1840–1870," *Bulletin of the History of Medicine, 46* (1972), 30–58.

83. See M. Jeanne Peterson, *The Medical Profession in Mid-Victorian London* (Berkeley: University of California Press, 1978), chapter I; Charles Newman, *The Evolution of Medical Education in the Nineteenth Century* (London: Oxford University Press, 1957); W. J. Reader, *Professional Men: The Rise of the Professional Classes in Nineteenth Century England* (London: Weidenfeld & Nicolson, 1966); Noel Parry and José Parry *The Rise of the Medical Profession: A Study of Collective Mobility* (London: Croom Helm, 1976); and Edwina C. Sherrington, "Thomas Wakley and Reform: 1832–62," D. Phil. thesis, Oxford University, 1973.

84. Erwin Ackerknecht, *Medicine at the Paris Hospital, 1794–1848* (Baltimore: Johns Hopkins University Press, 1967); W. H. McMenemy, "Cellular Pathology, with Special References to the Influence of Virchow's Teachings on Medical Thought and Practice," in F. N. L. Poynter ed., *Medicine and Science in the 1860's* (London: Wellcome Institute, 1968), pp. 13–43; William Bulloch, *The History of Bacteriology* (London: Oxford University Press, 1960); Hubert A. Lechevalier and Morris Solotorovsky, *Three Centuries of Microbiology* (New York: McGraw-Hill, 1965); and J. K. Crellin, "The Dawn of the Germ Theory: Particles, Infection, and Biology," in Poynter, pp. 57–76.

85. Peterson, passim.

86. See William Frazer, *A History of English Public Health, 1834–1939* (London: Bailliere, Tindall & Cox, 1950), chapters 1–7; C. Fraser Brockington, *Public Health in the Nineteenth Century* (Edinburgh: E. & S. Livingstone, 1965); Jeanne L. Brand, *Doctors and the State: the British Medical Profession and Government Action in Public Health, 1870–1912* (Baltimore: Johns Hopkins University Press, 1965); and Roy M. Macleod, "The Anatomy of State Medicine: Concept and Application," in Poynter, pp. 199–227.

87. See William F. Bynum, "Chronic Alcoholism in the First Half of the 19th Century," *Bulletin of the History of Medicine, 92* (1968), 160–185; and Amy A. Pruitt, "Approaches to Alcoholism in Mid-Victorian Britain," *Clio Medica, 9* (1974), 93–101.

PART THREE

Narcotic Drugs as Social Menace, 1910–1930

CHAPTER EIGHT

Agents of Corruption

In the period between 1910 and 1930, it would have been virtually impossible for a literate Briton to have avoided the subject of narcotic drugs. In newspapers, fiction, and films, the public was deluged with a mass of fact and opinion (often the latter masquerading as the former) about drugs. The perception of danger, expressed in a clear but controlled way in the previous four decades, gave way to near hysteria. Narcotic drugs, it seemed, were no longer confined to a handful of grimy opium dens in Limehouse, serving Asian seamen and a few offbeat Englishmen; their corrupting influence reached out into London's West End and beyond. Moreover, there was a subtle but significant shift in the portrayal of those characters who used narcotic drugs. In the representations of drug-takers in late nineteenth-century fiction, opium-smoking was a mark of their existing depravity. By contrast, the fictional drug-takers of the early twentieth century were often young innocents—confused, perhaps, but not depraved—whose demise was the result of their involvement with opiates or cocaine. Narcotic drugs were the agents of their downfall. This changed depiction of drugs in popular literature rested on two developments in the decade and a half prior to the outbreak of World War I: the influx of Chinese into London and other seaports, and the emergence of cocaine as a recreational "street drug."

Although there had been Chinese in Stepney as early as the 1780s, and a Chinese presence in East London and other ports

throughout the nineteenth century, their number was so small
as to make them rare items of interest. As late as 1901, there
were only 387 persons living in England and Wales who had
been born in China. By 1911 their number had grown to 1,319,
and by 1921, it had reached 2,419.[1] Compared with communities of Chinese in parts of the Empire or in America, this
was a miniscule number. But it was enough to populate a tiny
Chinatown along two streets in East London—Pennyfields and
the Limehouse Causeway. The Chinese community was large
enough to be visible and, in the eyes of some persons, to consti-
tute a social threat.

Chinese immigrants to Britain were, for the most part,
sailors who had grown tired of the sea, had jumped ship, or had
simply gotten stranded in a port city. They were overwhelmingly
male. According to the three censuses between 1901 and 1921,
men outnumbered women by seven to one.[2] They kept close ties
to their seafaring origins, opening boarding houses, shops, and
occasionally restaurants that catered to the large flow of Oriental
sailors that came through British ports. Gradually, in the twenties, they began to open laundries throughout the country. Because of the shortage of Chinese women, the men often con-
sorted with Caucasian women. The Chinese also imported their
own recreation, in the form of gambling games like puk-a-poo,
and opium smoking.[3]

The combination of miscegenation, strange gambling
games, and an exotic vice, all publicized in the popular press,
aroused the curiosity and often the hostility of Britons. After the
First World War, the housing shortage in East London provided
still another flashpoint between Chinese immigrants and English
residents of Limehouse. This hostility to the Chinese, and disapproval of their ways, was reflected in the London County Council by-laws, passed in 1909, which prohibited opium smoking in
licensed seamen's boarding houses, and in occasional race riots
that broke out in the East End after the war.[4] Then as now, the
combination of colored immigrants and native Cockneys, living
side by side amidst the squalor of the East End, proved to be a
volatile mixture.

The narcotic effects of coca leaves, when chewed by South

American Indians, had been observed by Europeans since the sixteenth century.[5] Yet it was not until 1855 that Gaedcke first isolated cocaine, the alkaloid derivative of coca, and it was not until the 1880s that cocaine was introduced into European medicine. In 1884, Carl Koller first discovered cocaine's use as a local anesthetic. One of the earliest and most enthusiastic proponents of its therapeutic use was a young Viennese physician, Sigmund Freud, who described the drug's stimulating powers in his cocaine papers, published between 1884 and 1887.[6] Although Freud eventually abandoned self-experimentation with the drug, and even expressed some misgivings about it, cocaine had nevertheless passed into the medical armamentarium of European and American physicians by the late 1880s. Cocaine's most significant medical use was as a local anesthetic in ocular and dental surgery.[7] It was also sold in patent medicines and in special concoctions in pharmacies as a "pick-me-up" for those in need of a cheap and effective stimulant. By the beginning of the 1890s, however, concern was already being voiced in the medical and pharmaceutical press that cocaine was becoming a dangerous drug of addiction.[8] The overdose deaths of two young actresses in 1901 created such a stir that there was some parliamentary discussion about limiting its sale.[9] While nothing eventually came of this incident, it is indicative both of the emergence of cocaine as a recreational drug among London's bohemian set and of the public's changed perceptions.

Despite this early cocaine scare, the Chinese, with their alleged involvement in the drug traffic, were the primary targets of popular journalists in the early twentieth century. Headlines reported "Opium Den Raid/Chinamen's Three Savage Guardians/Drug Heavy Air," or "Limehouse Secrets/Barred Doors, Trap Flaps, and Hidden Bell in Opium Raid."[10] The presence of women in opium dens charged the accounts with a further sense of danger. Gone was the Victorian reporters' depiction of the half-comic, half-sad, middle-aged wife of the Chinese opium master, resigned to her lot of preparing pipes for an endless succession of Oriental smokers. She was replaced by the much more potent symbol of the young white virgin, drawn to her demise by rigged gambling games and opium. Headlines told the stories of "White Girls 'Hypnotised' by Yellow Men;" "East End Dens of Vice/Babies of Every Colour;" or "The Lure of the Yellow Man/English Girls' 'Moral Suicide'/Fatal Fascination."[11] Even more sinister and frightening, however, was the specter of a Chinese syndicate, "backed by millions in money and powerful, if mysterious, influences" dedicated to the propagation of vice. Its leader was reputed to be a "Chinese Moriarity," a criminal mastermind who spoke familiarly to one reporter of prominent people and their whereabouts while smoking opium.[12]

These same themes—opium, seduction, and villainy—were echoed in postwar popular fiction. In *The Laughter of Fools* (1920), Lady Dorothy Mills told the story of orphan Louise Verith, who, after a disastrous affair and then early widowhood abroad, returns to London in search of pleasure and escape. It is wartime. Louise resumes acquaintance with a group of rich young people who are avid hedonists and call themselves "the Binge Club." Finding "nothing but champagne to drink, nothing but coronas to smoke, nothing but women to love," they seek out an opium den. The description of Louise's first opium dream rests solidly on De Quincey: she has complete recollection of the distant past; time and space are infinitely extended; the sound of music is "thrillingly, unbearably sweet;" she is at one with the universe.[13] The opium den is like the Underworld; the girl who prepares the opium looks like a "little witch," and the proprietor dabbles in witchcraft.

Eventually, Louise's eyes are opened to her folly, as she narrowly misses a raid on an opium den she frequents:

> It was sure to be an unsavoury case. Supposing her name were dragged in. Every one would blame her, probably cut her. She had been warned a dozen times. . . . She had always known in her saner moments that it was a place no decent woman had a right to go.[14]

Her wild days over, Louise sets out, at the close of the novel, to join a friend doing volunteer work among the wounded in France.

The most important popular fiction of the period was those stories and novels which were set in London's Chinatown and which mirrored the themes of popular journalism. Thomas Burke established his reputation as a short-story writer with *Limehouse Nights* (1917). What Burke knew about opium he learned from De Quincey. He admitted that the *Confessions,* the first book he ever bought, made a profound impression on him. Furthermore, Burke's description of opium's effects is almost identical to De Quincey's.[15]

Most of the tales in *Limehouse Nights* concern the intense passion of Chinese men for Cockney girls. There is usually an opponent to the Chinaman—whether father, husband, or other lover—and the plot revolves around methods of Oriental revenge. In "The Chink and the Child," for example, Chen Huan carries off the beautiful child Lily and adores her as a goddess. Her brutal father finds her and beats her to death, whereupon Chen Huan sends him a venomous snake as a "love token." Burke's stories are cast in a hazy, dreamlike cocoon in which fantasy and reality are often indistinguishable. In "The Perfect Girl," John Sway Too tells of cheating at cards and being found out and beaten. Suddenly, a beautiful white maiden with shining black hair drives away his attackers and takes him to her "palace." There she heals his wounds, feeds and loves him. In the morning she presses on him money and provisions as parting gifts. Where does one find this perfect maid? In little white pellets of opium.

In Burke's stories the Chinese are, if not exactly heroic, then often admirable characters. At worst they are unfortunate victims. By contrast, in the fiction of Sax Rohmer, the Chinese are villains. In the Fu Manchu stories (first published in 1913), Rohmer created an antihero of surpassing genius and limitless evil. In *The Yellow Claw* (1925), an international drug syndicate is controlled from Limehouse by the invisible Mr. King, a fictionalized version of a real-life drug dealer, Brilliant Chang (see Chapter 11). Throughout the novel, Rohmer echoes De Quincey's injunctions about the power of opium to devour a person's entire life. One addict-character admits:

One may drink opium or inject morphine; these and other crude measures may satisfy temporarily, but if one would enjoy the delights of that fairy land, of that enchanted realm which bountiful nature has concealed in the heart of the poppy, one must retire from the ken of goths and vandals who do not appreciate such exquisite delights; one must dedicate not an hour, snatched from grasping society, but successive days and nights to the goddess. . . .[16]

All of the fictional elements—conspiratorial Chinese, ruined virgins, and tenacious police inspectors—that characterize Sax Rohmer's work came together most forcefully in his immensely popular mystery, *Dope: A Story of Chinatown and the Drug Traffic* (1919), which was inspired by the Billie Carleton case of the previous year (see Chapter 9). Rita Dresden, an aspiring actress, becomes the girlfriend of Sir Lucien Pyne, director of a major theatrical syndicate. She does not submit to his advances, but on opening night, abject with fear, she sniffs Sir Lucien's proffered cocaine and thus is in his power. Quickly Rita becomes addicted to cocaine and then to veronal, and then, inevitably, to opium.

But if she had walked blindly into the clutches of cocaine and veronal, her subsequent experiments with chandu [smoking opium] were prompted by indefensible curiosity, and a false vanity which urged her to do everything that was 'done' by the ultra-smart and vicious set of which she had become a member.[17]

Rita is introduced to Mrs. Sin, half-Cuban, half-Jewish wife of Sin Sin Wa, who controls illegal drugs in London from an underground warehouse in Limehouse. Mrs. Sin arranges "chandu parties" at her exclusive and expensive "House of a Hundred Raptures." "Not to know Mrs. Sin was to be outside the magic circle [of] . . . smart people who practised the latest absurdities."[18] Rita's initiation into opium is strongly reminiscent of De Quincey, whom Rohmer mentions several times. She experiences the distortion of space and time, heightened sense perceptions, and feelings of "infinite repose." Rohmer has several characters mention that opium has "impaired Rita's will"

and weakened her moral sense. Inspector Kerry, who eventually
uncovers the drug syndicate, is more explicit: "It's bad enough
in heathens, but for an Englishwoman to dope herself is down-
right unchristian and beastly."[19]

Through Rita's addiction Rohmer also explores the evils of
the drug traffic. As her addiction becomes more insistent, Rita
finds that her sources for drugs suddenly disappear or refuse to
supply her any longer. Finally her only source is one Kazmah,
who poses as an Egyptian fortuneteller, but is in fact part of the
drug syndicate controlled by Sin Sin Wa, Mrs. Sin, and Sir Lucien Pyne. Rohmer's comments on this drug subculture resonate
with De Quincey's comment about the "one true church of
opium." "Drug-takers form a kind of brotherhood, and outside
the charmed circle they are as secretive as members of the Mafia,
the Comorra, or the Catouse-Menegant."[20]

In the closing chapters of the novel there are interesting
depictions of the operations of a drug monopoly. Sin Sin Wa, a
shrewd businessman, discovers lead shots in a shipment of
opium balls and lowers his payment without fear of reprisal. Sir
Lucien, attempting to stop the blackmail against Rita, is mur-
dered by Mrs. Sin. Rohmer even suggests that "the authorities"
either refuse to accept the existence of a drug syndicate, or
worse, are in the syndicate's pay and turn a blind eye.

But opium was not the only drug which, in the stories of
thriller-writers, threatened Britain. Journalists periodically discovered "the cocaine menace." The drug was allegedly pushed
by a "Vice Trust" in London, through female agents: "The
woman drug fiend is almost invariably a missionary of her vice.
She wishes to communicate the habit to her friends and to her
clients. The more converts she makes the better the trade and
higher the profit to the Vice Trust." Young and innocent girls,
naively seeking adventure, are introduced to cocaine by "interesting and apparently wealthy bohemians." Then "moral infection takes place." The traffic exists in all the fashionable neighborhoods of the West End: "You will find the woman dope fiend
in Chelsea, in Mayfair, and Maida Vale. An obscure traffic is
pursued in certain doubtful teashops. The sale of certain beauty
specifics is only a mask for the illicit traffic in drugs."[21]

The traffic in cocaine was a theme that ran through popular fiction. John Rhode's popular mystery, *A.S.F.: The Story of a Great Conspiracy* (1924) focused on the international illicit traffic in cocaine. William Westwood, the Home Secretary, is under intense political pressure to uncover the source of the cocaine supply that has resulted in a recent alarming rise in addiction. Westwood's secretary, Frank Clements, unwittingly discovers that Richard Westwood, William's brother, living in seclusion in France, is head of the operation which smuggles cocaine into England, mixed with the sawdust of a cheap but distinctive pottery. Cocaine customers buy the pottery for £50 per piece, and the drug is delivered in it. Code letters for all dealings are "A.S.F."—variously "Asiatic Soap Factory," "A Sincere Friend," and so on.

The novel makes use of heavy ironies to underscore the personal and social toll of cocaine addiction. Richard's daughter, Thérèse, unknown to him, is dying of an unexplained cocaine toxemia, but she cannot resist the fatal lure of the drug. A former addict is killed by inhaling a deadly vegetable poison at the very moment he intends to expose the smuggling operation to Frank Clements. The Secretary himself has only risen to his position with the extensive financial backing of his brother, the drug dealer. In short, cocaine is not confined to a few fashionable decadents who choose to enter the forbidden world of Limehouse, but penetrates the very fabric of English social and political life.

As late as 1934, Dorothy Sayers made use of cocaine in one of her Lord Peter Wimsey mysteries, *Murder Must Advertise*. Lord Peter assumes the role of a copywriter to ferret out a murderer at an advertising firm. In the course of his investigation, he discovers that an employee is using the firm as a cover in a complicated plot to distribute smuggled cocaine. Sayers paints a number of lurid scenes in which Lord Peter penetrates the circle of wealthy and decadent young thrill-seekers surrounding one Dian de Momerie. They use cocaine supplied by Major Tod Milligan, who keeps an open house for parties on weekends. But Milligan is merely a small fish; the entire traffic is run by far more powerful and wealthy figures who smuggle cocaine into the country on speedboats by way of the Norfolk coast. The "brains" behind the entire operation is an unprepossessing fellow who runs a tobacconist's shop in the West End. Lord Peter, of course, unravels the mystery and brings the crew of villains to justice.

The most notorious "dope novel" of the postwar period was Aleister Crowley's *Diary of a Drug Fiend* (1922). Crowley, who was a mystic, a satanist, and an all-around poseur, had already been publicly described as "the most evil man in all of England." The *Diary*, with its celebration of the effects of cocaine and heroin, cemented his dubious reputation. Unlike the novels by Rhode and Sayers, the plot of the *Diary* is simple, bordering on artless. Peter Pendragon, a wealthy and personable young Englishman and former fighter pilot, is introduced to cocaine by a group of London bohemians after the war. He and his beautiful young bride travel the Continent on their honeymoon, blissfully snorting kilograms of cocaine and heroin. In Naples, they run out of both drugs and money, and they begin the painful process of facing up to their addiction and to rehabilitation. The real focus of the novel is not the plot, however, but the effects of cocaine and heroin. Pendragon recounts the heightened sexual response to his fiancée that comes from his first sniff of cocaine:

> I stopped her song at last. My mouth was on her mouth. We were driving in the chariot of the Sun through the circus of the Universe. We didn't know where we were going, and we didn't care. We had no sense of time at all. There was a sequence of sensations; but there was no means of regulating them. It was as if one's mental clock had suddenly gone mad.
> I have no gauge of time, subjectively speaking, but it must have been a long while before our mouths separated, for as this happened I recognised the fact that we were very far from the club.
> She spoke to me for the first time. Her voice thrilled dark unfathomable deeps of being. I tingled in every fibre. And what she said was this:—
> 'Your kiss is bitter with cocaine.'[22]

The book is studded with other descriptions of the effects of drugs, which range from clinical to rapturous. For example, Pendragon describes his first experience with "H":

> The heroin had begun to take hold. We felt ourselves crowned with colossal calm. We were masters; we had budded from nothingness into existence! And now, existence slowly compelled us to action. There was a necessity in our natures which demanded expression and after the first interpenetration of our individualities, we had reached the resultant of all the forces that composed us.[23]

The young couple's miseries, when they realize their addiction, are detailed in the same lush, overblown prose. And Pendragon's rehabilitation comes through an agency that is as nonsensically mystical as his earlier drug experiences. Yet, despite its excesses, the book is a cautionary tale. Pendragon and his bride are not depraved characters. Rather they are representatives of the lost generation of young men and women whose lives were shattered by the war. They are the "Best of Britain"—lost but not evil—who are lured to a hideous fate by their first euphoric experiences with drugs. It is their innocence, not their malevolence, which has led to their entanglement with drugs.

The sense of danger of drugs was communicated to an even wider audience through the cinema. D. W. Griffith transformed one of Thomas Burke's stories into the popular 1919 film, "Broken Blossoms." Many of Sax Rohmer's Fu Manchu stories were made into films, as was "The Yellow Claw." "Cocaine" was the title of a feature produced by the Astra Film Company in 1922. It purported to be an exposé of the drug traffic in West End night clubs. The main supplier of the drug is called "Number One," ostensibly a respectable West End physician. Through an ironic twist of fate, Number One's innocent young daughter is introduced to cocaine and seduced by a Chinese seeking revenge on her father. Number One discovers this, shoots his enemy, and then commits suicide. His daughter, dishonored but now sobered, comes to her senses and marries a man who rescues her from narcotics. It is interesting that the promotional posters for the film depict an unsavory-looking Oriental grasping for a young girl. The poster is an acknowledgment of the extent to which, by the early 1920s, Chinese had become identified with the social danger of drugs in the public consciousness.[24] "Frailty" (1921) is a melodramatic film about love and temptation among the rich and beautiful. Morphia addiction is one of the trials endured and overcome by the hero and heroine in their twisted path to a happy ending. Noel Coward used an unnamed drug—either morphia or cocaine—to symbolize the ultimate step in self-destructive decadence in his play, and later film, "The Vortex" (1928).

Through journalism, fiction, and films, a picture of narcotic drugs was firmly fixed in the public mind by the 1920s. Drugs were a part of the moral deterioration of postwar upper-class society in its search for mindless escape and forbidden pleasures. Behind the trade in drugs stood a single figure— powerful, evil, and often Oriental—who controlled the entire drug traffic, from the dark haunts of Limehouse to the fashionable parlors and night clubs of the West End. Thus De Quincey's Oriental dream was reincarnated and extended. When he was adrift in an opium fantasy, De Quincey had feared for the safety of his soul. Still the drug held a powerful fascination for him. In the popular literature of the early twentieth century, the power of the drug is acknowledged, and so is its danger. The soul that is endangered is not that of a single individual, but of England herself.

Popular literature, journalism, and films had an increasing role in shaping public opinion on social and political issues in early twentieth-century Britain. A newly literate public found in cheap newspapers, books, and films a source of both information and entertainment, often inextricably mixed. The impact of the media on public opinion about narcotic drugs was even more significant than about other issues because so few people had ever tried them. Unlike comparable "moral issues," such as gambling, alcoholism, or prostitution, the great majority of Britons had no personal experience against which to measure media presentations about narcotic drugs. What most people knew about the effects of cocaine or opium, or about the traffic in drugs, they knew from the morning newspaper, the latest Sax Rohmer thriller, or the film showing at the local cinema. Regardless of their accuracy, these media depictions were of great importance in shaping the public image of narcotic drugs. While public opinion cannot introduce regulatory legislation, especially in its particular form, it can provide a climate of opinion which affects its chances for passage. This is what happened in early twentieth-century Britain. The regulatory legislation affecting narcotic drugs was shaped by bureaucratic and professional considerations, as well as by Britain's international commitments. But the sense of menace posed by narcotic drugs, which had been so vividly portrayed in the media after 1910, created a widespread feeling that "something must be done."

Notes

1. Ng Kwee Choo, *The Chinese in London* (Oxford University Press, 1960), p. 6.

2. Ng Kwee Choo, p. 11.

3. Puk-a-poo is played with a sheet of paper which is marked with a number—usually fifty—of Chinese characters. The player draws a black mark through ten of these and places his bet. He wins if a certain number of his marks are the same as the winning marks. The more correct marks chosen, the higher his payoff. It was alleged that a bet of one shilling could bring £500 if all the marks were correct. In structure the game bears an uncanny resemblance to that most English of all gambling games, the football pools.

4. Virginia Berridge, "East End Opium Dens and Narcotic Use in Britain," *The London Journal, 4* (1978), 3–28.

5. L. Grinspoon and J. B. Bakalar, *Cocaine: A Drug and its Social Evolution* (New York: Basic Books, 1976), Chapters 1 and 2.

6. Sigmund Freud, *Cocaine Papers*, R. Byck, ed. (New York: Knopf, 1974).

7. See "Cocaine in General Medicine," *Lancet*, May 20, 1893, 16; "The Method of Using Cocaine as a Local Anaesthetic in Operations," *BMJ*, May 18, 1889, 1113; "Cocaine in Dentistry," *C&D*, January 15, 1885, 36; and "The Use of Cocaine," *C&D*, August 17, 1901, 314.

8. See J. B. Mattison, "Cocaine Dosage and Cocaine Addiction," *Lan-*

cet, May 21, 1887, 1024–1026; "The Abuse of Cocaine," *Lancet,* May 7, 1892, 1041–1042; "On the Cocaine Habit in Diseases of the Throat and Nose," *BMJ,* April 27, 1889, 1186; "A Cocaine Slave," *C&D,* December 2, 1899, 892; and "The Cocaine Habit," *C&D,* September 12, 1903, 453.

9. "Cocaine-Poisoning," *C&D,* July 27, 1901, 151, 190.

10. See *Daily Express,* January 23, 1919; *Ideas,* January 1, 1919; *Star,* February 18, 1930; and *Daily Telegraph,* April 25, 1932. These newspaper articles are part of the collection of clippings on the Chinese community in Limehouse at the Tower Hamlets Borough Library.

11. *Evening News,* October 4 and 5, 1920, Tower Hamlets collection.

12. "Yellow Peril in London," *Daily Express,* October 1, 1920, Tower Hamlets collection.

13. Dorothy Mills, *The Laughter of Fools* (London, 1920), pp. 167–170.

14. Mills, pp. 217–218.

15. Thomas Burke, *The Ecstasies of Thomas De Quincey* (New York: Doubleday, 1929), pp. 21–24.

16. Sax Rohmer, *The Yellow Claw* (London: Methuen, 1925), pp. 127–128.

17. Sax Rohmer, *Dope: A Story of Chinatown and the Drug Traffic* (London: Cassell, 1919), p. 87.

18. Rohmer, p. 110.

19. Rohmer, p. 71.

20. Rohmer, p. 144.

21. "The Vice Trust in London," *Daily Express,* December 9, 1918. See also *Daily Chronicle,* August 12, 1922; *Daily Express,* March 21, 1922; and *Daily Mail,* November 12, 1925.

22. Aleister Crowley, *Diary of a Drug Fiend* (London: W. Collins Sons, 1922), p. 28.

23. Crowley, p. 60.

24. "Film of London's Night Life," *Daily Express,* May 4, 1922. A Home Office official viewed "Cocaine" before it was released. He was convinced that "the film seemed calculated to create a morbid interest in the use of cocaine at a time when the Police are doing all they can to stamp out the illegitimate use of it in this country, and its effect is likely to encourage rather than dissuade a girl from experimenting

with the drug." Malcolm Delevingne, of the Home Office, tried to persuade the Boards of Censors in various cities to forbid its showing. He succeeded in London (although it was shown in private cinema clubs there), but failed elsewhere, notably in Manchester and Cardiff. The film was eventually closed in the latter city, however, because the advertising posters were deemed objectionable to the local Chinese. Two years later, an American film about drugs, "Human Wreckage," was "totally rejected" by all local Boards of Censors (Public Record Office, HO 45/11599/433067).

Medical dispatch; or, Doctor Doubledose killing two birds with one stone. Etching by Thomas Rowlandson (1756–1827). *Courtesy of the National Library of Medicine.*

MEDICAL DISPATCH OR
Doctor Double dose Killing two Birds with one Stone.

Advertising card for "Mrs. Winslow's Soothing Syrup." *Courtesy of the National Library of Medicine.*

Illustration by Mahlon Blaine in Thomas Burke's *Limehouse Nights* (1926).

"O li'l Lucia .... White Blossom .... Twelve years old!"

A scene from D. W. Griffith's 1919 film, *Broken Blossoms. Courtesy of the Film Stills Archive, Museum of Modern Art, New York.*

A scene from the 1924 film, *Human Wreckage. Courtesy of the Film Stills Archive, Museum of Modern Art, New York.*

Another scene from *Human Wreckage. Courtesy of the Film Stills Archive, Museum of Modern Art, New York.*

Portrait of Aleister Crowley
from the frontispiece to his
1911 book of verse, *Amber-
gris*.

CHAPTER NINE

Regulating Narcotic Drugs

Not until 1916 did Britain regulate opium and cocaine as narcotic drugs rather than as poisons. The impetus to action came from a convergence of both international and domestic factors. Between 1909 and 1914, a series of conferences laid the groundwork for the international control system that came to maturity in the 1920s. At the instigation of the Americans, who were deeply concerned about opium-smoking in the Far East, a conference of interested powers was convened in Shanghai in 1909 to try to bring an end to the opium traffic. The British position was ambivalent. Throughout the nineteenth century, British India had been the largest supplier of opium to China, and the resultant revenues had been one of the stable financial supports of the Indian government. By the early twentieth century, however, those revenues had fallen considerably, and a vocal anti-opium lobby in Britain had maintained strong pressure on Britain to pull out of the trade altogether. The 1906 election returned a Liberal government pledged to ending the trade. The Liberals produced the Anglo-Chinese Agreement of 1907, which committed Britain to phase out opium exports from India to China over a period of ten years. In spite of this step, Britain participated in the Shanghai Conference reluctantly. The grating moralism of the Americans, set against Britain's rather dubious past history, made the British delegates wary and uncomfortable.[1]

By the time of the Hague Conferences (1911–12, 1913, and

1914), however, the government's position had become much more clear-cut. An alarming increase in smuggling of drugs into India and British colonies in the Far East moved the government to make it a condition of their participation that the conference "thoroughly and completely deal with the question of restricting the manufacture, sale, and distribution of morphia and cocaine."[2] The Americans readily agreed to the British condition. The Germans, fearing that their cocaine industry would be placed at a competitive disadvantage, insisted that signatories to the treaty be bound by its restrictions only if, and when, the treaty was ratified by all participants. The "International Opium Convention" was signed at The Hague on January 23, 1912, and then circulated for ratification.[3] Part III dealt with medicinal opium, morphia, and cocaine (Articles 9–14). In Article 9, the "contracting powers" agreed to restrict the trade and consumption of drugs to "medical and legitimate uses." In Article 13, they agreed to prohibit the export of dangerous drugs to other countries except when the importer had been issued a license by the authorities in the importing country. In Article 14, they agreed to apply these regulations to all preparations which contained more than 0.2 percent morphia, or more than 0.1 percent of either cocaine or heroin. These specific commitments strongly influenced the shape of British drug regulation over the next decade.

By the spring of 1914, most of the major powers had ratified the Opium Convention (as it was hereafter called). In Britain, an interdepartmental committee of bureaucrats met in May to frame the legislation which would ensure British compliance with the guidelines. But discussions were desultory because none of the participating departments showed much interest in taking the initiative. Within months the war intervened and the whole issue was suspended.

A second problem, somewhat closer to home, again raised the issue of narcotic drugs. By 1916, it had become apparent that Britain was the source of a considerable amount of smuggled drugs. Representations from government officials in both India and Burma indicated that cocaine seized in those countries had been posted from Britain.[4] Prepared (i.e., smoking) opium that turned up in Hong Kong had originated in Liverpool and London.[5] And British-manufactured morphia was reaching Chinese addicts in massive amounts (see Chapter 10).

Added to the Hague commitments and the evidence of British involvement in international narcotics smuggling was a sensational domestic case of drug trafficking. In February 1916, an ex-convict and a prostitute were convicted of selling cocaine to Canadian troops in Folkestone under Regulation 40 of the Defence of the Realm Act, which made it illegal to supply "intoxicants" to members of the armed forces in order to make them drunk or disabled.[6] This case, which brought together the three elements of cocaine, prostitutes, and soldiers, created a great deal of publicity. The officer in charge of the barracks hospital admitted that forty Canadian soldiers were cocaine addicts. Was "coke," previously portrayed in the popular press as the downfall of thrill-seeking young girls, now threatening the armed forces?

Meanwhile, the Metropolitan Police investigated narcotics trafficking in the West End. Thanks to a tip, the police learned of men selling cocaine to prostitutes along Charing Cross Road and Shaftesbury Avenue. Two police sergeants, carrying out undercover surveillance, apprehended one William Johnson, a former porter, whom they had seen approach several women in the area. He was carrying eleven small boxes, each containing one and a half grains of cocaine hydrochloride. At his trial in the Bow Street Police Court on May 11, Johnson testified that he was employed by a man called Alf Benjamin. Johnson received the boxes from Benjamin and sold them to prostitutes for 2s.6d., on which he received a commission of 9d. per box. (As the cocaine in each box was worth about 1d., the police report noted, the profit was "considerable.") A police surgeon testified that the girls usually "snuffed" it, although some injected it hypodermically. Despite his being caught red-handed, Johnson was released. The judge ruled that mere possession of cocaine was not an offense, and, since the police officers had not actually seen Johnson sell it (but only *try* to sell it), he did not violate the Poisons and Pharmacy Acts.[7]

Perhaps it was a result of this dramatic demonstration of the impotence of present legislation, or perhaps it was mere coincidence, but on the same day that the Johnson case was dismissed, the Army enacted Regulation 40B of the Defence of the Realm Act (DORA 40B), which made it an offense for anyone to supply a member of the armed forces with cocaine or any other narcotic drug, except for a dispensing chemist acting on a doctor's written prescription. However important this initial measure was as a first step toward narcotic drug control, it quickly became obvious that it had not solved, or even addressed, many of the outstanding issues. Prepared opium and cocaine continued to be exported from Britain to India and the Far East.[8] The 1914 proposals for compliance with the Opium Convention were still unfinished. And, despite the army order, cocaine trafficking continued.[9]

These were the cardinal points of a Home Office memorandum which served as the basis of discussion for an interdepartmental committee meeting on the subject of narcotic drug control in July 1916. The memorandum noted that one way of dealing with these problems was by extending the DORA 40B Regulation to civilians. That raised certain difficulties, since "its [i.e., narcotics trafficking] bearing on the 'Defence of the Realm' is neither very direct nor important. It would have to be justified on the grounds that opium is an article required for war purposes; that its exportation has been prohibited by Proclamation; and that the smuggling causes serious difficulties and delays to our overseas' trade." Although this solution was problematic, the memo noted that "the only alternative method would be legislation which may be difficult to get and would possibly not be regarded as uncontroversial."[10]

Expediency won out. The civil servants convinced their masters of the necessity of extending DORA 40B, which was done by an order-in-council on July 28, 1916. The salient features of the new regulation were: (1) cocaine and opium were to be sold only by a dispensing chemist on the written, nonrepeatable prescription of a qualified medical man; (2) cocaine and raw opium were to be imported only by persons holding a license from the Home Office; (3) records of cocaine and opium sales were to be kept by chemists and by dispensing doctors; (4) prepared opium was absolutely proscribed; and (5) cocaine preparations were to fall under the new regulations if they contained more than 0.1 percent cocaine, the limit set by the Hague Opium Convention.

These regulations were clearly directed at the immediate problems of opium and cocaine smuggling from Britain and cocaine trafficking among the troops. The Home Office circular on their enforcement to chief constables instructed them to keep especially close watch "in districts where troops are stationed," and "in seaport towns and districts frequented by persons of Chinese extraction."[11] Morphia, which had been of such concern to the British delegates to the Hague Conference, was not even included in the Regulation. It was clear to the bureaucrats who urged its enactment that DORA 40B was a wartime stopgap, but that "a permanent measure would have to follow at a later date."[12]

The police were pleased. A Home Office memorandum of March 1917, summarizing police response to the Regulation, noted that "as a whole . . . the Regulation is working well," and that "infringements [are] mostly technical and minor."[13] Some years later, Sir Basil Thomson of Scotland Yard explained police methods and their success under the Regulation: "Traps had to be set; the traffickers fell into them without more ado, and a few exemplary sentences did the rest. Therefore the price [of cocaine] rose a hundredfold, and though the traffic is not dead, few people could be found to take the risk of a long-term imprisonment."[14] While this appraisal turned out to be overly sanguine, it is easy to understand why Sir Basil was pleased with the new Regulation: The ambiguities of enforcement under the Poisons and Pharmacy Acts, which had been so embarrassingly apparent in the Johnson case, were resolved for the police by DORA 40B.

Professional opinion about DORA 40B was divided along traditional lines. The *British Medical Journal* said that, given the spread of the "vicious habit" of cocaine-taking among the troops, the restrictions "have not come too soon." The *Lancet* also welcomed them enthusiastically.[15] The *Pharmaceutical Jour-*

nal, however, was considerably more restrained, while the *Chemist and Druggist* claimed that "the Army Council order is a bad precedent for medicine and pharmacy."[16] For doctors and pharmacists, the DORA 40B Regulation was one more skirmish in their ongoing war over control of access to drugs in general. Since, for the first time, the Regulation made certain drugs available only with a doctor's prescription, it was not surprising that medical men should favor it while pharmacists should have reservations.

Besides pharmacists, unregistered dentists were unhappy about DORA 40B. In 1916, over half of the country's practicing dentists were unregistered. They were especially prevalent in the north of England, where they treated working-class patients, and in rural areas, where they treated the entire population. Despite the recent introduction of novocaine, cocaine was still widely used as a local anesthetic in dentistry. To deprive unregistered men of the drug would, in effect, deprive them of the ability to practice. The issue was so significant that the Home Secretary appointed a "Cocaine in Dentistry Committee" to investigate. In their report of February 1917, the Committee split along professional lines. The lay majority recommended that local authorities have the right to allow unregistered dentists in their areas to have access to cocaine, while the representative of the registered dentists strongly disagreed. He argued, unsuccessfully, that only registered dentists had the training and skill to administer cocaine properly; their unregistered competitors could make do with novocaine.[17]

With the coming of peace in 1918, and the eventual expiration of the Defence of the Realm Act, the issue of narcotic drug control arose once more. As in 1916, it was the convergence of international and domestic factors that produced the Dangerous Drugs Act of 1920. Article 295 of the Treaty of Versailles committed its signatories to honor the agreements made in the prewar Hague Conferences. In order to adhere to those agreements, Britain had to enact permanent legislation to replace the wartime regulation and to widen the scope of legislation to include morphia and heroin as well as cocaine and opium. Furthermore, despite the choking off of morphia exports to Japan through the unilateral imposition of the "certificate system," British morphia was still reaching Chinese addicts by way of America (see Chapter 10). And finally, the popular press once again seized the opportunity to give narcotic drug cases lurid publicity. Revelations about "dope dens," "cocaine smuggled in pianos" by wily Chinese, and forlorn young widows overdosing on morphia became standard fare in popular newspapers by 1918.[18]

It was the Billie Carleton case, however, that focused public attention firmly on the issue of narcotic drug use. Billie Carleton was a beautiful young actress who was found dead in her flat after attending a Victory Ball at the Albert Hall in November 1918. It was originally thought that she died of an overdose of cocaine, although this was never confirmed. Nevertheless, the testimony at the coroner's inquest revealed a wealth of sordid details. Billie Carleton had begun by smoking opium at fashionable West End haunts, and had progressed to using cocaine and heroin. Her supplier was allegedly her friend, Reginald de Veulle, a professional dress designer and bon vivant with a dubious reputation and a shadowy past. The "dope" supposedly came from a Chinese source in Limehouse. Testimony revealed that Billie Carleton and de Veulle had attended opium-smoking parties in the early hours of the morning, at which the women wore filmy negligees and the men wore lounging pyjamas. Billie Carleton and de Veulle, a married man, were rumored to be having an affair, although de Veulle strenuously denied this. No matter. His suspect job, his lounge-lizard good looks, and his French name were enough to convict him in the court of public opinion, if not in a court of law. The publicity generated by the case helped to create the archetypal myth of drug abuse, which was exploited and embroidered by journalists, novelists, and filmmakers. The essential elements were a beautiful young girl led to her ruin and perhaps her death by drugs; a malevolent male supplier with a sexual interest in the victim; a Chinese source of both opium and cocaine; and a setting that alternated between elegant West End drawing rooms and squalid Limehouse dives.[19] Novelists like Crowley and Rohmer, and a legion of newspaper reporters, later mixed these elements in various combinations to their great profit. The fate of Billie Carleton was the touchstone of public consciousness which made their writings credible. Moreover, the case had political consequences. The publicity that trailed in its wake, stressing the depravity of drug-taking, made the public and politicians more willing to accept the stringent controls that were proposed in 1920.

The Dangerous Drugs Act of 1920, the capstone of British narcotics legislation, was born amidst a sharp interdepartmental squabble. The newly created Ministry of Health attempted to define narcotics control as its own responsibility.[20] In a memo to the Home Office of June 11, 1919, Dr. G. F. McCleary of the Ministry of Health reviewed the three Hague Conferences, Britain's commitment through the Versailles Treaty to enact legislation, and the DORA 40B Regulation. He proposed that his department should draft legislation which would place narcotics control on a more regular footing. He was opposed, however, by Sir Malcolm Delevingne of the Home Office, who had seized control of the issue of narcotic drugs when no one else was interested in it, and had been the prime mover behind the DORA 40B Regulation. Delevingne bluntly replied to McCleary that "the control of opium, cocaine, and other dangerous drugs should remain with the Home Office [as] the matter is very largely a police matter." The Ministry of Health bureaucrats, in an internal memo, reluctantly agreed that they had to give in, since they had no one who could match Delevingne in "obstinancy" and knowledge. Delevingne proceeded to draft the bill, which he circulated back to Ministry of Health officials for comments. They suggested only minor changes, but insisted that Delevingne formally recognize their joint responsibility in drawing up the detailed regulations provided for in the bill. Delevingne agreed to this. Thus was born the arrangement between the Ministry of Health and the Home Office that ensured that Britain's narcotic drugs policy would reflect both medical and police perspectives on the issue.[21]

The Dangerous Drugs Bill was introduced into Parliament in May. It was greeted with apathy bordering on complete disinterest. Indeed, when the Bill was scheduled for committee discussion, after its second reading, the chairman was barely able to muster a quorum. Such parliamentary discussion as there was centered on the moral evil of the trade in British-manufactured morphia in the Far East. Major Baird, speaking for the Bill on behalf of the government, shrewdly stressed its potential to bring this traffic under control. The Bill passed, with no significant opposition, on its third reading on July 30.[22]

The Dangerous Drugs Act of 1920 came into force on September 1. It was basically DORA 40B expanded and extended to conform to the guidelines set down by the Opium Convention. The import of prepared opium was absolutely prohibited. The import, export, and manufacture of raw opium, cocaine, morphia, and heroin were prohibited except under license. Narcotic preparations fell within the Act if they contained more than 0.2 percent morphia, or more than 0.1 percent of either cocaine or heroin. Sale of regulated drugs was limited to dispensing chemists acting on a doctor's written prescription, and to medical men. Persons engaged in the sale of narcotic drugs were required to keep a record of every transaction in books that would be open to inspection. Contravention of the Act was punishable by a fine of up to £200, or imprisonment for as long as six months, or both. The Act promised that more specific regulations would shortly be laid before Parliament.[23]

Professional opinion about the Act was not sharply defined. Pharmacists were annoyed at not having been consulted when the Bill was first presented in May.[24] When the Bill was amended to incorporate the suggestions of the Pharmaceutical Society, however, they became cautiously optimistic. "Even at the cost of some circumscription of their liberties," the *Pharmaceutical Journal* commented, "we are confident that pharmacists as a class will loyally co-operate in making the new law effective." The *British Medical Journal* struck much the same tone in its perfunctory editorial approval of the Bill.[25]

This cautious professional approval soon turned sour. In 1921, the government drafted regulations spelling out specific details of the Act's enforcement without consulting pharmacists, medical men, dentists, or veterinarians—the groups most affected by the new restrictions. Only after considerable protest were the draft regulations amended to incorporate a few of their suggestions. Pharmacists felt themselves to be most aggrieved, for they were subject to a plethora of regulations which, if breached, even inadvertently, could lead to a conviction that would result in a large fine or even a jail sentence. From their point of view, the Act, and especially its regulations, worked completely against their interests. It severely restricted their right to sell an important class of drugs; it imposed on them an additional burden of bookkeeping; and it made them liable to criminal prosecution for the most routine oversights. Ministry of Health officials were unsympathetic to pharmacists' complaints—a reflection, undoubtedly, of their own medical background. Dr. G. F. McCleary claimed that chemists wanted to undermine the most basic goals of the DDA:

> The chemists want to be free to go on with their counter-prescribing of drugs of this kind [i.e., preparations containing cocaine, opium, and morphia] of whatever strength. . . . The practical effect of this would be to give them the complete monopoly which they desire of the supply of these preparations while still leaving them free to supply them themselves to the public, without any medical prescription, and subject only to the very limited restrictions which the Poisons and Pharmacy Acts impose.[26]

In the face of this hard line, the Pharmaceutical Society was unable to wring any major concession from the government on the Act's regulations or amendments.[27]

Pharmacists were politically impotent; medical men were not. The latter were professionally established and politically and socially connected. They had vocal and articulate supporters in Parliament. And they could cause serious trouble, as was shown by the resistance of general practitioners to participation in the National Health Insurance in 1911–12.[28] The DDA gave doctors the exclusive right to prescribe narcotic drugs, an important precedent that would later be extended to other drugs as well. The Act required only that dispensing doctors, like chemists, keep a register of their sales. So long as the Act imposed only this minimal inconvenience on them, in return for an important concession, medical men supported it, albeit somewhat unenthusiastically. In 1923, however, the government attempted to tighten controls by two new regulations. The first limited the right to prescribe narcotic drugs to medical men "in actual practise;" the second prohibited medical men from prescribing narcotic drugs for themselves. Physicians were incensed. They protested particularly against the second regulation which, they claimed, was both unenforceable, since doctor-addicts will find a way to supply themselves with narcotics regardless of the law, and insulting, since it cast aspersions on the entire profession because of the actions of a few "degenerates."[29] The doctors won. A Home Office memorandum, written eighteen months after the fact, laconically summarized the fate of the proposals: "This Regulation, however, was objected to by the medical profession, and in view of the opposition the Regulation was subsequently withdrawn."[30]

In fact, the government did introduce and pass some noncontroversial amendments to the DDA in May 1923. These were, however, primarily intended to clarify some minor problems in the original Act and to strengthen the hand of the police in cracking down on illicit dealers in cocaine and opium. The power of search was increased in suspected drug cases; maximum penalties for conviction under the DDA were increased to £1000 and ten years' penal servitude; and it was made illegal to engineer international smuggling operations from Britain, even if the drugs involved never touched British soil.[31] Despite the passage of the DDA (Amendment) Act of 1923, the government had run into serious opposition in its attempt to extend and resolve some of the Act's enforcement ambiguities, especially as they touched on medical men. By 1923, it was clear, even to Malcolm Delevingne, that further extension of the Act would require their prior approval.

British narcotic drug legislation was shaped by a variety of conditions and commitments. While cocaine had been used as a recreational drug at least since 1900, it was not until it was seen as a threat to the armed forces, during the war, that there was any serious attempt to regulate it. Publicity generated by the Folkestone case in 1916, and the Billie Carleton case in 1918, was important in creating a climate of opinion which was favorably inclined to regulation. But events in Britain did not occur in a vacuum. Rising worldwide concern about narcotic drugs led to the international conferences at Shanghai and The Hague. The *specific* shape of British drug regulation, especially in 1920, was the result of British commitment to the guidelines formulated by the Hague Opium Convention. Finally, British narcotic drug policy, particularly on its enforcement side, was influenced by bureaucratic tussles between the Home Office and the Ministry of Health, and the political clout that could be mustered by affected professional groups. It was no small accomplishment that the child born of so many parents emerged so comparatively well-formed and healthy.

Notes

1. Bruce Johnson, "Righteousness Before Revenue," in Arnold H. Taylor, ed. *American Diplomacy and the Narcotics Traffic, 1900–1939* (Durham, N.C.: Duke University Press, 1969).

2. "Instructions to the British Delegates to the Internation Opium Conference held at The Hague, December 1911–January 1912" (Public Record Office, HO 45/10500/119609).

3. There is a copy of this document in PRO, MH 58/51.

4. See HO 45/10601/189271.

5. "Report of Metropolitan Police Commr. on the Investigation of 'Jack May'" (PRO, HO 45/10500/119609). See also the reports on smuggling in PRO, PC 8/803.

6. *The Times*, February 10 and 12, 1916. See also Francis Chester, *Shot Full: The Autobiography of a Drug Addict* (London: Methuen, 1938).

7. See PRO, HO 45/10813/312966.

8. On June 19, 1916, an interdepartmental committee, with representatives from the Foreign, Home, Colonial, and Privy Council Offices, and the Board of Trade and Customs met to consider what measures could be taken "to prevent illicit dealings in opium, especially as regards the smuggling of opium prepared for smoking (known as *chandu*) from the United Kingdom to the Dominions, Colonies, and Foreign Countries." This was the core of the group

that recommended the extension of DORA 40B one month later (PRO, HO 45/10500/119609).

9. On July 18 and 19, as a result of the undercover investigations of Sgt. Gilbert Smith of the Canadian Military Police, seven men were convicted of selling cocaine to soldiers. The *Daily Chronicle* echoed popular feeling on the subject in its articles of July 19 and 20: Because of the DORA 40B Regulation, the drug traffickers have recruited prostitutes to act as go-betweens. "The method of distribution is borrowed from the counterfeiters—one woman acts as 'carrier,' and is in possession of a number of boxes of the drug, and another undertakes the actual sale, in small boxes." The paper called for an extension of the Regulation, noting that so long as cocaine were freely available to civilians, soldiers "will eventually get it."

10. See PRO, HO 45/10500/119609.

11. See PRO, HO 45/10813/312966.

12. Home Office memorandum in PRO, HO 45/10500/119609. See also Virginia Berridge, "War Conditions and Narcotics Control: The Passing of Defence of the Realm Act Regulation 40B," *Journal of Social Policy,* 7 (July, 1978), 285–304.

13. See PRO, HO 45/10814/213966.

14. "The Cocaine Habit," *C&D*, December 3, 1921, 47.

15. "Restrictions on the Sale of Cocaine," *BMJ*, July 22, 1916, 117; "The Regulations with Respect to the Sale of Cocaine," *Lancet,* August 6, 1916, 238.

16. "Cocaine and Opium: The New Regulations," *Pharm. J.*, August 5, 1916, 132; "Traffic in Narcotic Drugs," *C&D*, June 17, 1916, 42–43.

17. "Cocaine in Dentistry Committee, 1916–17" (PRO, HO 45/11013/323566).

18. *Daily Express*, December 23, 1918; *Daily Telegraph*, December 12, 1918; *Yorkshire Post*, September 26, 1918.

19. The Carleton case was publicized from November 1918, through April 1919: *Daily Telegraph*, December 13 and 14, 1918; *Daily News,* January 24, 1919; *The Times,* November 30, December 4, 13, and 21, 1918; January 3, 17, 24, and 25; February 1, 6, 8, 15, 19, and 22; March 1, 6, and 8; April 3, 4, 5, and 8, 1919; *News of the World,* January 5, 19, and 26, 1919. The *Daily Express* used the Billie Carle-

ton case as an excuse to launch an investigation of London's illicit
drug traffic, which produced some sensational headlines, if little
actual information: November 30; December 4, 7, 9, 10, 13, 14, 16,
17, 18, 21, 23, and 24, 1918.

20. On the background of the Ministry of Health, see Frank Honigs-
baum, *The Struggle for the Ministry of Health*, Occasional Papers on
Social Administration, No. 37 (London: G. Bell & Sons, 1970).

21. The memos are in PRO, MH 58/51.

22. The parliamentary debates on the Bill were published in the *C&D*,
June 19, 1920, 46–48; July 31, 52; August 7, 61; and *Lancet*, June
19, 1920, 1338–1339.

23. There are copies of this and all subsequent Dangerous Drugs Acts
and regulations in the Public Record Office (PRO, HO
45/19983/402179).

24. "The Dangerous Drugs Bill," *C&D*, May 15, 1920, 60–61; "The
Dangerous Drugs Bill," *Pharm. J.*, May 15, 1920, 468–469; "The
Dangerous Drugs Bill," *Pharm. J.*, May 22, 1920, 502; "The
Dangerous Drugs Bill," *C&D*, June 26, 1920, 207.

25. "The Dangerous Drugs Act," *Pharm. J.*, September 4, 1920, 246–
247; "The Dangerous Drugs Bill," *BMJ*, May 22, 1920, 714.

26. Memo by G. F. McCleary to Dr. J. Smith-Whitaker, dated February
17, 1921 (PRO, MH 58/51).

27. See "Dangerous Regulations," *C&D*, January 15, 1921, 64–65;
"Dangerous Drugs Act," *C&D*, January 22, 1921, 49; "Failure of
the Dangerous Drugs Act," *C&D*, June 24, 1922, 160; "Administration of the Dangerous Drugs Act," *Pharm. J.*, March 18, 1922, 211–
212; and "The Draft Regulations Under the Dangerous Drugs
Act," *Pharm. J.*, January 29, 1921, 84.

28. See Jeanne L. Brand, *Doctors and the State, 1870–1912* (Baltimore:
Johns Hopkins University Press, 1965).

29. See "Restrictions in Prescribing Dangerous Drugs," *Lancet*, March
31, 1923, 659–660; "The Dangerous Drugs Regulations," *BMJ*,
February 10, 1923, 260–261; and "Self-Prescription of Dangerous
Drugs," *Lancet*, August 19, 1922, 406. At a debate at the Medico-
Legal Society on March 20, 1923, Dr. Burridge said that "the
Dangerous Drugs Act seemed as if it might become known as the
'Dangerous to Doctors Act,' and half the members of the Medico-
Legal Society might presently be employed in keeping the other

half out of prison." ("The Problem of Drug Addiction," *BMJ*, March 31, 1923, 565–566.) See also "Dangerous Drugs/Doctors Objections to New Bill," *Morning Post*, March 28, 1923.

30. "Memorandum prepared by the Home Office for the Information of the [Rolleston] Committee," October 12, 1924 (PRO, MH 58/277).

31. "The Dangerous Drugs and Poisons (Amendment) Act, 1923," *BMJ*, June 2, 1923, 939.

CHAPTER TEN

British Morphia, Chinese Addicts: The International Connection

The passage of the Dangerous Drugs Act of 1920 had an enormous impact on Britain's role in the international trade in opium and opiates. Within two years, opium imports (in absolute terms) declined to the level of the 1850s, which (in per capita terms) was smaller than at any time since the 1830s. Since most of the imported opium was used for alkaloid production, morphia manufacture declined from an average of 596,000 ounces per annum in 1919 and 1920, to 111,600 ounces per annum from 1921 through 1923 (see Fig. 4). The DDA permitted manufacture of dangerous drugs, including morphia, heroin, and cocaine, but only by government license. Furthermore, it permitted the export of dangerous drugs only if the exporter could produce a certificate from the government of the importing country, attesting that the drugs would be used "only for medicinal and scientific purposes." The certificate system was designed to insure that narcotic drugs would not be "consigned to persons engaged in illicit traffic."[1]

There was no reason why the certificate system should have impaired the legitimate trade in narcotic drugs. A manufacturer or an exporter simply had to demonstrate that his consignment was intended for medical or scientific purposes. Thus the sharp drop in opium alkaloid manufacture after the enactment of the DDA inevitably leads one to wonder about what had been the destination of the millions of ounces of morphia manufactured up to 1920. Certainly some of it was intended for domestic consumption, but how much? In the late 1920s, when domestic sales of drugs were carefully monitored, the Home Office was able to produce a very accurate profile of the legitimate British demand for narcotic drugs (see Table 7 in the Appendix). Between 1924 and 1929, the average yearly consumption was 19,120 ounces of morphia (plus 3911 ounces of heroin and 9,120 ounces of cocaine).[2] But the manufacturing and export figures for morphia in the nonwar years just previous to 1920 show that the average amount of morphia produced per annum was 533,900 ounces, and the average exported for those years was 340,100 ounces, leaving an annual difference of 193,800 ounces for the domestic market—approximately ten times the amount consumed legitimately a decade later (see Fig. 4). It is inconceivable that domestic demand could have changed so radically within a decade and a half. The inescapable conclusion is that from 1911 to 1920, approximately 175,000 ounces of morphia per year, which could not be accounted for either by export or by domestic demand, was funneled into the nonmedical market, either in Britain or abroad. The point is reinforced when one considers the sudden contraction, between 1921 and 1923, of the difference between morphia produced (averaging 111,600 ounces per annum) and morphia exported (averaging 102,600 ounces per annum): 9,000 ounces per year were left to satisfy the entire domestic market which had previously "absorbed" an annual 193,800 ounces.

But that is not all. Surely a large proportion of the morphia exported during the period was also intended for a nonmedical market. One cannot, of course, estimate international demand with the same precision and certainty that one can gauge domestic demand. There are several factors which could have accounted for a drop in the international demand for British morphia from one decade to the next, but the sharpness of the decline after 1920 (from 340,100 to 102,600 ounces per annum) leads one to suspect that much of it—perhaps amounting to 200,000 ounces per year—was destined for a nonmedical market.

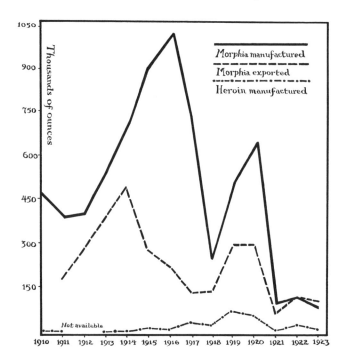

Figure 4.
Manufacture and export of morphia and heroin, 1910–1923.
(*Source:* Home Office data published in *British Medical Journal,*
November 1, 1924, p. 830.)

But what of the war years, 1915 to 1918? During that period
morphia production expanded, to an average of 751,600 ounces
per annum, while exports dropped to only 195,700 ounces per
annum, leaving a yearly difference of 555,900 ounces (see Fig.
4). What happened to this immense amount of morphia? At first
glance, the answer seems obvious. The morphia was needed at
the front, where millions of men were engaged in a savage conflict. Undoubtedly some of it was, but did war needs really account for over half a million ounces each year? A closer look at
the morphia production figures raises some doubts about the
"war needs" interpretation. First, production began to expand

in 1913, after three years of relative stability. In fact, 1915, the first year in which production figures would reflect war-caused demand, appears to be less a starting-point than the penultimate step on an upward curve that began in 1913 and peaked in 1916. Second, the production figure for 1918 is clearly anomalous. The war still raged for ten months of that year, yet morphia production was at its lowest point by far since 1910. Only if one accepts the highly improbably conjecture that British morphia manufacturers radically overproduced in the early war years, and then sold off socks in 1918, can the "war needs" interpretation be maintained.

There is an alternative interpretation. Throughout the decade, but especially in the years 1913 to 1917, the massive amount of British-produced morphia was destined, not for Flanders Field, but for China. The infamous traffic in smoking opium that was exported from British India to China throughout the nineteenth century is well-known. Suffice it to say that the revenues that were generated from this opium, grown on state monopolies, provided 18 percent of the annual revenue of the Indian government in the late nineteenth century. From the 1880s these revenues began to decline, and the whole trade came under acute criticism in Britain. The election of 1906 returned a Liberal government pledged to end the traffic, which it did in 1913. As Chinese opium imports waned, however, a new danger arose.

From the late eighties onward there were reports that Chinese opium smokers were switching to morphia injections. Morphia was first introduced into China by Western physicians who touted it as a cure for the opium-smoking habit. An English pharmacist described how, by the nineties, a thriving commerce in morphia was carried on in many Chinese cities:

> The smoker finds it cheaper and far more convenient to carry a morphine preparation in his pocket, and take an occasional dose, than to have to lie back and go through the slow process of smoking. Ghouls, with dirty hypodermic syringes and morphine solutions made with any water are to be seen in the teashops (or restaurants) in Soochow giving injections at the low rate of seven

cash (one-fifth of a penny) each. As their victims pass before them
each gets his allowance in succession without the needle being
even wiped after the previous one.[3]

In Hong Kong, a medical student in a mission hospital in
the 1890s set himself up in a shop with morphia and hypodermic syringe. Within weeks, business was flourishing and
rivals had appeared "in back alleys all over the city of Victoria."
Coolies found that they could get a bigger kick from a ha'penny's worth of morphia than from two pennies' worth of opium.
Profits were enormous. On a capital of $100, these shops were
reported showing a profit of $500 per month. The members of
the Hong Kong "Opium Farm," the colonial government's
licensed monopoly, found that the spread of the morphia habit
had severely cut into their business.[4] The morphia was alleged
to be of British manufacture. Indeed, one report from the
1890s claimed that "the Chinaman buys his morphia by the
pound, and his predilection is for Macfarlan's, which he must
have in original pound bottles."[5] According to G. S. Muir of the
Edinburgh Committee for the Suppression of the Indo-Chinese
Opium Traffic, "2000 chests of opium are made into morphine
in Edinburgh and London annually, and this constitutes about
half the world's supply. A large proportion of this finds its way,
directly or indirectly, to the East."[6] In one early report of morphia-injecting it was alleged that "the vendors [in Amoy] are said
to obtain their supplies direct from London."[7]

Attempts by the Chinese government, in 1902, to tax morphia prohibitively and then, in 1909, to prohibit its importation
and manufacture altogether simply had the effect of trans-
forming it from a licit to an illicit trade.[8] In 1913, nationalist
revolutionaries finally overthrew the Manchu dynasty, bringing
a puritanical fervor to the anti-opium campaign, which had been
conducted rather laconically by the previous government. In the
same year, the British government finally stopped shipping Indian opium to China. By the twenties, the central government
was enveloped in such chaos that its anti-opium policies were
virtually unenforceable, and illicit Indian opium and domestically produced opium flooded back into the Chinese market.
But in the seven or eight years after 1913, the drop in opium

supplies, combined with more rigorous enforcement policies, induced many opium-smokers to switch to morphia-injecting, since morphia was easier to transport and use without detection.[9] Smugglers were receiving fees of $20 per pound for carrying the drug into the country. Morphia was described as "fetching a higher price than gold."[10] In 1920, one pound of morphia, which sold at £10 to £13 from a pharmaceutical manufacturer in Britain, brought £210 in China.[11] Such powerful financial rewards inevitably attracted smugglers, the most important of whom were Japanese.

Between 1898 and 1907, Japan imported an average of 20,000 ounces of morphia per year, which may stand as a rough measure of the maximum legitimate Japanese demand. Before 1913, Japanese imports of morphia never exceeded 30,000 ounces in any one year. Yet Japanese morphia imports rose to 359,000 ounces in 1915; to 559,000 ounces in 1916; and to 600,000 ounces in 1917, or about thirty times the legitimate domestic demand.[12] Virtually all of this morphia was of British manufacture, and, according to an investigator for the *Japan Chronicle*, it was intended for the Chinese market.[13] Once in the hands of Japanese smugglers, the drug entered China by several routes. The center of activity was Manchuria. In 1917, the British consul in Mukden asked a local British businessman, one Mr. S. F. Drakeford, to make discreet inquiries about the drug trade in Manchuria. Drakeford replied that the Japanese openly encouraged opium-smoking in Manchuria among the Chinese.

> [Morphia] is openly sold to Chinese in the Japanese concession and in so-called drug-stores just outside the city walls. . . . Its distribution is either winked at or encouraged by those in authority as part of the policy for the peaceful penetration of Manchuria by the Japanese.

Apparently this trade had been in existence for some years. Drakeford continued:

> A gentleman travelling for a home firm of surgical instrument manufacturers told me in 1914 that he had ascertained that it was possible in many places to buy from Japanese chemists and others

a morphia syringe and dose of morphia for 30 cents (7½ d.), and Dr. Colman, of Changchun, told me about the same time that jinriksha coolies could obtain an injection of morphia for 10 cents.[14]

An article in the *Japan Advertiser* for April 3, 1917, quoted from a Chinese government official posted in Manchuria:

Almost every Japanese drug dealer or peddler in Manchuria sells it [morphia] in one form or another, and does so with impunity, because no Japanese can be arrested without first informing the consul. From these agents the drug may be passed on to disreputable Chinese who frequent the coolie depots and inject a solution, usually very dirty, with a hypodermic syringe, which may be made with glass, metal, or even bamboo. Rigorous imprisonment for two years is a common sentence for Chinese found with morphine in their possession, but I fear that the principal culprits usually escape punishment.[15]

From Manchuria the morphia moved into China proper by railroad. Still another route used by the Japanese smugglers was through Korea, from which "by a regular system of motor-boats it is clandestinely distributed along the northern coast of China."[16] Formosa was used as a similar entrepôt farther south. While the Japanese were the most important smugglers, they were not the only ones operating in China. Hong Kong was a center of the morphia traffic for south China, and morphia also entered the country overland from French Indo-China. Furthermore, until 1922, morphia was sent quite legally by post from Europe to China, the only risk being the occasional confiscation by an alert, or lucky, Chinese postal inspector.

Over all these routes, British-manufactured morphia poured into China. By 1917, the trade had reached embarrassing proportions. The indefatigable Mr. Muir, on behalf of his anti-opium committee, wrote the Foreign Secretary long and detailed letters, accurately summarizing the nature of the trade. The Foreign Office circulated one of these, in January 1917, for comments from interested parties. One staff officer from the Far East section bluntly stated the department's position.

The prohibition of morphia exports would preclude a considerable number of Japanese from earning their living by poisoning the inhabitants of Manchuria and would therefore add fuel to the fire of Japanese irritation. In fact it seems essentially a question to be postponed until the end of the war.[17]

His colleagues agreed. Mr. Muir was put off with a noncommittal reply. But the anti-opiumists were not so easily defeated. In February 1917, Sir William Collins, a Member of Parliament, a medical authority on addiction, and an anti-opiumist, asked a parliamentary question about the amount of British morphia exported to Japan and its ultimate destination. This was, according to Sir William Langley, an assistant under-secretary of state in the Foreign Office, "a very awkward question since it is undesirable to discuss the infamies of the Japanese morphia traffic in Manchuria, and we cannot, on the other hand, deny its existence." After assembling the damning figures, Langley noted sourly that because of all the pressure, "we shall never be left alone until something definite has been done."[18]

Hectored by the anti-opiumists, the government finally moved. After consultations with the Japanese, the British government decided to restrict the issue of licenses to export morphia or cocaine to holders of certificates from the Japanese government, attesting that the morphia was intended only for medicinal uses within Japan and her territories. As a result, Japanese imports of British morphia "came to a complete standstill."

In 1918, British morphia production fell to 295,000 ounces despite the medical demand created by the last year of the war, and the worldwide influenza, the most devastating pandemic in modern history. But the morphia trade was too lucrative for manufacturers and smugglers to give up so easily. By 1919, they had discovered that the law could be evaded in two ways: morphia could be shipped directly from Britain to Japan without securing the necessary forms (which accounts for the vast discrepancy between British export figures to Japan and Japanese import figures from Britain); or it could be shipped indirectly to Japan, by way of Switzerland, France, and especially America.[19]

This interpretation—that British-manufactured morphia reached Chinese addicts by way of Japanese smugglers—makes the figures on British morphia manufacturing from 1913 to 1918 more comprehensible. Put simply, it accounts for the steady growth from 1913 to 1916 on the basis of Chinese demand, and the precipitous fall in 1918 by the imposition of export controls. The enormous quantity of morphia produced between 1913 and 1917 was not destined for the battlefield wounded, but for Chinese addicts. In the nonwar years between 1911 and 1920, an estimated average of 375,000 to 400,000 ounces per annum of British-produced morphia was sold into the nonmedical market, mostly in China. In the period 1914–1918, the quantities were much larger, averaging about 700,000 ounces per annum.

But what of the years before 1910? The British government did not keep records on morphia production before that date, but it is possible to speculate, from fragmentary records, about quantities produced. Mr. Deric Bolton, a retired chemist formerly employed by Macfarlan-Smith pharmaceutical manufacturers, wrote an article in 1976 in which he claimed that J. F. Macfarlan's yearly production of morphia reached 250,000 ounces in the 1890s.[20] The records that Bolton used, according to the managing director of Macfarlan-Smith, have been lost or destroyed, but Bolton's figure seems not unreasonable. From the extant records of a second morphia manufacturer, T. Whiffen of London, we know that that firm produced an average of 142,000 ounces between 1893—when it began morphia production—and 1900 (see Table 8 in the Appendix). A third firm, T. & H. Smith, also produced morphia at this time, but its records have not survived. If one estimates, conservatively, that T. & H. Smith produced 100,000 ounces per year, then it is possible to project total annual British morphia production during the later 1890s at approximately 492,000 ounces.

Less is known about the first decade of the twentieth century because of the missing Whiffen ledger books for that period, and the complete dearth of information from Macfarlan and from Smith. Nevertheless, the value of all drugs and medicines exported from Britain continued to rise gradually during this period, and it seems reasonable to believe that the level of morphia production and export did not dip significantly (see Table 9, Appendix). Any severe disruption of the trend would surely have been noted in such professional journals as the *Chemist and Druggist*, and there is no evidence of it. It is reasonable to infer that the high level of morphia production in Britain from the 1890s onward primarily served the large and growing population of Chinese addicts. Until 1909, the trade was legal and direct. After that date, however, the illegality of morphia imports to China induced Japanese smugglers to intervene. And after 1913, when Indian-grown opium was at least temporarily taken off the Chinese market, Chinese demand for morphia grew and smugglers profited enormously. Increasing controls, in 1917 and again in 1920, only had the effect of pushing prices still higher, and thus making smuggling even more lucrative. In 1921, the *Japan Chronicle* reported that the same quantity of morphia which could be bought in London for the equivalent of about 100 yen could be sold on the illicit market in China for 1000 yen.[21]

Manufacturers as well as smugglers profited from the trade. T. Whiffen was the last of the three British morphia manufacturers to begin production, but by 1912 it was the largest, controlling over 50 percent of the market (see Fig. 4 and Table 8). At the height of its production, in 1916, Whiffen manufactured 650,000 ounces of morphia, two-thirds of the British total. Not only did the quantity of morphia produced increase during the war, but also its selling price increased. In 1911, Whiffen sold 185,400 ounces of morphia for £72,500, or 8s. per ounce. In 1916, Whiffen sold 650,000 ounces for £469,000, at the nearly doubled price of 14s. 5d. per ounce. And after 1917, when the government's action temporarily closed the China market, the selling price continued to climb. In 1918, Whiffen sold only 100,000 ounces of morphia, but at a record price of 25s. 10d. per ounce. The passage of the Dangerous Drugs Act, which effectively made the "export certificate" system universal for British morphia manufacturers and exporters, had a drastic effect on both Whiffen's gross profits and its profit margin. In 1922, Whiffen sold 57,000 ounces of morphia for £21,000, a

drop to the prewar price of 8s. per ounce. One can only speculate about the effect on Whiffen's net profits of the virtual collapse of a manufacturing line which, at its height, had generated
revenues ranging from a third to a half million pounds sterling
per annum. It must have been considerable.

After World War I, the British government's attitude
toward the international narcotics traffic changed significantly.
The evasion of the 1917 regulation—which of course was
brought to its attention by the vigilant Mr. Muir and his colleagues on the Edinburgh anti-opium committee—embarrassed
the government and laid it open to charges of hypocrisy. Believing that it could shut down the traffic by sealing off smuggling
routes, the British government sought a series of bilateral agreements with other major countries—especially France and the
United States—to impose the certificate system on narcotics imports and exports.[22] Under the auspices of the League of Nations, this arrangement was expanded by the early 1920s to include all countries involved in the narcotics trade except Turkey
and Peru.

The establishment of the "export certificate" system
throughout most of the world, and the passage of the DDA in
1920, did not eliminate the morphia traffic to the Far East, but it
did change its character. For decades, British morphia manufacturers had operated entirely within the law. They sold their
morphia, without restriction, to agents and exporters. If these
consignments turned up in Far Eastern ports in the possession
of smugglers with fair regularity, which they did, the manufacturers and the government could disingenuously claim perfect
innocence, which they did. However, the DDA posed manufacturers a difficult dilemma. If they adhered to the spirit as well as
the letter of the law, and sold only to agents who dealt in morphia for legitimate scientific and medical purposes, they would
sacrifice a lucrative business. But if they continued to deal with
agents who were involved in smuggling morphia to China, they
risked violating the spirit of the law, even if they adhered to its
letter by requiring their agents to procure certificates. Macfarlan
and Smith opted for the first course; but for Whiffen the temp-

tations of the second were too great. The firm's involvement came to light in the wake of a spectacular drug-smuggling case.

On October 11, 1922, a Japanese subject, Tieu Yiu Kim, was arrested in Hong Kong in illegal possession of 2500 ounces of cocaine and 2400 ounces of morphia. He was also carrying correspondence and other documents which implicated other members of a complex smuggling network that moved European narcotic drugs into the Far East. Among Tieu Yiu Kim's papers was an offer by one H. M. F. Humphrey, a 32-year-old English businessman, to sell drugs to Tieu's employers, Messrs. Tong Say of Amoy.

Humphrey was nothing if not bold. A copy of a letter from Humphrey to Loo Benn Tan, the managing director of Tong Say Brothers, dated January 31, 1923, eventually turned up in the Foreign Office files. Humphrey noted that Tieu had been captured but was convinced that he would not "talk." (He was obviously unaware that Tieu had been carrying the implicating documents at the time of his arrest.) Humphrey wished to continue doing business and reminded Mr. Loo that "the Manufacturers are personal friends [of mine]." He proposed a deal:

We buy say 50,000 ounces [of morphia] at 16/- an ounce . . . £40,000. We ship this quantity and I will arrange personally to come out with the parcel to see the safe delivery at your end *if you cannot make the arrangements I can.* I am sure that we could easily sell this quantity in China at 48/- which would raise £120,000, the expenses to deliver to you safely would be about £1000 including my Passage, therefore we could make a profit of about £79,000 if the goods were sold at this very cheap figure, we might even get as much as 200/- per ounce and then we should of course make very much more.

The quoted price of 16s. per ounce, Humphrey assured Mr. Loo, "includes the movement from Country to Country [within Europe]." As an alternative, Humphrey proposed simply to procure the goods for Tong Say, charging them a flat fee of 1s. per ounce over cost. But if they want him to arrange delivery, then they must send him a bank draft for the entire amount:

I must have your financial assistance, owing to heavy expenses incurred in protecting myself against the same fate that overtook Mr. Tiewe [sic], in other words I must PAY FREELY to get the goods FREE OF CONTROL.[23]

This particular caper never came off. Unbeknownst to Humphrey, the Home Office had opened an investigation which led to his arrest and conviction in March 1923, and to the discovery of the smuggling ring.[24] Humphrey was associated with two other Englishmen: F. L. Baker of Messrs. Baker, Golwynne & Co., a London firm, and A. L. Baxter, Baker's partner. These three men regularly purchased morphia and cocaine, either directly from manufacturers or, more commonly, from licensed European dealers in pharmaceuticals. The narcotics were then moved to Basle where they were hidden in innocent consignments of goods shipped to the Far East.[25]

In Europe, the problem for the smugglers was how to circumvent the system of government certificates necessary for the import and export of narcotic drugs. In Germany and Switzerland, where authorities were notoriously lax, Baxter was occasionally able to buy directly from pharmaceutical manufacturers—Merck and Boehringer in Germany, and Hoffman-LaRoche in Switzerland.[26] But he was able to obtain British narcotics only by working through continental agents. The morphia manufactured by Whiffen and its subsidiary, J. A. Wink, was the most highly prized by Chinese addicts, and thus fetched a premium price. When Baxter could not buy the real thing, he employed a Berlin printer to forge Whiffen labels for him.[27] Genuine Whiffen-produced narcotics were available, however, from at least two sources: John Laurier, Whiffen's licensed agent in Paris (and President of the British Chamber of Commerce there), and Camille Honhon in Brussels.

Laurier bought narcotics on such a scale from Whiffen that only the most naive or conniving company director could fail to appreciate its significance. In 1922, Laurier bought 21,144 ounces of morphia, over 40 percent of Whiffen's total manufacture, and one-third of all the morphia imported into France that year.[28] Some of this Laurier sold to Humphrey, although not directly. On paper, Laurier sold the narcotics to a French firm, Messrs. Weil, who obtained the necessary export licence, and shipped the goods to Humphrey in Basle. In this way, Humphrey did not appear on Laurier's books, and the entire transaction, from England to Basle, was covered by government-issued import and export certificates.[29]

The other connection between Humphrey and his associates was through Camille Honhon in Brussels. Like Laurier in Paris, Honhon ostensibly sold the narcotics to a local firm, one Seldeslachts, who obtained the necessary export license, and were paid a commission by the English smugglers.[30] The most important European link in the drug traffic was the Swiss firm of Bubeck and Dolder in Basle. Bubeck and Dolder obtained the Swiss import license for the smugglers' narcotics and allowed them to repack the drugs at their warehouse for shipment to the Far East.[31] Since export licenses were not required by the Swiss government, all of these European transactions fell within the letter, if not the spirit, of existing laws. From Switzerland the narcotics were sometimes shipped directly to China, where they passed customs hidden in ordinary goods. The English smugglers arranged with a French chemicals firm, Kaempf & Co., to pack their narcotics in consignments of chlorate of potash. On another occasion, Humphrey and Baxter concealed the drugs in a load of furniture.[32]

More often, however, the smugglers shipped their narcotics to Japan, whence they were sent, often by way of Vladivostok, to their final destination. Well into the twenties, Japanese smugglers continued to function as the final link between European morphia manufacturers and Chinese addicts. Reports from British diplomats in both China and Japan continually emphasized Japanese complicity in the traffic after 1920. In 1922, the British ambassador in Peking, in a letter to Lord Curzon, enclosed a report from A. H. Harris, Commissioner of Customs in Canton, about the illicit morphia trade conducted there by Japanese:

> The most noted and popular brand is that labelled T. & H. Smith Ltd. of Edinburgh and London. [Although he noted that some

heroin manufactured by J. A. Wink had recently been seized.]
The present market price in Canton is Hk$420 per lb., whilst the
price in England now is 8/6 per oz. = 136/- per lb. or $53 per lb.,
showing tempting gains for smugglers. As opium is easily obtained nowadays the consumption of morphia in Canton at Present is estimated at not more than 200 lbs., but a lot of this would
be distributed to other places.[33]

Sir Charles Eliot, the British ambassador to Japan in the
early 1920s, wrote to the Foreign Secretary in 1923, describing
the situation. "The Japanese authorities have not as yet dis-
played any great zeal in the execution of the recommendations
of the Opium Advisory Committee [of the League of Nations],"
he wrote with diplomatic understatement. Of course, Eliot said,
the Japanese government gives official assurances of compliance.

But the lamentable lack of interest which the competent authorities display in the ultimate destination of the drugs stored in
their bonded warehouses, the practical impunity with which
smuggling operations on a large scale can be carried out, the
failure to verify bills of lading even in *prima facie* suspicious cases,
the readiness with which the Japanese consul at Vladivostok
certifies import licenses, and the attitude of the Government monopoly officials in Formosa towards all inquiries into the disposal
of their products, are facts which cannot be ignored.[34]

Humphrey and his associates had been dealing with continental agents and shipping firms at least since the passage of the
DDA in 1920.[35] But papers confiscated from Baxter's residence
indicated that on the eve of Humphrey's arrest, the English
smugglers had put together a formal syndicate, consisting of
themselves, Dundas Simpson and Joe Kahan of R. Fuller & Co.
(an American firm also involved in smuggling morphia into
China), the Basle firm of Bubeck and Dolder, and one Macdonald, an American shipper and drug trafficker operating out
of Freiburg-Baden.[36] It seems, then, that the arrest of Tieu Yiu
Kim and the subsequent investigation of Humphrey's connec-

tions interrupted the establishment of a formidable alliance of experienced drug smugglers.

The investigation was less successful, however, in halting smuggling in Europe. Marginal notes on the documents indicate that Foreign Office officials felt that there was little they could do other than bringing the facts to the attention of European governments. The prospects for a clampdown seemed bleak. A Foreign Office memorandum of late 1923 noted that the German and Belgian governments had prosecuted Macdonald and Honhon respectively, although without apparent success. The French authorities delayed and, at the time of writing, they had not taken any action against Laurier, Weil, or Kaempf. Swiss pharmaceutical firms, responding to their government's inquiry, claimed that the British government was acting cynically in trying to close down continental firms engaged in the drug trade in order to make the position of the British firms stronger.[37] (The Swiss position is easy to understand, and even to sympathize with, given the British government's inaction until 1917.) Malcolm Delevingne noted that when the Humphrey case broke, Baxter fled to Paris and wrote to Macdonald, asking him to direct his business to Baxter at the offices of Kaempf & Co. in Paris.[38]

One concrete result of the investigation was that Whiffen was put out of the morphia business. On April 25, 1923, William George Whiffen, the managing director, was interviewed at the Home Office about the extent of his company's involvement in the illicit drug trade. He was not criminally prosecuted, but Whiffen's license to manufacture and export morphia and cocaine was revoked that same day. One can only speculate about what was said during the interview, since the relevant Home Office file is still closed to researchers. However, a Home Office memorandum of 1923 made reference to "the firm of Whiffen whose complicity in the illicit transactions was established."[39]

Of course, smuggling went on. Humphrey was given the maximum sentence of six months in prison, which the judge noted was scarcely fitting for the crime, and certainly not much of a deterrent for others. Baxter was back in business immediately. One lasting result of the case was that Whiffen's highly prized morphia was finally out of the illicit drug market. In a larger perspective it meant that Britons were no longer in the ignominious business of selling opium and opiates to Chinese addicts.[40]

Another result of the Humphrey case was that the Home Office became more sensitive to the problems of international narcotics smuggling and pursued certain important cases tenaciously. In November 1923, Scotland Yard arrested Yosukichi Miyagawa, a 35-year-old Japanese businessman who had been living in London for the past four months. While Miyagawa was ostensibly trading in legal articles, he was in fact buying morphia from Bubeck and Dolder in Basle, and shipping it to Marseilles where it was consigned to his family's firm in Kobe, Japan. Scotland Yard detectives received permission from French authorities to enter a bonded warehouse in Marseilles, where they found 500 pounds of morphia belonging to Miyagawa. He was extradited back to Britain and stood trial there for engineering the deal, an offence under the Dangerous Drugs (Amendment) Act of 1923. In the course of his trial it was revealed that he had paid £6,282 for the Swiss morphia, and in October he had paid £37,590 for heroin from a firm in Hamburg. Miyagawa, whom the prosecutor called "the largest trafficker in drugs who has ever been brought to justice," was sentenced to three years' imprisonment and recommended for deportation.[41] The tenacity of the police pursuit and the severity of the sentence convinced other drug smugglers that operating from London was too risky. By the end of 1923, Britain was no longer connected to the international narcotics traffic.

The British government's record on the international traffic in narcotic drugs through the nineteenth and early twentieth centuries was far from exemplary. As late as 1917, Foreign Office officials strenuously resisted any attempt to interfere with the Anglo-Japanese morphia trade, even though they were clearly aware of the drug's ultimate destination. Yet change did come, quickly and decisively, as a result of several factors. The Shanghai and Hague Conferences signaled a new international mood which strongly favored the control of narcotic drugs through adherence to common guidelines. The British government at first balked at, and then embraced these controls, in large part because of the alarming evidence that drug addiction was increasing in British colonies from India to Hong Kong. Furthermore, the Edinburgh Anti-Opium Committee and Sir William Collins, through private letters and parliamentary questions, relentlessly attacked the government's hypocritical narcotics policy. Finally, Sir Malcolm Delevingne of the Home Office, and later the League of Nations' Opium Advisory Committee, worked skillfully to insure British compliance with the spirit as well as the letter of the new controls. By 1923, in a complete reversal of its past position, the British government had become the leading European advocate of international narcotics regulations, uniformly enacted and strictly enforced.

Notes

1. "Control of Export of Dangerous Drugs from UK," PRO, HO 45/16176/415349/44A.

2. PRO, HO 45/14213/482142. These figures may include some small quantities used for nonmedical purposes.

3. "Morphine in China,"*C&D*, September 27, 1902, 560.

4. "Morphine in China," *C&D*, September 20, 1902, 528.

5. "Morphine in the Far East," *C&D*, September 26, 1896, 479.

6. "The Trade in Morphine to the East," *BMJ*, January 22, 1910, 240.

7. "Intelligence," *Pharm. J.*, July 11, 1885, 57. See also "Export of Morphia from Great Britain," *Pharm. J.*, December 3, 1910, 658; "The Morphia-Habit in China," *C&D*, October 21, 1893, 592; "Opium in China," *C&D*, January 30, 1909, 158; and "A Rival to Opium-Smoking," *BMJ*, October 7, 1893, 803.

8. "Morphine in China," *C&D*, October 11, 1902, 630.

9. "The Passing of the Chinese Opium Trade," *BMJ*, May 17, 1913, 1078.

10. "Opium Suppression and the Chinese Trade," *Pharm. J.*, July 18, 1914, 79.

11. "The Opium and Morphine Traffic," *C&D*, June 19, 1920, 56.

12. "The Opium and Morphine Traffic," 56.

13. "Morphine Smuggling," *C&D*, August 30, 1919, 68. A report from the British Chamber of Commerce in Turkey explained why Japanese demand for Turkish opium had, until recently, been so great: "The Japanese are employing large numbers of Chinese labourers in Manchuria and elsewhere for cultivation purposes. It was noticed during the war that unless this labour was supplied with opium very little work was done. The Japanese found it necessary to give each workman an injection of morphine before work was started, and another at the end of the day; in this way very good results were obtained." Quoted in "Turkey Opium," *C&D*, September 11, 1920, 82.

14. PRO, FO 371/2914/10262/239. Letter from P. O'Brien-Butler, Consul-General in Mukden, July 24, 1917, to B. Alston, Ambassador to Peking.

15. Copy enclosed in letter from Sir C. Greene, Ambassador to Tokyo, to Mr. Balfour, April 29, 1917 (PRO, FO 371/2914/10262/127).

16. Extract from the *Times*, March 27, 1920 (PRO, FO 371/5305).

17. See PRO, FO 371/2914/10262/50–52.

18. See PRO, FO 371/2914/10262/62,70.

19. Two long letters by government officials discuss the morphia trade after 1917: M. Delevingne to Sir Eric Drummond, August 4, 1920 (PRO, HO 45/19978/402144); and Sir C. Eliot, Ambassador to Tokyo, to Lord Curzon, January 9, 1922 (PRO, FO 371/8025/47–51).

20. Deric Bolton, "The Development of Alkaloid Manufacture in Edinburgh, 1832–1932," *Chemistry and Industry*, September 4, 1976, 702.

21. *Japan Chronicle,* June 30, 1921 (copy in PRO, FO 371/8025/43). The paper mistakenly quotes the price of morphia in London as 20s. per pound; in fact it was about 16s. per ounce. The comparison between the London and China prices of morphine is thus not 8 to 1000 yen, but about 100 to 1000 yen.

22. The files concerning British efforts to secure international agreement on the certificate system are in the Public Record Office (PRO, FO 371/5305–10).

23. See PRO, FO 371/9248/127–40.

24. The Home Office files on the Humphrey case are still closed. However, in 1923, Malcolm Delevingne of the Home Office sent a series

of letters to the Foreign Office, setting out the facts revealed by the investigation and trying to enlist the Foreign Office's cooperation in urging European governments to crack down on their subjects involved in the illicit drug traffic (PRO, FO 371/9247/24–50).

25. See PRO, FO 371/9247/26.

26. See PRO FO 371/9247/32–33.

27. See PRO, FO 371/9247/27.

28. In 1922, the French government issued import licenses for 1814 kilos (63,853 oz.) of morphia. See "Dangerous Drugs: Figures for Leading Countries," *Pharm. J.*, December 20, 1924, 658.

29. See PRO, FO 371/9247/45.

30. See PRO, FO 371/9247/37–39.

31. See PRO, FO 371/9247/30–31.

32. See PRO, FO 371/9247/30–31.

33. See PRO, FO 371/8026/50; also FO 371/8025 and 8027.

34. See PRO, FO 371/9247/263.

35. See PRO, FO 371/9248/144.

36. See PRO, FO 371/9248/26–28.

37. See PRO, FO 371/9248/26–28.

38. See PRO, FO 371/9248/49–50.

39. See PRO, FO 371/9248/49–50.

40. Macfarlan and Smith both continued to produce morphia, although at considerably reduced levels. In the 1930s, for example, Macfarlan averaged 10,000 ounces per annum. Codeine-manufacture, which previously had accounted for less than 10 percent of all opium-alkaloid production, expanded rapidly as worldwide demand grew. Eventually codeine replaced morphia as Macfarlan's largest-selling opium alkaloid (see Bolton, p. 708).

41. "Illicit Drug Traffic," *Times*, November 7, 1923.

CHAPTER ELEVEN

Illicit Drug Use in the Twenties

By the end of 1923, strict enforcement of the Dangerous Drugs Act meant that British drugs were largely eliminated from the illicit international traffic in narcotics. But what was the effect of DDA enforcement on the domestic traffic in illicit drugs? Was the picture of the drug traffic as it was drawn by popular novelists and journalists a reflection of reality? Were their stories isolated and atypical or were they fairly representative of drug trafficking in the twenties?

The social historian always looks at reality through the prism of his sources. Distortion, which occurs under the best of circumstances, is magnified when the subject is an illegal activity like drug trafficking. Furthermore, the best sources—contemporary police reports—are presently closed to researchers under the 75-year rule covering certain Home Office records. Nevertheless, there are some available sources which can bring us closer to an understanding of the reality of drug trafficking than the few cases that made headlines.

Britain was an original and enthusiastic member of the League of Nations' Opium Advisory Committee, established in 1920. The British government submitted to the OAC annual reports on narcotic drugs in the United Kingdom, which included complete statistics on persons prosecuted under the Dangerous Drugs Acts.[1] In addition to these statistics, we have the summaries of several hundred individual DDA prosecutions published in the *Times*. These summaries, while brief, provide enough information about individual cases to flesh out the statistical skeleton. From these two sources it is possible to construct a fairly complete profile of DDA offenders and to understand how policemen and magistrates dealt with them. Nevertheless, though these data bring us closer to the reality of drug trafficking than the fictional or journalistic accounts, they are still skewed in certain ways.

First, since drug addiction *per se* was never a crime, and doctors continued to have the option of maintaining addicts on nondiminishing doses of drugs, a certain amount of drug-taking was not reflected in prosecution records. A person who had become addicted to morphia might be able to find a doctor who would be willing to continue prescribing it for him, especially if his habit were therapeutically induced. As long as the addict did not try to obtain morphia from a second doctor, or with a forged prescription, he would not run afoul of the law. In contrast to morphia, heroin was rarely used therapeutically in Britain, and cocaine's legitimate medical uses had declined drastically by the 1920s. It was unlikely that a doctor would ever see a patient who had become therapeutically addicted to either heroin or cocaine, and thus very unlikely that he would be willing to prescribe those drugs to addicts. While morphia addicts had a good chance of maintaining their addiction legally, heroin and cocaine addicts did not, and so were forced into situations where they would have to commit illegal acts in pursuit of their supplies. Thus morphia addicts were certainly underrepresented relative to cocaine or heroin addicts in the prosecution statistics.

Second, since smoking opium was a proscribed substance, mere possession of it was an illegal act. Furthermore, the smoking of opium was usually limited geographically to the tiny Chinese quarter of a few port cities, and was easy to detect because of opium's pungent odor. Virtually all of the offenders were Chinese, who often did not speak English and were not familiar with British narcotics laws. All of these factors made Chinese opium smokers likely targets for arrest and prosecution, and thus assured that they would be overrepresented in the prosecution statistics.

Third, since police and prosecutors traditionally treat the
wealthy and powerful more gingerly than the poor and weak,
the latter were more likely to be arrested; and if arrested, they
were more likely to be prosecuted than the former. To some
extent, this was a function of visibility. Cocaine might be dis-
creetly sniffed at an upper-class country house by weekend
guests with fair assurance that the local constable would not
come snooping around the premises. But cocaine being traded
in the streets of Soho was a much more public act. And especially
if the traders were prostitutes and thugs, they were likely to be
arrested and prosecuted. Even if a well-to-do person were arrested for a drug violation, there was a good chance that his
influence and his money would protect him from prosecution.
Only in the event of a highly publicized drug death would the
resulting inquest turn up tidbits of information about upper-
class drug-taking. This is what happened in the cases of Billie
Carleton, in 1918, and Freda Kempton, in 1922. One can speculate that some drug-taking probably occurred among the upper
classes, particularly in those social niches where the privileged
flirted with bohemianism: the universities, literary circles like
Bloomsbury, and upper-class clubs and brothels in London. But
the sources appear too insubstantial to support anything more
than speculation. In any case, the rich and powerful are certainly underrepresented in the prosecution statistics.

Given these qualifications it is possible to generalize about
the patterns of drug use and drug trafficking in the twenties
from the available data. The most dramatic development was
the steep decline in total DDA prosecutions after 1923 (see Fig.
5). From 1921 to 1923 there were between 200 and 300 cases per
year; after 1923 there was never more than 100 in any year. All
categories of drugs were affected. Opium cases declined from
an average of 148 per annum in 1921–23 to a yearly average of
36 in 1927–29. Cocaine, which figured so prominently in the
fictional and journalistic representation of drug trafficking, declined from an annual average of 65 cases in 1921–23 to a mere
five cases per annum in 1927–29. Even morphia cases declined,
although much less dramatically, from an average of 32 cases
per year in 1921–23 to 17 on average between 1927 and 1929.

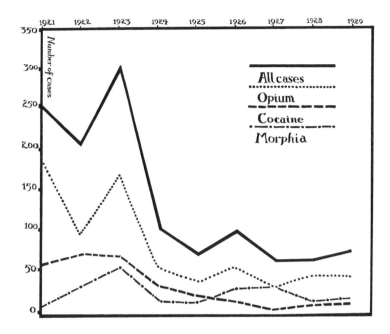

Figure 5.
Cases prosecuted under the Dangerous Drugs Acts, 1921–1929.
(*Source:* Reports of the British Government on Opium and
Other Drugs, 1921–1929, League of Nations Library, Geneva.)

One could argue that this decline reflects an addict population
which did not change its rate of drug consumption, but which
had learned, after a few years, how to avoid arrest. While that
may be partially true, the decline is simply too substantial for
that explanation to carry full weight. Surely this decline in DDA
prosecutions reflects the reality of declining use of narcotic
drugs after 1923.

The sudden increase in DDA prosecutions in 1923 and the
subsequent decline thereafter was the result of two interrelated,
but separable, factors: the police crackdown on drug dealers in
1922–24 and the social demography of narcotic drug users.

Through 1920 and 1921, police arrested and prosecuted drug users, but the really significant campaign against narcotic drugs in Britain did not begin in earnest until March 1922, when the death of another young woman made headlines. The connection of cocaine, sex, and the perception of social menace went back to the Folkestone case of 1916 and the Billie Carleton case of 1918. The death of Freda Kempton once again brought drugs into the public eye.

Freda Kempton collapsed and died on March 7, 1922. She was a beautiful young woman with "bobbed golden hair," who worked as a dance instructress in a West End night club. The inquest revealed that Freda Kempton has occasionally taken cocaine. A few phials of the drug were found in her flat. She had been depressed the night before her death because of a broken love affair, and she had spoken to a girl friend about committing suicide. The postmortem revealed that her stomach contained a residue of cocaine. Where did Freda get the drug? According to the same girl friend, it came from "Billy," an apparent reference to a Chinese restaurateur, one Brilliant Chang. Chang was quite unlike the majority of unlettered Chinese who found their way to London. The scion of a wealthy family, Chang was a smooth and dapper young hustler, well connected to London's "fast" night club set, whose restaurant was located just off the fashionable Regent Street. Under questioning Chang admitted that he had known Freda Kempton and had seen her the night before her death, but he denied that he had supplied her with cocaine. Chang was universally disbelieved.[2]

The case touched off a massive investigation into the narcotics traffic by popular newspapers. Reporters discovered London's "dancedope dens," where "the same sickening crowd of undersized aliens" mingled with "pretty, underdressed" young English girls.[3] This sort of lurid publicity stimulated a police campaign directed at suppliers and smugglers, as well as street dealers. Undercover detectives, posing as cocaine buyers, made contact with major dealers. In April 1922, an Indian, S. S. Gaikwar, aged 27, was convicted of offering 28 ounces of cocaine for sale to a detective for £30 an ounce—about 25 times the legitimate price of pharmaceutical cocaine.[4] In October, after a long investigation, police arrested three Chinese and charged them with bringing cocaine from Limehouse to the West End, where they broke it into "retail-sized" packets and offered it for sale to prostitutes. Two of the three—who were eventually convicted of the charge—were employed in Brilliant Chang's Regent Street restaurant.[5]

Police kept certain suspicious persons and places under surveillance. In December 1922, Mary Roberts, a 31-year-old Englishwoman, was followed by detectives from the Limehouse Causeway to the Strand. There she met Albert Ellis, aged 33, a commercial traveler, who gave her a package and hurriedly left. The police closed in and arrested Roberts, whose package was found to contain £100 worth of opium. At her trial, a police witness testified that Roberts had been cohabitating with a Chinese, and "was known to the Liverpool police as an associate of opium smugglers, being engaged in carrying opium for Chinese in Liverpool."[6] In August 1923, London police arrested Jack Kelson, an American seaman, after following him from Oxford Street to a Chinese restaurant in Pennyfields and back to Southampton Row. The package that Kelson picked up at the restaurant contained cocaine. According to police testimony at his trial, Kelson had been running cocaine from Limehouse to West End clubs for the last 18 months.[7] Cases similar to these appeared in the press throughout 1922 and 1923. This police campaign against London's drug traffic accounts in part for the sudden rise in prosecutions in 1923 and the decline thereafter. To a considerable extent the police were successful. They went after suppliers and dealers, and they got results. In addition, the Dangerous Drugs (Amendment) Act of 1923 provided for much stiffer sentences for first-time, and especially for repeat, offenders. By December 1923, the *Times* reported that this combination had drastically reduced the amount of cocaine trafficking in the West End.[8]

But while it may have been reduced, the cocaine traffic was very much alive so long as Brilliant Chang was still in business. On April 11, 1924, the *Daily Express* screamed out a front-page story under the headline: "Dope King Sent to Prison/Brilliant Chang to be Deported." "Efforts have been made for years by

London police to hold this elusive, cunning Chinaman, who was
without doubt the most devastating figure behind the scenes of
the illicit drug traffic, and a leader of organised Oriental vice."

   Chang was convicted as a result of either good honest police
work or a convincing police frame-up. After being arrested for
illegal possession of cocaine, one Violet Payne testified that she
had sought out Chang in a Limehouse restaurant and expressed
interest in buying some cocaine. Chang disappeared, but shortly
thereafter a hand appeared over a nearby wall and presented
her with a packet of cocaine. She placed a pound note in the
same hand—never seeing the person to whom it was presumably
attached—and left. Police swooped down on Chang's house and
searched it, finding in a kitchen cupboard a small quantity of
cocaine. He denied that it was his. Was the cocaine planted by
the police? It is difficult to believe that a shrewd operator like
Chang would have made such an elementary mistake as to leave
cocaine lying around his house. Certainly the police were frustrated, since two earlier searches of Chang's house had yielded
nothing. Nevertheless, despite these suspicious circumstances,
Chang was convicted. After the conviction, but before his sen-
tencing, a detective testified to Chang's activities. He had arrived
in Britain in 1913, and had been involved in the narcotics traffic
since 1917, "but he was so crafty that it was almost impossible to
catch him." The police, however, claimed to have extensive
knowledge of his dealings:

> Chang was a dealer in five [sic] kinds of dope—cocaine, or 'white
> snow,' heroin, opium, and hasheesh. He obtained his supplies
> from Chinese and other foreign sailors, and had agents in Paris,
> Brussels, Berlin, and Antwerp as well as China. His Paris agent
> was a woman, who is believed to have smuggled drugs into this
> country by using a little child, and sewing the drugs into her
> bloomers.
>   He would never deal direct with any drug-taker unless the
> person was a girl, with whom he made his own conditions. The
> girls he corrupted he used time and again as his selling agents.
> They knew where they could get the drugs, and acted as passers
> on for Brilliant Chang. He used to sit in the Chinese restaurants
> of Limehouse, and clients would come to him. His motorcar

would take him on mysterious journeys to the West and to the suburbs.

Many girls, during the last few months, have been arrested by the police for having cocaine and other drugs in their possession, and when asked where they obtained their supplies have said Brilliant Chang, but never until the present charge could police find Chang with any drug in his house.[9]

He was sentenced to 14 months' imprisonment and deported. It is necessary to discount the police summary of Chang's activities for some embroidery, but surely he was one of the most important links between Limehouse and the West End, between opium and cocaine, and between foreign smugglers and English users. His conviction, along with the conviction of smaller fry in 1922–24 and the change in the Dangerous Drugs Act, broke the spine of the flourishing drug traffic in London. After 1924 there was only one recorded case in which a Chinese was convicted of illegal possession of any drug other than opium.[10] After Chang, the prosecution summaries reveal a pattern of narcotics trafficking and use that had—except for a few operations like Chang's—been dominant throughout the 1920s: opium users, cocaine users, and morphia users were three distinct groups, and very rarely mixed with one another.

Opium cases constituted 57 percent of all DDA prosecutions during the twenties decade. Over 80 percent of the opium cases were prosecuted in London, Liverpool, and Cardiff—all ports of call for ships engaged in trade to the Far East. The mean age of opium offenders was 38.1, reflecting an age distribution of an adult, working population. The offenders were 98 percent male; throughout the entire decade only twelve women were prosecuted for opium offenses. Fifty-five percent of opium offenders listed their occupation as seamen; another 22 percent were laundrymen.[11] The opium offenders that appeared in the summaries of prosecutions almost always had Chinese names. Opium prosecutions were usually for simple possession or for smoking of opium. The punishment for opium offenses ranged from small fines of £5 or £10 to fines of £100 and deportation. Opium offenders were not regularly sentenced to jail terms.

Opium smoking in Britain was confined, for the most part, to Chinese, most of whom were transient seamen. They smuggled in small amounts of opium and rarely dealt in other drugs, especially after 1924. Opium "dens" usually consisted of a room in a Chinese restaurant or in a rooming house frequented by Chinese sailors in Limehouse or in similar Chinese settlements in Liverpool and Cardiff.

Magistrates, realizing perhaps that opium-smoking was both geographically and socially confined, dealt rather leniently with opium offenders, especially if they were merely smokers. In July 1922, the police raided an opium den in Limehouse when they smelled the distinctive odor of smoking opium. Six Chinese were found in a room either smoking or preparing opium to be smoked. The proprietor was Low Ping You, whose deceased English wife had been connected to the Billie Carleton circle four years earlier. Police called Low Ping You "one of the principals in the opium traffic" and recommended him for deportation. The others, who were merely smokers, were fined £5 each.[12] Magistrates dealt more harshly with those Chinese they suspected of dealing in opium. In February 1924, police raided four Chinese laundries in Manchester after receiving a tip that they were the bases for the opium traffic in the north of England. The police arrested nine Chinese and seized a "considerable" amount of smoking opium. The ringleader, Jou Sing, aged 61, who had lived in England for 22 years, was sentenced to jail for six months and fined £100, and his eight associates were sentenced to terms of from three to four months' imprisonment. All nine were recommended for deportation.[13] While deportation meant virtually nothing to a transient seaman, it could be a significant deterrent to a Chinese who had established a business and perhaps a family in Britain. Surely the fates of men like Jou Sing, Low Ping You, and Brilliant Chang must have caused other Chinese living in Britain to think twice before entering into the opium traffic.

The data on cocaine offenders reveal quite a different demographic profile from opium offenders. Cocaine offenders had a mean age of 32.7 for the entire decade, but only 26.9 for the three years at the beginning of the decade, when the street traffic in cocaine was at its height. Nineteen percent of cocaine offenders were women. The occupations of cocaine offenders varied so widely as to be virtually unclassifiable. In general, however, cocaine offenders were much more likely to have a working-class occupation, or no occupation at all, than were other drug offenders. In contrast to opium offenders, only 24 percent of cocaine offenders were seamen or ships' officers. Although a number of foreigners were prosecuted for cocaine offenses, almost no Chinese were, and none after 1925. If we turn to the summaries of individual prosecutions, we can bring these statistics to life.

Cocaine was by far the most popular street drug in Britain in the twenties. It was peddled by men, and occasionally by women, in the streets of Soho. Then as now, the Soho–Leicester Square area was given over to entertainment: restaurants, theaters, clubs and brothels were packed cheek-by-jowl. Most of the cocaine cases in the early 1920s began with arrests in this area. Typically, a detective would see a young man offering something for sale to a prostitute. The detective would make an arrest, and the suspect would be found to be in possession of "retail" sized packets of cocaine—diluted by 25 to 50 percent—which sold for 5s. to 10s. a packet. The defendant would be convicted and sentenced to jail, usually for three to six months. There were, however, variations on this standard scenario.

Often the street dealers were women. In April 1922, Britannia Yettram, aged 33, was convicted of offering to sell and being in unauthorized possession of cocaine. The undercover policeman's testimony provides a glimpse of Yettram's operation:

Police-sergeant Marks stated that the prisoners were seated on Thursday evening the the lounge of the Shaftesbury Tavern, a public house on Shaftesbury Avenue, and altogether four women approached Yettram and went upstairs with her, remaining a few minutes and then leaving the premises. The first-comer said to Yettram 'Got it?' while another inquired 'Any snow, Gipsy?' and Yettram, who is also known by the name 'Gipsy,' replied that she had.[14]

It was difficult for police to obtain evidence against drug suppliers. Max George Rosenz, aged 32, arrested for selling cocaine in Soho, summed up his precarious situation in answer to a magistrate's question: "I am working for the biggest man in London. You know him quite well, but I can't split on him, can I?"[15] Occasionally, however, the police managed to turn a street dealer into a prosecution witness. William Henry Stewart, aged 43, was given the maximum sentence of six months at hard labor in 1922 for supplying cocaine to unauthorized persons on the testimony of Sophia Marlow, a young cripple. She said that "the defendant give her cocaine to sell to girls in the streets. She sold the packets for 5s. each. At first she gave the defendant 2s.6d. and kept 2s.6d., but later gave him 2s. and kept 3s. She was supplied with packets of 10 or 20 at a time."[16]

Even more rarely, a supplier would be caught with drugs in his possession. In 1921, Frederick Masters, aged 28, was sentenced to six months' imprisonment, with hard labor, for unauthorized possession of cocaine. Masters was descibed by the arresting policeman as one of the "principals" behind the Soho cocaine traffic. He was caught holding 21 separate packages of the drug. Masters had previously been convicted once of cocaine trafficking and twice for living on "immoral earnings" (of a prostitute).[17] Occasionally, an entrepreneur would find a way to divert cocaine from the licit into the illicit market. In June 1921, Miss Doris Burton, a musician, was convicted and sentenced to three months' imprisonment for offering to sell cocaine to actors in the Vaudeville Theatre. Miss Burton got her supply from pharmaceutical distributors through her father, a chemist. She simply placed orders in her father's shop for cocaine for a fictitious German doctor, then took the drug herself. The bottle of white powder which she was trying to sell as cocaine was found to be adulterated by Epsom salts and morphia.[18]

The adage *caveat emptor* applied particularly to buyers of illicit drugs which were, and are, often adulterated or totally misrepresented. Detectives, like other buyers, could be victims of fraud. In December 1921, two men were charged with illegal possession of cocaine. However, the package with which they were seized, when analyzed, turned out to be only flour, containing no trace of cocaine. According to Detective Inspector Wise, "the police had confidential information that the defendants had offered 40 oz. of cocaine for sale, and in consequence of that observation was kept, and they were found to be in possession of this parcel which, funnily enough, weighed exactly 40 oz."[19] Occasionally prosecutors could convict fraudulent drug dealers on a lesser charge. A detective was accosted in the Holland Park tube station by a man offering to sell him three-quarters of an ounce of cocaine for £1. However, the "cocaine" turned out to be nothing more than sugar. The vendor was sentenced to six weeks of hard labor for attempting to obtain £1 under false pretenses.[20]

Usually the drug traffickers are simply names; we can glean precious little about their lives from the short prosecution summaries. One notable exception, however, is Edgar Manning, a musician from Jamaica. In 1923, at the age of 37, Manning was sentenced to three years' penal servitude for illegal possession of cocaine and opium-smoking apparatus. Manning's unusually harsh sentence was the result of his past record:

> In 1920 he received a sentence of 16 months' imprisonment for shooting at and injuring other men in a restaurant, and at that time was trafficking in drugs and living on the immoral earnings of a woman. In 1922 a man died in Manning's flat from an overdose of heroin, believed, no doubt rightly, to have been obtained from him. In 1922 he was sentenced to six months' imprisonment for the possession of opium and cocaine after being arrested in the house of a Greek woman also carrying on a business in cocaine. A woman had died in 1922 from taking drugs believed to have been obtained from him. The police stated at the Old Bailey that Manning used the drug himself, while supplying it to others.[21]

Manning also owned a revolver and an intricate hollow cane which was allegedly used to transport drugs.

Clearly, Manning was a hoodlum whose various indiscretions guaranteed that he would come to the attention of the police. His drug-dealing was only a part of a wider pattern of criminal behavior. In this regard Manning personifies the whole

cocaine traffic in the early part of the decade. Centered in the
West End, it was in the hands of young street hustlers whose
customers were prostitutes, actresses, criminals, well-to-do bohemians, night club habitués, and others on the fringes of London's underworld.

Where did the cocaine come from? How did dealers obtain
and distribute it? Some cocaine was stolen or diverted from
legitimate suppliers, as in the case of Miss Burton, the chemist's
daughter. In 1926, an undercover policeman, posing as a
cocaine buyer, was led through an intermediary to Frank Allday,
aged 48, who offered to sell him cocaine at £5 an ounce. Allday
was a dentist who had been in practice for 30 years and who had
lived at the same address for 20 years. Unlike Edgar Manning,
Allday was an established professional who was unable to resist
the enormous profit to be made by diverting cocaine from his
practice.[22] But under the system of licensing and registration
established with the DDA, government inspectors kept track of
cocaine orders, especially in large amounts. Thus the quantity
that could be diverted without arousing suspicion was very
small, and this source accounts for little of the cocaine in the
illicit traffic.

Most of the illicit supply had to be smuggled into the country. In 1922, the *Evening News* ran a series of articles on cocaine
smuggling into Britain. According to these reports, the "snow"
was moved from the Continent in small quantities in a variety of
goods: French flowers and vegetables, German sausages, bri-
quettes and fire-lighters, opera hats, cheeses and other articles,
including, to the horror of the reporter, hollowed-out models of
the Whitehall Cenotaph ("Only the German mind could have
sunk to this level . . .").[23] While the specifics of this article may be
suspect, the general thrust of it was surely true.

Because of lax controls, and a large cocaine manufacturing
industry, much of the smuggled cocaine that ended up in Britain did in fact come from Germany, and most of it entered the
country in small packets. Heinrich Mayer, an elderly German,
was arrested in Folkestone for attempting to smuggle six ounces
of cocaine into the country. Mayer's ingenuous protest that the
cocaine was "medicine," intended for personal use, was some-

what undercut by his admission of having made forty recent trips between Germany and England.[24] Cocaine, like opium, was often smuggled in small quantities by seamen and ships' officers. In 1924, a cook and an engineer on board a German ship offered to sell five grams of cocaine to an undercover customs' officer for £4. One of the defendents had claimed that the next time they could bring in five ounces.[25] Some criminals smuggled cocaine as a sideline to other business. In 1926, Henricus Augustus Boom, a 29-year-old Dutch citizen, pleaded guilty to unauthorized possession of cocaine. According to police testimony, Boom had been living in London for twelve months, during which time he had traveled frequently to Holland and France "in order to bring cocaine to this country and to arrange for the journeys of undesirable foreign women."[26]

There were occasional indications of large-scale cocaine smuggling. In 1922, a first-class Australian passenger from Hamburg was arrested in Grimsby when it was discovered that his false-bottomed trunk contained 3½ pounds of cocaine in 100 bottles. The drug, which he claimed he had purchased in Germany for £60, had a value on the illicit market of £3000.[27] Two Swedish merchants were convicted of cocaine trafficking when they offered to sell 3½ kilos of cocaine to a detective for £1800 per kilo. They claimed that the prospective buyer could sell it at more than double that price in a certain night club in the West End.[28]

Cocaine was attractive to smuggle because it had a high value and was relatively easily concealed. It could be purchased for £1 per ounce in Germany and sold for up to fifty times that price in England. When diluted with boric acid or some other adulterant, an ounce of cocaine could yield 400 packets which, by late 1923, could be sold for 10s. each on the street, for a total of £200. With profits of this magnitude it is not surprising that cocaine attracted dealers and smugglers in the early twenties. Yet despite the glimpses of the cocaine traffic afforded us by the prosecution summaries, its structure is not entirely clear. Above the level of street dealers there were suppliers like Stewart or Masters, who probably were in direct contact with smugglers. And surely the larger operators, like Brilliant Chang, must have tried to maintain a steady supply of cocaine, either by smuggling it themselves or by making arrangements with smugglers. Since the police reports on drug trafficking during this period are still closed, we can only speculate. The prosecution records do not reveal any trace of a single, massive drug-smuggling ring, with the possible exception of Brilliant Chang's operation. It is most likely that there were several wholesalers operating in the early 1920s, none of whom could control the entire traffic and all of whom relied, for the most part, upon smuggled cocaine that flowed into Britain in numerous trickles rather than in a single torrent.

The statistics on morphia offenders suggest still a third distinct group of drug users. The mean age of morphia offenders was 41.8, considerably older than cocaine or even than opium offenders. Twenty-three percent of all morphia offenders were female, a higher proportion than either of the other two groups. In sharp contrast to cocaine and opium offences, which occurred predominantly in London, morphia offences were geographically scattered: only 24 percent of all morphia cases originated in London. The occupational profile of morphia offenders was also unique: less than 10 percent were seamen, but 62 percent were either chemists, doctors, or nurses. Fully 25 percent of morphia offences were technical; that is, they usually involved the failure of a doctor, a chemist, or a firm to keep records properly. This means that the number of serious morphia offences was even smaller than the total suggests.

Nearly all serious morphia offences involved an individual addict trying to obtain the drug illegally from a chemist or doctor. Forging prescriptions was the most common offence. In 1924, a husband and wife, Patrick and Winnifred McKay, both aged 37, were charged with illegal possession of morphia. McKay had become addicted to morphia in 1904, while he served in the Royal Navy and had suffered extreme pain in an attack of appendicitis. From 1904 to 1907 he took 40 grains per day, but eventually was able to reduce his daily dosage to four grains. During the war, he again began using drugs very heavily when he contracted tuberculosis. His wife, a nurse, became addicted to morphia when her husband suggested that she use it for neuralgia. They obtained morphia by forging prescriptions in the name of Dr. J. J. Levins. In a ten-month period prior to their arrest, Mr. and Mrs. McKay had consumed 4,054 grains of morphia.[29] Katharine Fryer, a 51-year-old nurse, was charged with obtaining morphia with a forged prescription. On this occasion, the prescription was made up for another person in the name of a nonexistent doctor, and sent to Nurse Fryer at Seaford.[30]

Occasionally addicts tried to pass themselves off as medical men, and thus obtain larger supplies from chemists, or even from pharmaceutical suppliers. But such impersonations, because they could easily be checked against the medical register, were doomed to eventual failure. In 1922, a Mr. Wolfe was sentenced to four months' imprisonment for obtaining supplies of heroin—to which he was addicted—by posing as an Austrian doctor. The chemist who was taken in by Mr. Wolfe's masquerade—to the point of allowing him a 10 percent professional discount—was fined £100 for his duplicity.[31] Another addict assumed a literal masquerade, dressing up as a naval surgeon and obtaining "large amounts" of morphia and cocaine from chemists in the port city of Southampton.[32] Finally, addicts sometimes tried to augment their supplies of morphia or heroin by obtaining prescriptions from two or more physicians simultaneously. After 1926 this became an offence under the Dangerous Drugs Act.

Magistrates generally dealt compassionately with morphia offenders, especially if they were therapeutically addicted, middle-aged women. Their sentences usually consisted of probation if the defendant promised to enter a convent or some other institution where she could undertake a drug cure.[33] Morphia addicts, then, tended to be middle-aged persons, often in health-related occupations, living outside of London, whose habits were therapeutically induced. Often they managed their habits under the care of a medical man, and only infrequently did they run afoul of the law.

The illicit traffic in morphia was almost nonexistent. Morphia was not available, for the most part, from the cocaine dealers in the West End or from the opium users in Limehouse.

(This was especially so after the demise of Brilliant Chang in 1924.) But even if it had been, the great majority of British morphia addicts would have been unwilling, and perhaps unable, to buy it in the streets. Middle-aged professionals were, both geographically and socially, worlds apart from Soho drug dealers. No matter how desperate she was for her morphia, it is difficult to envision Nurse Fryer queuing up with prostitutes at the Shaftesbury Tavern to buy drugs from "Gipsy" Yettram. Morphia users thought of themselves, and were largely regarded by others, not as recreational drug users, but as unfortunate victims who had succumbed to addiction in the course of medical treatment. When they were unable to obtain their drug through legal means, they turned to expedients which were illegal extensions of their usual means of supply: forging prescriptions and impersonating doctors.

The prosecution records suggest that there was an element of truth in the literary and journalistic depictions of drug addiction, at least for the immediate postwar years and the early twenties. Billie Carleton, Freda Kempton, and Brilliant Chang were visible manifestations of a submerged social reality. Even so, it was strictly limited. The drug subculture was based on cocaine and did not embrace, for the most part, opium smokers or morphia takers. It was so small and tentative that it was virtually harassed out of existence by concerted police action and stiffer sentences for convicted drug dealers. After 1924, illicit drug use in Britain was on the wane.

Notes

1. The complete British reports to the Opium Advisory Committee for 1921–1923 are available in the Public Record Office. For subsequent years, however, those reports that exist are missing the section containing information about DDA prosecutions. This section consists of several tables which summarize how many cases were prosecuted, the offences and disposition of the cases, and the ages and occupations of the offenders. Names are never given except in summaries of extraordinary cases like those involving Humphrey,

Chang, or Miyagawa. The location and document numbers of the reports are as follows: Public Record Office, Kew: for 1921—HO 45 19982/402144; for 1922—FO 371/9238; and for 1923—FO 371/10325/07762. League of Nations' Archive, UN Library, Geneva: for 1924—Registry file 1919–27; 12A/44903/18661; for 1925—O.C.23(b)4(2); for 1926—O.C.23(e)8; for 1927—O.C.23 (m)11(a); for 1928—O.C.23(h)15; and for 1929—O.C.23(e)19.

2. *Daily Express*, March 6, 8, and 10, 1922; *Times*, March 10, 1922.

3. *Daily Express*, March 11, 13, 14, 15, 16, and 21; April 18 and 25; *Evening News*, March 10, 12, 13, 14, 16, 17, 20, 22, 23, and 29.

4. "Dope Agent's Secret," *Daily Express*, April 3, 1922; "Indian Cocaine Trafficker," *Times*, April 3, 1922.

5. "The Cocaine Traffic," *Times*, October 30 and November 7, 1922.

6. *Times*, January 1 and 8, 1923.

7. "Alleged Possession of Cocaine," *Times*, August 6, 1923.

8. "Cocaine Traffic. The Evil Checked," *Times*, December 5, 1923. See also "Cocaine Traffic Suppression: Effect of the Police Campaign," *Times*, December 3, 1923, and "The Cocaine Traffic," *Times*, July 29, 1922.

9. *Daily Express*, April 11, 1924. See also *Daily News*, April 14, 1924; *East End News*, April 15, 1924; and *Times*, April 11, 1924.

10. "Chinese with Opium," *Times*, May 23, 1925.

11. All of these, and subsequent, statistics were compiled from the annual British reports to the Opium Advisory Committee.

12. "Raid on an Opium Den," *Times*, July 30, 1922.

13. "Opium Traffic in Manchester: Chinese Laundrymen Sent to Prison," *Times*, February 25, 1924.

14. "Women's Cocaine Traffic," *Times*, April 8, 1922.

15. "Prison for a Cocaine Trafficker," *Times*, November 13, 1922.

16. "Street Sales of Cocaine," *Times*, September 17, 1922.

17. "Man in the Background," *Times*, June 6, 1921.

18. *Pharm. J.*, July 9, 1921, 41.

19. "Not Cocaine, but Flour," *Times*, December 31, 1921.

20. "Sugar as Dope," *Daily Express*, May 2, 1922.

21. *Lancet*, August 4, 1923, 247.

22. "Cocaine at £5 per Ounce," *Times,* October 1, 1926.
23. "Drugs Hidden in Flowers," *Evening News,* March 29, 1922.
24. "German Charged with Cocaine," *Times,* July 18, 1925.
25. "Cocaine Importers on the Docks," *Times,* February 27, 1924.
26. "Trafficking in Cocaine," *Times,* July 29, 1926.
27. "Cocaine Smuggler Sentenced," *Times,* June 24, 1922.
28. "Bloomsbury Cocaine Charge," *Times,* September 17, 1923.
29. "Morphine Victims," *Times,* August 27, 1924.
30. "A Drug Victim," *Times,* July 18, 1923.
31. *Pharm. J.,* March 11, 1922, 200.
32. "Drug-Taker Sent to Prison," *Times,* February 27, 1922.
33. See "Woman Drug Victim," *Times, February 8, 1922;* "A Drug Victim," *Times,* July 18, 1923; and "A Morphia Victim," *Times,* January 1, 1924.

CHAPTER TWELVE

Evaluating Drug Abuse:
The Rolleston Committee Report

The Rolleston Committee Report of 1926 is often hailed as a model of dispassionate analysis and judicious recommendation on the subject of narcotic drug abuse, especially in juxtaposition to the hardening enforcement situation in contemporary America. In part it was. However, in a retrospective appraisal of the Rolleston Committee, one may lose sight of the fact that its findings were shaped by a variety of factors which grew out of the history of drug use and control in Britain: the "loose ends" of previous legislation; the development of the disease model of addiction; the social realities of the British addict population; and the professional interests and political power of medical men. In appreciating the Rolleston Committee's work, and especially in trying to apply its findings to other places and other times, one must remember that is was addressed to the very particular needs of Britain in the 1920s.

The Rolleston Committee—or the Ministry of Health Departmental Committee on Morphine and Heroin Addiction, to give it its proper name—owed its inception to a small but persistent problem in enforcing the Dangerous Drugs Act. What was to be done about doctors who prescribed large amounts of narcotic drugs for patient-addicts without in any way trying to "cure" them of their addiction? And what was to be done about doctor-addicts who prescribed for themselves? In the first two years of the DDA, a small number of both types of cases had come to the attention of Malcolm Delevingne at the Home Office. An example of the former was Dr. Donald J. Grant, a general practitioner in Glasgow. Dr. Grant, according to a report filed by the Glagow Chief Constable, was unkempt, eccentric, and alcoholic, and was known locally as "the daft doctor." He had previously come to the attention of the Scottish Board of Health for the strange combination of medicines he had prescribed for certain patients. The Chief Constable noted that large amounts of narcotic drugs were being supplied to Dr. Grant, which he admitted administering to a Mr. George Ellis. Ellis was a masseur whose leg had been amputated fifteen years before. Thereafter, he had "suffered from time to time from neuralgic pains in the stomach," which he relieved by taking large doses of narcotic drugs. Between August 30 and December 30, 1922, Ellis took 4,360 grains of morphia and 620 grains of cocaine, all supplied by Dr. Grant. Ellis admitted that he was an addict, although not a "degenerate," and claimed that he could not work without the drugs.[1]

An example of the latter was Dr. J. A. A. Boddy, a medical man in general practice with his father in a working-class district of Manchester. A routine investigation of the ledgers of a local manufacturing chemist showed that substantial amounts of morphia were being supplied to the Drs. Boddy. An inspection by the Divisional Medical Officer revealed that the elder Dr. Boddy used morphia suppositories nightly for a rectal complaint, and the younger Dr. Boddy, "a nervous and emaciated man," regularly took large hypodermic injections of morphia.[2]

In seeking legal advice, Delevingne found that he probably would not be able to make a case against Dr. Grant, or even the Drs. Boddy. A doctor could claim that supplying drugs to a patient, even if he were an addict, was a form of "medical treatment," and thus lawful according to the DDA. Moreover, unless a doctor were actually convicted of an offence under the DDA, he could not be deprived of his right to prescribe and dispense narcotic drugs. In the end, Delevingne sent the wayward doctors stern letters, threatening to prosecute them unless they stopped supplying and taking narcotic drugs. But he knew full well that, if it actually came to legal action, a prosecution would probably fail.[3]

There was, then, this anomaly created by the DDA: an addict could be prosecuted if he bought his drugs from a dealer on the streets in Soho or on a forged prescription in a chemist's shop. But if he managed to find a down-and-out doctor, like Dr. Grant, who would write prescriptions with few questions asked, he could have his drugs quite legally. Even worse, in Delevingne's view, was the fact that a doctor-addict could supply himself. The absolute number of such cases was small, but for Delevingne, the archetypal bureaucrat, such legal untidiness was disturbing. What he needed was a definition of the legitimate medical use of narcotic drugs which would exclude addiction and be of sufficient authority that it would stand up in court. That would allow him to prosecute culprits like the Drs. Boddy and Grant while not interfering with those medical men who used narcotic drugs for therapeutic purposes.[4]

In November 1922, Delevingne sent a memo to the Ministry of Health, asking for a medical opinion on the treatment of addiction by sudden or gradual withdrawal, and enclosing a copy of South African legislation which specifically prohibited doctors from maintaining addicts on nondiminishing doses of narcotic drugs. A second letter, sent two months later by A. J. Eagleston of the Home Office, was even more forward in spelling out the Home Office's dilemma. Finally, Delevingne suggested that the Royal College of Physicians, as an authoritative medical body, be asked to deliver an opinion on addiction.[5] But Delevingne did not get the clear-cut ruling he was hoping for. E. W. Adams, of the Ministry of Health, responded to Delevingne's request with an investigation of medical opinion on the sudden withdrawal method of treating addiction. Although this method is preferred in America, he noted, it "cannot usually be adopted except as part of institutional treatment, and would therefore only be practicable in a relatively small number of cases in this country, in view of the limited institutional accommodations available. It would seem, therefore, unnecessary to trouble the Royal College of Physicians by asking them to appoint a committee of investigation."[6]

In reply, Delevingne conceded that sudden withdrawal as an exclusive therapy was "impracticable," but he still wanted an authoritative statement on addiction. While Ministry of Health officials were anxious to mollify Delevingne, they were nevertheless reluctant to accept addiction of the patient as a factor which would justify limiting the doctor's right to prescribe.[7] Faced with this opposition of his colleagues, and the failure to carry through the regulation prohibiting a doctor from prescribing for himself, Delevingne finally accepted a compromise in 1924. A departmental committee, appointed by the Ministry of Health, would investigate the issue of drug addiction and make recommendations which would clarify the ambiguities that troubled Delevingne. This represented a small defeat for Delevingne in the guerrilla wars of bureaucracy. He had been unable to secure the definitive medico-legal opinion he sought; instead he had to take a chance on a committee that was not even responsible to his department. Still, it seemed like the only way to resolve the enforcement problem.[8]

The creation of the Committee, and its composition, reflected the greater willingness of the Ministry of Health than the Home Office to take cognizance of medical opinion in framing dangerous drugs legislation. Delevingne had been content to draft the original legislation, as well as the 1921 regulations, with no prior consultation with medical men or pharmacists, much against the wishes of Ministry of Health officials. The primary purpose of dangerous drugs legislation, he believed, was to codify Britain's commitments to the Hague Opium Convention and succeeding international agreements. This usually meant drafting legislation which took a much "harder" line toward narcotic drugs than would have been supported by interested professional groups. Only when he was confronted by the defeat of his policy in 1923 did Delevingne surrender the initiative to the Ministry of Health.

Dr. Smith-Whitaker of the Ministry of Health suggested

that the Committee be chaired by Sir Humphry Rolleston, distinguished physician and President of the Royal College of Physicians, who had previously acted as a consultant for the Ministry. Delevingne agreed and confined himself to nominating as a member of the Committee Dr. G. M. Cullen of the Scottish Board of Health, who "has seen a number of morphine addicts in Scotland."[9] The Committee was formally appointed on September 30, 1924. It was composed entirely of medical men and was heavily weighted toward recognized experts on addiction. For example, besides Rolleston himself, the Committee included William Willcox, W. E. Dixon, and R. W. Branthwaite, all of whom had ties to the Society for the Study and Cure of Inebriety, and had written and lectured on the subject of drug addiction. There were two Ministry of Health officials on the Committee, in addition to the two secretaries, and only one general practitioner, who had been nominated by the British Medical Association. There was no representative of pharmacists (unless one counts W. E. Dixon, Reader in Pharmacology at Cambridge), and only Dr. Branthwaite from the Home Office on the Committee. This virtually guaranteed that the Committee would be more sympathetic to medical than enforcement issues and that it would reflect the theory of addiction that had been developed in the professional medical literature.[10]

Once constituted, the Committee met fortnightly from October 1924, through October 1925, in a total of 23 sessions. As if to underscore its medical predisposition, the Committee took evidence from 34 witnesses, all of whom, save two, were either medical men or connected to the drug trade. One of the exceptions was Malcolm Delevingne. His testimony, given at the Committee's second meeting, revealed a great deal about his concerns. Delevingne touched on many specific issues, but his overriding intention was to tidy up loose ends efficiently and cautiously. Several times he turned back suggestions from individual Committee members for more extensive controls over addicts because of the practical problems involved. For example, when one member suggested that the Inebriates' Act be extended to include drug addicts, Delevingne, perhaps remember-

ing past defeats, replied that it was not "practical politics" at the
moment.[11] And when another Committee member raised the
possibility of legislating for the involuntary incarceration of
drug addicts, similar to the process provided for the mentally ill
by the Lunacy Acts, Delevingne said that it would probably be
rejected by Parliament as being too expensive. Thus Delevingne's attempts to influence the Committee members were
limited to laying the problems before them and steering them
away from controversial and expensive solutions.[12]

The Committee tried to call all the representatives of one
group of witnesses before moving on to another. It began by
interviewing prison medical officers, then hospital consultants,
then pharmacists and druggists, and finally general practitioners.[13] The specific questions asked of the witnesses varied somewhat from one group to the next, but they fell into four broad
categories: What is the pattern and extent of drug addiction?
What is the most effective method of treating drug addiction?
Are further regulations necessary in order to curb drug abuse?
And, should the status of certain drugs within the DDA be
changed?

Questions about the pattern and extent of addiction were
particularly important in light of the sensationalized accounts of
drug cases that had appeared in periodicals and popular literature, and the police crackdown of 1922–23. The evidence of the
witnesses was unanimous on three critical points: Drug addiction was not nearly so prevalent now as it had been before and
during the war; the absolute number of cases was tiny and diminishing as a result of the DDA; and the major drug of addiction was not heroin (as it was in the United States), or cocaine
(which was featured so prominently in the popular literature),
but morphia, which was used in 80 percent or more of the recorded cases. All of the witnesses who commented on the relationship between alcoholism and drug addiction stressed that
the former was a much more dangerous social problem than the
latter. One witness, Sir James Purves-Stewart, was able to draw
on extensive patient records in constructing a tabular summary
of the 62 cases of addiction that he had seen in private practice:

Drug Taken	*36 Men*	*26 Women*
Morphia 39	15 medical practitioners	17 married
Morphia and alcohol 8	5 military/naval officers	(12 society women)
Heroin 5	4 businessmen	9 unmarried
Chlorodyne 2	3 politicians	(5 'demi-mondaines')
Cocaine 1	2 professors	
Other 7	2 barristers	
	1 explorer	
	1 artist	
	3 no occupation	

Daily dose of morphia
  in men varied from gr. 30 to gr. ¾; average 7.2 gr.,
  in women varied from gr. 40 to gr. 1; average 10.3 gr.[14]

Purves-Stewart's data reinforced the assertion made in the medical literature on drug addiction that it was a disease of "brain workers," the professional classes, and especially medical men.

The less systematic observations of other witnesses supported this demographic profile of drug-takers. The only physician whose experience was substantially different was Dr. E. M. Niall, who reported that of sixty to eighty cases of addiction that he had seen, most were either travelers, "who had picked up the disease abroad," or "ladies of easy virtue" of either "French or American nationality."[15] Most of the addicts they saw, witnesses agreed, were not young pleasure-seekers, but rather weak-willed or sickly persons of middle or advanced years who had slipped into addiction in the course of therapeutic treatment. Moreover, many witnesses were reluctant to agree that a normal person could become a drug addict if he did not have a predisposing psychopathic condition. In nearly every respect, then, there was a sharp disparity between the nature and extent of addiction as depicted in popular literature and that experienced by medical practitioners. (Indeed, several witnesses commented on this point.) The typical drug addict was not the thrill-seeking young innocent, rapidly transformed into a dope fiend after a few snorts of cocaine, but a rather unfortunate, middle-aged gentlewoman—or gentleman—whose dependence on morphia was therapeutically induced.

With regard to treatment, witnesses confirmed the view that E. W. Adams had put forward in his memo of 1923: sudden withdrawal of drugs was practical only in an institutional setting. All of the prison officers used and favored sudden withdrawal on their convict-addicts, but they agreed that it was only the total control afforded by the prison setting that made this possible. Consultants and general practitioners had even stronger opinions on the subject. With only a few exceptions, they favored gradual withdrawal. They denounced sudden withdrawal as "barbarous and inhumane," claiming that it sometimes led to fatal collapse. Opinion was more divided on the question of whether some addicts should be maintained on their drugs. A small majority favored maintenance, although most agreed that the number of cases in which a cure was impossible, and maintenance therefore necessary, was relatively small. In answer to the specific question of whether hyoscine injections could be substituted for opiates in effecting a successful sudden withdrawal, most witnesses demurred. Individuals cited a plethora of specific treatments, from belladonna to bromides to psychotherapy, but there was no clear consensus on the issue.

Interesting data about Chinese opium users emerged in the testimony of prison medical officers and general practitioners. Contrary to the popular image, which linked Limehouse opium smokers to West End cocaine users, the witnesses mentioned Chinese only in the context of opium smoking. Some prison officers noted that Chinese opium smokers, in contrast to Caucasian drug users, seemed to suffer no withdrawal pain when deprived of their drug. Nor did witnesses cite a single instance of a cocaine or morphia user who had been introduced to drugs by a Chinese.

The Committee asked witnesses to comment on several proposed regulations to control drug abuse. Two of these, compulsory consultation and notification, were intended to make it impossible for a doctor, like the "daft" Glaswegian, Dr. Grant, to prescribe indiscriminately for addicts or for addicts to garner large stocks of narcotics by going from one doctor to another. Compulsory consultation meant that a doctor must call in a fellow practitioner for a second opinion on every new addiction case; and compulsory notification meant that he must notify the Home Office of the name of every addict he was seeing as a patient. The great majority of witnesses strongly disapproved of the compulsory nature of these proposals, on professional, ethical, and practical grounds. They argued that compulsory consultation impinged upon a practitioner's professional prerogative; that notification violated the confidentiality of the doctor-patient relationship; and that drug addiction was such an insignificant social problem in Britain that it did not warrant *any* further legislation that might inconvenience medical men. When the Home Office continued to press for some way to deal with doctors who supplied addicts, or who were addicts themselves, the British Medical Association proposed a "Medical Tribunal," composed entirely of medical men, who would sit in judgment on their colleagues who were suspected of impropriety in drug cases.

Finally, the Rolleston Committee made recommendations about two particular drugs—heroin and chlorodyne. In response to a question from the League of Nations, the Home Office asked the Committee, as well as established medical bodies like the British Medical Association, to consider whether heroin was of such negligible medical value that it could be proscribed. With only two exceptions, every questioned individual and group replied that heroin was essential for certain kinds of medical problems and should on no account be banned. Chlorodyne was a more complicated problem. Several cases of chlorodyne addiction had come to the attention of the Home Office. Since chlorodyne contained morphia in amounts smaller than 0.2 percent, it was not regulated by the DDA Dangerous Drugs Act.[16] Some observers felt that drug addicts were turning to the diluted proprietary preparations as it became more difficult for them to obtain narcotic drugs in stronger forms.[17] Yet professional interests on this issue were strong. Pharmacists and druggists, as well as some medical witnesses, argued that chlorodyne was an extremely useful household remedy, and the extent of abuse was so limited that it did not justify bringing it within the DDA.[18]

The Committee finished taking evidence in October 1925, and presented its findings on January 26, 1926. The Report was intended to fill three functions: it summarized witnesses' testimony; it presented the Committee's recommendations; and it laid down guidelines for medical men on the treatment of addiction. The Committee's recommendations closely followed the general opinions expressed by witnesses. On issues on which there had been a lack of consensus among witnesses, the Committee invariably opted for the "softer" option. For example, the Report favored gradual withdrawal over sudden withdrawal and came out against compulsory consultation and notification, despite the fact that the last was favored by many witnesses, including Malcolm Delevingne.[19]

One of the most useful contributions of the Report was to define the term "addict" to mean

> a person who, not requiring the continued use of the drug for relief of the symptoms of organic disease, has acquired, as a result of repeated administration, an overpowering desire for its continuance, and in whom withdrawal of the drug leads to definite symptoms of mental or physical distress or disorder.[20]

The Committee thereby detached the term from its pejorative associations with the "dope fiends" of popular literature, and expressed it entirely within a medical context.

On the "nature and causation" of addiction, the Report stated that "the condition must be regarded as a manifestation of disease, and not a mere form of vicious indulgence. In other words, the drug is taken not for the purpose of obtaining positive pleasure, but in order to relieve a morbid and overpowering craving."[21] Thus the Committee clearly decided that addiction must be seen as a disease rather than as a vice. Furthermore, the *Report* stated flatly that "addiction to morphine or heroin is rare in this country and has diminished in recent years."[22] This general picture of drug addiction in Britain—of a waning disease which afflicts very few people—conditioned the recommendations made in the remainder of the Report. Having determined that drug addiction was not a serious social problem, it was natural that the Committee would eschew drastic solutions. The section of the Report dealing with treatment was obviously intended to be educational. It spelled out the relative advantages and disadvantages of alternative therapies, often in minute detail. The practitioner was reminded that every case of drug addiction is peculiar and must be treated individually. Although the goal in every case must be the complete "cure" of the addiction, there are two classes of persons who might justifiably be maintained on nondiminishing doses of morphine or heroin: (1) "those in whom a complete withdrawal of morphine or heroin produces serious symptoms which cannot be treated satisfactorily under the ordinary conditions of private practice," and (2) "those who are capable of leading a fairly normal and useful life so long as they take a certain quantity, usually small, of their drug of addiction, but not otherwise."[23] Before undertaking such a course of action, however, medical men were strongly urged (although not required) to obtain a second opinion.

The Report rejected every suggestion for further controls except for the Medical Tribunal, which was to be composed of three medical men, nominated by medical organizations, to hear cases in which a doctor had been accused of prescribing or supplying dangerous drugs improperly, either for himself or for his patients.[24] On only one issue did the Report make a recommendation which contravened the suggestions made by most witnesses. Chlorodyne, the Report noted, was a mixture which had been abused. If the maximum morphia content were halved, from 0.2 percent to 0.1 percent, the danger would be practically nil. The fact that it was pharmaceutical witnesses whose suggestions about chlorodyne were overridden is significant. Although the Committee showed no particular solicitude for the professional interests of druggists and pharmacists, it turned back every suggestion which would have interfered legislatively with the right of medical men to prescribe and administer narcotic drugs. Even the acceptance of the Medical Tribunal was a manuever to keep disciplinary control over wayward doctors within the profession. The justification for these rebuffs to more regulation was that the incidence of drug addiction was so rare that it did not warrant closer controls.

Although he would have preferred a report which would have advocated a more punitive position, Delevingne was reasonably satisfied. He had got a definitive medical statement on addiction, and, in the Medical Tribunal, a body which would solve his enforcement problems. Moreover, he had got recommendations which were neither expensive nor controversial, so that ambiguities of existing drug legislation would be resolved with ruffling parliamentary feathers. Despite some grumbling from both camps over minor issues, professional opinion about the Report and its recommendations from medical men and pharmacists was restrained and not overtly antipathetic.[25] In July 1926, new regulations under the DDA were issued which incorporated the recommendations of the Rolleston Committee Report.[26]

The Rolleston Committee Report must be analyzed, and understood, on two different levels. On one level, it was the end of a process of narcotic drug regulation that had begun in 1916. For the most part, the entire issue was subpolitical. Despite the odd parliamentary question or sharp exchange on the floor of Commons, narcotic drug legislation was not an issue which touched raw political nerves. Titillated by sensational journalism and pulp fiction, most Britons felt that something should be done. But narcotics abuse did not affect their lives so significantly that they much cared about *what* was actually done. The issue was thus relegated from Westminister to the warrens of Whitehall. Here Malcolm Delevingne came to the fore, initially by default. Then, as the result of his growing expertise and his personal tenacity, Delevingne consolidated his position as the prime shaper of British drug policy. Because of his growing involvement in League of Nations drug control activities and his penchant for legal tidiness, Delevingne believed that British drug regulation should implement the international controls to which Britain was pledged. Yet he did not have an entirely free hand in the matter.

The general public may not have felt strongly about the

specifics of drug regulation, but interested professional groups did. Medical men, dentists, pharmacists, and drug dealers were all variously affected by it. Although Delevingne tried to block them, they maneuvered to influence the particulars of regulation—doctors successfully, pharmacists not. Furthermore, Delevingne had to compromise with his colleagues in the Ministry of Health who, in 1924, finally forced him to rely on a departmental committee over which he had little real influence to solve an enforcement problem. Yet despite these setbacks, Delevingne succeeded in the end in completing British drug regulation in a way which was noncontroversial and inexpensive. Pharmacists might complain, but politicians did not. Delevingne maintained drug addiction at the subpolitical level, and confined conflicts to nonessential issues. Moreover, by enforcing tough legislation, he had shown the rest of the world that Britain was serious about its transformation from the foot-dragger of the 1909 Shanghai Conference to the strong supporter of international controls of the 1920s.

On a second level, the Rolleston Committee's Report must be analyzed as the only national inquiry, however limited, into the extent and nature of drug addiction in Britain. The exclusively medical composition of the Committee had an enormous influence on the way in which Committee members perceived the problem. They extrapolated from their own and their witnesses' experiences with patients to conclude that the incidence of addiction was rare and diminishing in Britain. But Chinese seamen, West End prostitutes, and Soho nightclub habitués—those drug users who had drawn the attention of both police and journalists since 1916—were among the groups least inclined to visit a doctor, especially for a condition which they did not necessarily accept as a sickness. If the Committee had included politicians (as had the 1917 "Cocaine in Dentistry Committee"), police officers, journalists, or clergymen, or if the Committee had interviewed such persons, the Report might well have reflected a rather different opinion about the extent of addiction in Britain.

Likewise, the background of the Committee members conditioned the way in which they perceived the nature of addiction. Not only were they all medical men who had been exposed to the disease theory of drug addiction that had emerged in the medical literature over the previous two decades, but several Committee members had contributed to its formulation. This accounts for the unequivocal definition of an addict as a sick person to be cured, rather than as a criminal to be punished. In this and in virtually every other particular, the Report embodied the disease model of addiction. This theoretical orientation had significant policy implications. The recommendations on drug maintenance meant that the addict did not have to choose starkly between complete withdrawal or a criminal career. In effect, the Committee deflected Delevingne from completing the criminalization of addiction that had begun in 1916 and 1920. On this second level, then, the Rolleston Committee Report represented a victory for the medical profession. Not only did medical men beat back the proposed challenges to their professional autonomy, but in a more subtle yet important way they triumphed by imposing on the Report both the medical definition and the medical solution to the problem of drug addiction.

By the end of the twenties, narcotic drugs had not entirely disappeared from British society. Patent medicines containing small amounts of drugs, plus low-strength opiates like paregoric and codeine, continued to be available over the counter for some time thereafter. Medical men continued to prescribe morphia and even heroin in cases where they thought it was necessary. Chinese continued to be arrested and convicted on opium-smoking charges. And undoubtedly, some cocaine continued to be sniffed by self-styled bohemians. But the magnitude of both medical and recreational drug use, and concern about it, was greatly diminished by 1930. Professional squabbles among medical men, pharmacists, and civil servants had been resolved, and exemplary regulatory legislation had been passed. The infamous trade in British opiates to China had ceased. The police had successfully shut down the small drug subculture in the West End. And the Rolleston Committee had laconically informed the British people that drug addiction was a problem that was rapidly disappearing.

Except for the *Times'* dutiful reporting of occasional police raids on Chinese opium dens, narcotic drugs virtually disappeared from the newspapers, then from the novels and films, and finally from the public consciousness. Billie Carleton and Reggie de Veulle, Freda Kempton and Brilliant Chang quickly became dim memories to Britons of the 1930s and 1940s, who had much more substantial threats to be concerned about. Indeed, it was perhaps only in the early 1920s, when the nation enjoyed a short period of peace and prosperity, sandwiched between two world wars and a major depression, that Britons could indulge themselves in the luxury of worrying about a social problem, like narcotic drugs, that touched so few of their lives.

Notes

1. Report dated January 6, 1923, in the Public Record Office (HO 45/11285/440177).

2. Report from the Chief Constable of Manchester, dated February 15, 1923, in PRO, HO 45/11285/440177.

3. See PRO, HO 45/11285/440177.

4. This position is most clearly set out in a Home Office memorandum that Delevingne forwarded to the newly formed Rolleston Committee on October 12, 1924. (Copy in PRO, MH 58/277.)

5. Copies of all of these memoes are in PRO, MH 58/275.

6. Memo by E. W. Adams, dated March 1923, in PRO, MH 58/275.

7. An interdepartmental memo, dated August 23, 1923, summarized a recent meeting between Dr. Smith-Whitaker of the Ministry of Health and Delevingne: "Dr. Smith-Whitaker had got into touch with the President of the Royal [College of] Physicians and other medical men such as Dr. Branthwaite, who have a special knowledge of the subject. As a result of his inquiries he was convinced that, although a person addicted to cocaine could at once be taken off the drug, morphine and presumably heroin could not in all cases be totally withdrawn from a person addicted to those drugs." (HO 45/408/10A.)

8. Most of the correspondence concerning the background to the Rolleston Committee's appointment is in PRO, MH 58/275. There are

also a few pieces of information in a file still held at the Home
Office: (HO 45/408/10A).

9. Correspondence in PRO, MH 58/275.

10. The complete Committee, as appointed by John Wheatley, Minister
of Health, included:

Members
  Sir Humphry Rolleston, Chairman
  Sir William H. Willcox, Honorary Medical Advisor,
    Ministry of Health
  Prof. W. E. Dixon, Reader in Pharmacology, Cambridge
  Dr. R. W. Branthwaite, Home Office
  Dr. G. M. Cullen, Scottish Board of Health
  Dr. John Fawcett, Guy's Hospital
  Dr. J. Smith-Whitaker, Senior Medical Officer,
    Ministry of Health
  Dr. A. Fulton, Divisional Medical Officer,
    Ministry of Health
  Dr. J. W. Bone, representing the
    British Medical Association
Secretaries
  Dr. E. W. Adams,
    Ministry of Health
  Mr. R. H. Crooke,
    Ministry of Health

The original terms of reference of the Committee were "to consider
and advise as to the circumstance, if any, in which the supply of morphine and heroin (including preparations containing morphine and
heroin) to persons suffering from addiction to those drugs may be
regarded as medically advisable, and as to the precautions which it is
desirable that medical practitioners administering or prescribing morphine or heroin should adopt for the advoidance of abuse, and to
suggest any administrative measures that seem expedient for securing
observance of such precautions." In February 1925, the terms were
extended "to consider and advise whether it is expedient that any or all
preparations which contain morphine or heroin of a percentage lower
than that specified in the Dangerous Drugs Act should be brought
within the provisions of the Acts and Regulations and, if so, under what
conditions." The Committee was appointed by John Wheatley, who was
Minister of Health in 1924, and reported to Neville Chamberlain, who
had replaced him, in 1926.

11. According to Delevingne, "The [Home Office] Departmental Committee on the Inebriates Acts which reported in 1908 recommended the extension of the provisions of the Inebriates Acts to persons addicted to the use of drugs, and a provision to this effect was included in the Inebriates Bill introduced by the Home Office in the House of Commons in 1914. No progress however could be made with the Bill and it is well known that the Inebriates Acts are now practically inoperative." (PRO, MH 58/277, October 12, 1924, p. 4.)

12. Copies of the minutes of the Committee meetings, and Delevingne's testimony, are in PRO, MH 58/276.

13. The testimony of all witnesses is included in two files: PRO, MH 58/277 and 278.

14. See PRO, MH 58/277.

15. See PRO, MH 58/277.

16. Prior to 1920, J. Collis Browne's Chlorodyne contained 0.19 percent morphia; after the passage of the Dangerous Drugs Act, the manufacturer lowered the morphia content to 0.15 percent, just to be on the safe side. (Private letter from Mr. C. D. Wilson, Managing Director, J. T. Davenport, Ltd.)

17. The sales figures of J. Collis Browne's Chlorodyne seem to bear this out. Beginning in 1915, after nearly a decade when domestic sales hovered around £17,000 per year, sales rapidly increased to over £50,000 per year by 1919. However, other factors, such as the worldwide influenza of 1918, may also have contributed to this rise (see Table 4).

18. Between 1926 and 1932 there was some sporadic concern in both the Home Office and the Ministry of Health about chlorodyne, partially sparked by outside pressure. In 1929, for example, Lady Astor asked a question in Parliament about why chlorodyne, as a well-known drug of abuse, was not regulated by the DDA (See PRO, MH 58/272).

19. At the last minute Delevingne tried to convince the Committee to support compulsory notifications, but they rejected it. (See the letter of R. H. Crooke to Delevingne, dated October 5, 1925, in PRO, MH 58/278.)

20. *Report of the Department Committee on Morphine and Heroin Addiction* (His Majesty's Stationery Office, 1926), p. 9.

21. *Report of the Departmental Committee,* p. 11.

22. *Report of the Departmental Committee,* p. 30.

23. *Report of the Department Committee,* p. 18.

24. *Report of the Departmental Committee,* pp. 24–35. There were actually to be two Medical Tribunals—one for Scotland and one for England and Wales. The three members of each were to be nominated by the Royal College of Physicians of London (or Edinburgh), the General Medical Council, and the British Medical Association. The Committee did agree that nondispensing doctors, who had previously not been obliged to keep any records of drugs purchased, should now be obliged to do so.

25. See "Morphine and Heroin Addiction," *BMJ,* February 27, 1926, 391–393; "Amendments of the Dangerous Drugs Regulations, 1921," *BMJ,* June 24, 1926, 1001; "Morphine and Heroin Addiction," *Lancet,* February 27, 1926, 448–449; "New Dangerous Drugs Regulations," *Lancet,* July 24, 1926, 203; "Drug Addiction," *Lancet,* July 31, 1926, 229; "DD Acts: A Tall Order," *Pharm. J.,* March 27, 1926, 380–381; "Dangerous Drugs Regulations, 1926," *Pharm. J.,* July 10, 1926, 53; "The Amending Dangerous Drugs Regulations," *Pharm. J.,* August 21, 1926, 276–277; and "Proposed Amendments to DDA Regulations," *Pharm. J.,* July 24, 1926, 82.

26. Copy in the Public Record Office (MH 58/51). In May 1926, the Home Secretary, after conferring with representatives of the Ministry of Health, the British Medical Association, the Pharmaceutical Society, issued an order-in-council, bringing "veronal and other drugs of the barbitone group" under Part III of the DDA. (See PRO, HO 45/15597/354321.)

AFTERWORD

Narcotic Drugs in Britain
and America

By 1930, the narcotic drug problem had assumed different proportions in America and Britain. In America, where the problem was visible and apparently worsening, narcotics law enforcement was entrusted to the newly created Federal Bureau of Narcotics, with a full-time staff of over 150 agents and a budget of over a million dollars a year.[1] In Britain, where the problem was waning rapidly, the enforcement agency was a four-man "drugs squad," directed part-time by a Home Office civil servant. The contrast between the respective enforcement agencies is a visible indicator of the different narcotic addiction problems in America and Britain. How did it happen that, by 1930, the experience of the two countries with narcotic drugs had diverged so significantly? Can we, by comparing their histories, pinpoint the factors which led to the success of the British and the failure of the Americans in dealing with their respective drug problems?

This is not the first time that these questions have been raised. They have been asked, and answered, as part of a liberal critique of narcotics policy that originated in the 1920s and has been revived periodically.[2] The short version of this position runs as follows. The "criminalization" of addiction in America has failed. It has, in fact, exacerbated the problem by forcing addicts to turn to illicit suppliers who charge exorbitant prices

for low-quality drugs. This, in turn, has forced the addict to
adopt the "junky" lifestyle of constant criminal activity in order
to support his drug habit; life in filthy corners of squalid slums;
and the ever-present dangers of disease and death from infected
syringes and drugs of variable quality. The alternative which the
liberals offer is the "medicalization" of the narcotics problem.
Addicts should be treated as sick persons rather than as criminals. If an addict does not wish to be "cured" of his addiction, he
should be maintained on his drug of choice by regular prescriptions from a physician. At a minimum, this would alleviate the
criminal activity connected with hustling junkies by supplying
them with drugs at a nominal cost.

The advocates of this position support it, in part, by their
interpretation of the comparative history of narcotic drugs in
America and Britain. Before 1914, they claim, when narcotic
drugs were legal and cheap, American drug addicts were law-
abiding and peaceful. With the passage of the Harrison Act
(1914), and the Supreme Court's interpretation of it that made
maintenance illegal (1919), addicts were forced into the arms of
underworld suppliers who raised the price and forced them to
become criminals to support their habits. Through the Harrison
Act and hard-line enforcement efforts, the federal government
created a class of criminals where none previously had existed.

In Britain, by contrast, the Rolleston Committee (1926) endorsed the medical model of treatment which allowed an addict
to be maintained on his drug if his physician deemed it appropriate. As a result of this judicious and humane policy, the traffic
in narcotic drugs was kept out of the underworld, and addiction
did not spread in Britain as it did in America.

In both cases, the different policies are assumed to have
created two different addict populations. The American addict,
driven by desperation, was transformed after 1914 into a
dangerous street junky, while the British addict, supplied with
cheap, legal narcotics, remained a responsible citizen, afflicted
with an unfortunate, but not necessarily incapacitating disease.
The conclusion of this critique is that if Americans adopted the
medical model of heroin maintenance, the American addict

would be retransformed from the hardened criminal into the harmless habitué of the British experience. The debate about heroin maintenance is complex and multilayered. I do not intend to go into it in detail, nor to advocate a position. However, as the liberal critique rests, at least in part, on a particular reading of the history of drugs in Britain and America, it seems appropriate to address it here. Except for casual reading, I have not done primary research on the history of narcotic drugs in America. I have relied on the recent work published by several American historians. I am particularly indebted to David Musto's pioneering study of the legal history of drug addiction in America, *The American Disease: Origins of Narcotic Control,* and David Courtwright's splendid epidemiological study, *Dark Paradise: Opiate Addiction in America Before 1940.*[3] By placing their research next to mine, I have tried to answer the questions I asked at the beginning of this section.

Two clarifications are necessary. Scholars and policymakers who are concerned about narcotic drugs customarily distinguish between the medical drug user and the recreational drug user. The prototypes are, for the former, a hospitalized patient who is given injections of morphia at a physician's direction because of a painful medical condition, and, for the latter, an urban teenager shooting up heroin in the company of his friends. The distinction is clear enough for these two prototypes, but how does one classify a housewife whose physician prescribed Valium when she was in a mild depression, but who is now dependent on these "calmer-downers" to make it through the day? Or how does one classify the turn-of-the-century bon vivant who popped into his local drugstore for a cocaine-laced pick-me-up whenever his spirits sagged? Given such anomalies, some scholars have suggested that we abandon the distinction altogether. That seems misguided to me. While I acknowledge that the distinction between the medical and the recreational drug user is not entirely clear, I think that it is nevertheless useful. It does distinguish between two very different types of drug users that exist today, and that existed historically.

Finally, a word about addiction. There is considerable literature—ranging across medicine, sociology, and psychology—
about what constitutes addiction. This is not the place to rehash
that debate. I propose, as a simple definition of addiction, the
regular use of narcotic drugs, the cessation of which causes the
user to feel physical discomfort and a craving to resume their
use. This definition allows me to distinguish between the use of
narcotics which does not lead to addiction (e.g., the periodic use
of laudanum as a specific for gastrointestinal difficulty) and that
which does. Some drugs, like the opiates, are more addictive
than others, like cannabis or cocaine; and some modes of administration, like the hypodermic syringe, are more addictive than
others, like smoking. Furthermore, one can become addicted
either through medical or recreational use. Likewise, neither
medical nor recreational use *necessarily* leads to addiction. One
can, for example, periodically smoke opium or marijuana, or
snort cocaine, without becoming addicted.

Medical Uses of Opiates in the Nineteenth Century

How much opium was actually consumed in nineteenth-century
Britain and America? The question is impossible to answer with
accuracy for several reasons. Periodic changes in the tariff on
opium imports in both countries either encouraged or dis-
couraged smugglers, thus often rendering import statistics
meaningless as a gauge of how much opium was actually consumed; inadequate reporting of imports left gaps in the record,
particularly in the early part of the century; and the rise of a
pharmaceutical industry, particularly in Britain, further distorts
the meaning of the import statistics since much of the opium
imported was manufactured and exported rather than consumed domestically. Nevertheless, it is possible to make some
comparisons between opium imports to Britain and America for
a few decades at mid-century when tariffs were low and manufacturing was negligible. According to Courtwright, opium imports to America averaged 27,238 pounds per annum between
1827 and 1842. In Britain, between 1831 and 1842, opium im-

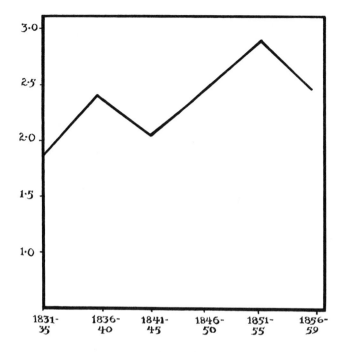

Figure 6.
Average annual amount of opium imported into Britain
for home consumption, 1831–1859, in lbs. per 1000 population.
(*Sources:* Annual Accounts of Trade and Navigation,
Parliamentary Papers; and B. R. Mitchell and P. Deane,
Abstract of British Historical-Statistics, Cambridge,
Cambridge University Press, 1962, p. 6.)

ports averaged 36,125 pounds per annum. A more meaningful,
although somewhat shakier statistic, is the change in the per
capita rate of consumption. Opium imports to America jumped
sharply from one pound per 1000 population in the early 1840s
to four or five pounds per 1,000 in the mid-1850s (see Fig. 6).[4]
By contrast, British opium imports grew much less dramatically
during a corresponding period. Part of the rapid increase in
these imports to America, according to Courtwright, may be

attributed to the opium imported by and for Chinese smokers, who first immigrated to America in substantial numbers during the 1850s. If, for example, 20 to 25 percent of opium imports in the 1850s were destined for this population (as was the case later in the century), then the rate of opium consumption among non-Chinese was only slightly higher in America than in Britain.

How was this opium used? With few exceptions, opiates were used medically in both Britain and America before 1850. Although there were substantial legal and status differences between orthodox medical men in the two countries, they shared a similar medico-scientific outlook, particularly in therapeutics. Discoveries and new techniques that were successfully introduced in one country were quickly transmitted to the other. The use of ether as a general anesthetic, for example, was first tried in America in 1846; within a year it was being used in Britain.

The common medical culture was facilitated by a common language. Discoveries announced in the *Lancet,* for example, would be known to subscribers in Philadelphia or New York within weeks. Standard medical texts, like Jonathan Pereira's *Materia Medica and Therapeutics,* were read and sometimes published on both sides of the Atlantic. Furthermore, the disease experience of the two countries was similar. Cholera epidemics broke out in America at about the same time that they occurred in Britain. And opium was used extensively in orthodox therapeutics in nineteenth-century America for much the same purposes that it was used in Britain: as an analgesic, a sedative, a febrifuge, an anti-diarrhea agent, and a cholera remedy.[5]

There were similar trends in self-medication. In America as in Britain, the last third of the century saw a rapid expansion in the sale of patent medicines, many of which contained opiates. "Between 1880 and 1910, the national population [of America] increased about 83 per cent, while the sale of patent medicines rose seven-fold."[6] Opiates were also widely available in America from the local druggist and from a variety of other sources, as they were in Britain. There is even an interesting parallel in the regional use of opiates. According to Courtwright, the incidence of opiate addiction in nineteenth-century America was highest in the South.[7] The part of Britain that is climatically most like the American South is the Fens, which was notorious for its high rate of opium consumption. Broad alluvial plains and wet swamplands made inhabitants of both places susceptible to malaria, fevers, and rheumatism. Opium's considerable power to alleviate pain and reduce fever made it as attractive to the Southerner as it was to the Fenman.

Opiate-based children's quieteners, which were widespread and visible enough in mid-nineteenth-century Britain to provoke considerable public discussion, stirred less controversy in America. Does this mean that they were used less frequently? Certainly soothing syrups and other children's opiate mixtures were available in America as they were in Britain. Yet the literature suggests that they were administered to children less commonly in America, although this is admittedly a speculation.[8] If it is true, this may be due to the different kinds of work done by women in the two countries. By the 1850s, Britain had a mature, industrialized economy. Women constituted a substantial part of the workforce, and they regularly worked outside the home, particularly in the North. Children of working mothers were usually placed in the care of a child-minder, who regularly dosed them with opiates. Often the mothers themselves, after an exhausting day at the workbench, administered opiates in order to secure some peace and quiet. In America, industrialization was still a generation away in 1850. Most women worked in their homes or in jobs where they did not have to leave their children with child-minders. Quieteners were not as commonly accepted as a natural part of the domestic culture in nineteenth-century America as they were in Britain. Thus Americans seem to have been somewhat less afflicted by the scourge of children's opium-poisoning that brought so many tragedies to Victorian Britons.

Although the two countries probably differed in their use of children's opiates, they had a similar experience with the medical use of injected morphia. After Dr. Wood announced the perfected hypodermic syringe in 1858, it quickly became popular with medical men in both countries. The syringe's most important use was in the subcutaneous injection of morphia. Throughout the 1860s, injected morphia was touted as a

panacea which had none of the unpleasant side effects of ingested opium. Courtwright explains the attraction of medical
men to the new therapy:

> For the first time in the entire history of medicine near-
> instantaneous, symptomatic relief for a wide range of diseases was
> possible. A syringe of morphine was, in a very real sense, a magic
> wand. Though it could cure little, it could relieve anything; doc-
> tors and patients alike were tempted to overuse.[9]

Physicians administered the drug at the slightest provocation,
completely unaware of its dangers. Injected morphia was ten
times stronger and much more addictive than ingested opium.
The coming of the Civil War during the period of morphia's
uncritical reception probably exacerbated its misuse in America,
but patients in both countries suffered the curse of iatrogenic
addiction in the two decades after its introduction.

The first articles calling attention to the dangers of morphia
addiction appeared in both American and British medical journals in 1869–70. The most influential warning was the English
translation of Edward Levinstein's *Die Morphiumsucht (The Morbid Craving for Morphia),* published in 1878. In the two decades
following the publication of Levinstein's book came a flood of
medical literature in both countries stressing the disease of addiction, or "morphinomania." Although physicians disagreed
somewhat about the etiology and cure of the disease, they
agreed unanimously that medical men were largely responsible
for its spread and that they must use extreme caution in administering morphia. Popularizers in both countries wrote articles and books, like Seymour Sharkey's "Morphinomania" or
H. H. Kane's *Drugs that Enslave,* which alerted laymen to the
drug's dangers. By the end of the century, medical men and
their patients were becoming more cautious about the use of
morphia. As a result, the number of iatrogenic morphia addicts
in both countries began to decline as an older generation died
off more rapidly than it was replaced.[10]

The profile of morphia addicts was similar in America and
Britain. According to Courtwright, the typical addict in

nineteenth-century America was a middle- or upper-class, white, middle-aged, native-born female, who had become addicted to morphia in the course of medical treatment. Female addicts were predominantly housewives; male addicts were predominantly medical men.[11] The demographic data on British addicts is not nearly so extensive or precise as the American data. Nevertheless, there are certain points of comparison. British morphia addicts tended to be middle-aged, middle-class persons, nearly all of whom were therapeutically addicted, largely concentrated in health-related professions. On only one point do the British data not correlate with the American data: while American morphia addicts were predominantly female, *reported* British morphia addicts were predominantly male.

Before seeking an explanation for this disparity in the differences between British and American culture, it will be well to recall that the British data were drawn from 51 cases of persons seeking treatment that were reported in the medical press, while the American data were drawn from extensive surveys of morphia addiction in a number of cities. It may be that men—especially professional men—were more willing to seek treatment for addiction because it interfered with their work, and there was less stigma attached to acknowledging their condition than there was for upper- or middle-class women. In other words, I suspect that the reported sexual balance among morphia addicts in Britain may not correspond to their actual sexual balance.

Increased medical caution about opiates was the most important, but not the only factor which led to the decline of their use; other factors were increasing regulation and the development of safer substitute drugs. In America, regulations which governed the conditions of the sale of narcotics were either municipal ordinances or state laws. As early as 1860 there was an anti-morphia law in Pennsylvania.[12]

> From 1895 to 1915 most states and many municipalities passed laws limiting the sale of narcotics (usually defined as cocaine and the opiates) to those possessing a valid prescription. Although these laws were unevenly and often inadequately enforced, their

net effect could only have been to reduce the number of unauthorized refills.[13]

In Britain there was no legal restriction on the sale of opiates and cocaine, save those minimal requirements imposed by the Poisons and Pharmacy Acts of 1868 and 1908, until DORA 40B in 1916. Even then, morphia sales were not regulated until the passage of the Dangerous Drugs Act in 1920. There is some indication, from the correspondence columns of *Chemist and Druggist* and the *Pharmaceutical Journal,* that ethical chemists would not sell morphia to customers without a prescription. However, pharmaceutical editors and correspondents agreed that they had no moral—nor legal—right to refuse to fill a prescription, even if it were several years old and the holder a known addict. With the passage of the DDA, narcotic drugs (opium, cocaine, morphia, and heroin) were legally available only with a physician's nonrepeatable prescription.

In America, the Pure Food and Drug Act of 1906 forced manufacturers of opiate-based patent medicines to list the ingredients on the label, which greatly reduced their sales.[14] In Britain, the 1892 legal case against the manufacturers of J. Collis Browne's Chlorodyne forced them to label each bottle "poison" in conformity to the Poisons Act of 1868. The sale of Chlorodyne dropped 13 percent, but there is no indication that other manufacturers followed suit or that their sales suffered. Not until 1920 were patent medicine manufacturers forced to restrict the amount of morphia in their products (to 0.2 percent). In 1905, after three and a half decades of expansion, patent medicine sales leveled off in Britain. All of this meant that from the 1890s through the 1920s the amount of opiates that Britons ingested through patent medicines began a very slow decline. In America, by contrast, 1906 was a much more definite turning point.

In America, the Harrison Act of 1914 regulated narcotic drugs at the federal level. All persons who dealt in narcotic drugs were required to register and to keep a record of the drugs they bought and sold. Although the wording of the Act made no mention of addiction, the Treasury Department, which was charged with its enforcement, interpreted it to mean that the maintenance of drug addicts on nondiminishing doses of their drugs was prohibited. After an initial setback (*U.S. v. Jin Fuey Moy*, 1916), the government finally received a Supreme Court decision which supported its position (*Webb et al. v. U.S.*, 1919). Within several years, the short-lived municipal maintenance clinics had been harassed out of business. The era of cheap, legal drugs in America was over.

In Britain, the DDA also forced dealers in drugs to register and to keep a detailed record of the amounts that passed through their hands. As in America, this allowed government agents to keep a much closer watch on addicts and on those persons who supplied them. Diverting legally manufactured drugs in large amounts became nearly impossible. Until 1926, addicts—and medical men who supplied addicts—were subject to harassment by local health officers, and by Malcolm Delevingne of the Home Office. Thus narcotic drugs, which had been cheap and readily available in both countries as recently as 1895, became, by the twenties, extremely difficult to procure.

Finally, the therapeutic range of narcotic drugs in both countries shrank rapidly from the 1890s onward. Better water sanitation and other public health measures made gastrointestinal complaints less widespread. Vaccination and chemotherapy provided cures for a few diseases, like syphilis and typhoid, for which opiates had previously been used as a palliative.[15] And new drugs, most notably aspirin and veronal, proved to be relatively safer substitutes for opiates.

Despite a few variations, then, the experience of nineteenth-century Britons and Americans with the medical use of narcotic drugs was remarkably similar. They used opiates for almost identical purposes, and took them in nearly identical form, although Americans may have taken them in somewhat greater quantity after 1860. Some medical users became addicted to opium and, to an even greater degree, to morphia. But the medical use of opiates in both countries peaked in the 1890s, and declined thereafter, as a result of greater medical caution, increasingly strict regulation, and the availability of safer substitute therapies. If we want to know why the American experience with narcotic drugs diverged so radically from the British, we will have to look to recreational drug users.

Recreational Drug Use in Britain and America

Narcotic drugs were used recreationally in both countries in the nineteenth century. From the 1830s through the 1860s there were occasional reports in Britain of being opium used as an intoxicant—in factory districts, seaports, and especially in the Fens. But by the 1880s, recreational opium use was waning rapidly. In America, however, recreational use of opiates and cocaine was expanding in the last two decades of the century. Morphia and cocaine were taken by prostitutes, and cocaine was reputedly being used as a cheap stimulant by blacks in the South. While a certain amount of the publicity about black cocaine-taking was undoubtedly exaggerated by racist hysteria, it did have a basis in reality.[16] In any case, morphia and cocaine were certainly being used recreationally much more widely in America than in Britain in the late nineteenth century.

The most important factor in the differential rate of recreational drug use in the two countries, however, was related to opium-smoking. Unlike the handful of Chinese seamen who floated up onto British shores, the Chinese who arrived in nineteenth-century America came in large numbers and for a specific purpose. They came in the 1850s to work as miners and laborers in California and the West. By 1900 there were about 100,000 Chinese immigrants in America. Most came from the area around Canton, where opium-smoking was more widespread than anywhere else in China. The typical Chinese immigrant was a very young man who expected to save a great deal of money in a short time and return to China. However, because these young men were encumbered by passage-money debts, and because the astronomical cost of provisions and supplies precluded savings, very few were able to carry through with their original plans. They were forced to remain in America, but they continued to think of themselves as sojourners. Living in separate quarters in the mining camps and cities of the West, they made little attempt to acclimate to American society. Nor would they have been accepted, for Chinese immigrants to America faced a solid wall of xenophobic hostility. As his dream of returning to the homeland disintegrated, the young man found solace in the entertainments of Chinatown:

> The most popular forms of recreation were gambling, prostitution, and opium smoking, often found together in a single or adjoining establishment. There the sojourner might lose his troubles in a game of fan tan, or in the company of a slave girl, or, what is of most concern here, in the familiar fumes of smoking opium.[17]

Gradually the Chinese spread out across America, first as laborers, and then as small entrepreneurs. Chinatowns sprouted up as they settled in one city after another. Almost invariably, the Chinese were permitted to settle only in or near the red-light districts of nineteenth-century cities. Given the racial and social polyglot and the immense size of many of these urban tenderloins, a few hundred—or even a few thousand—Chinese residents were hardly cause for concern. With the Chinese came the familiar opium den. It was ensconced next to the saloons, gambling establishments, and brothels of tenderloins from mining camps to large Eastern cities. Opium-smoking became one more vice to be sampled by the district's residents and visitors alike. According to one report, the first white man smoked opium in America in 1868. Whether or not this particular story is true, it is clear that opium smoking spread rapidly through the underworld in the 1870s. The opium den often became a "rogue's paradise" where thieves, pimps, prostitutes, and saloonkeepers could enjoy conversation and relax over a few pipes in the wee hours of the morning, knowing that the informal code of honor prohibited violence or robbery within the den.

Although state and municipal regulations against opium smoking were enacted in most places where the Chinese settled, the importation of smoking opium was not actually banned until 1909. The effect of this ban was to reduce (although not eliminate) the supply, thus driving up the price of smoking opium.

Furthermore, increasingly strict narcotics enforcement made opium smokers particularly vulnerable, since the odor of the burning drug makes it especially difficult to conceal. After 1909 Caucasian opium smokers began to switch to "white drugs"— cocaine, morphia, heroin—and especially to heroin, as it became much more expensive and dangerous to smoke opium. By contrast, heroin was cheap, easily concealed, and quickly taken by sniffing or injection. By 1930, according to Courtwright, injected heroin and morphia had replaced smoking opium as the predominant drug among addicts. Only a few wealthy Caucasians and some Chinese continued to smoke opium.

The characteristics of recreational drug addicts were completely different from those of the nineteenth-century medical addict. Recreational heroin users were young, urban, lower-class hustlers—and overwhelmingly male. By 1930, the transformation of the American addict population was complete. As Courtwright so aptly puts it, Mrs. Henry Lafayette Dubose, the elderly, upper-class, morphia addict of Harper Lee's *To Kill a Mockingbird* had been replaced by Frankie Machine, the tough, young heroin addict of Nelson Algren's *Man with the Golden Arm*. He was not to be pitied but to be feared.

Why was there no comparable transformation of the British addict population? To begin with, the size and location of the Chinese community were different. While there were about 100,000 Chinese in America in the late nineteenth century, there were never more than a few hundred in Victorian Britain, and only a few thousand in the early part of this century. Fewer Chinese meant fewer opium dens. Furthermore, the largest Chinese community in Britain—Limehouse in London's East End— was near the waterfront, miles from the vice district around Soho. Of course, this did not stop some Britons from visiting Chinese opium dens, but they were neither so prevalent nor so accessible as they were in America. Furthermore, the social structure into which opium smoking was introduced differed significantly. Mining camps and many cities of the American West were "wide open." A man did not lose caste because he frequented an opium den in Carson City or even San Francisco. Smoking was simply an extension of the drinking, gambling, and whoring that was taken for granted as a man's prerogative in those tumultuous communities. In London the situation was rather different, as is suggested by *Edwin Drood* or *Dorian Gray*. A gentleman might furtively consort with a prostitute, or even smoke opium; but if he did so openly, he risked censure and a loss of status. Besides the Chinese communities in the two countries, there were other factors which surely contributed to their different addict populations, although these are admittedly speculative.

American cities between 1880 and 1920 were undergoing tumultuous social changes, as industrialization coincided with the largest wave of immigration in American history. The core of the industrial American city became an expanding polyglot of foreign-born workers. Jews, Italians, and Poles mixed uneasily with the Irish, Germans, and blacks who had preceded them into cities like Detroit, Boston, and New York. Informal social controls often disintegrated in these rapidly changing slums. Drug-taking by gangs of boys and young men, which would not have been tolerated in more traditional communities, flourished in these circumstances of ethnic heterogeneity and social dislocation. British cities, by contrast, were mature and relatively stable between 1880 and 1920. They had undergone rapid growth and industrialization a century earlier. While working-class neighborhoods were hardly prosperous, they were fairly stable and homogeneous (except for the Irish populations in London and a few west coast cities). For example, in *The Classic Sum*, Robert Roberts has written a memoir of his boyhood in turn-of-the-century Salford, Lancashire, one of the worst slums in the country. Life was hard, but the lines of authority in the community were clearly demarcated. Codes of dress, language, and behavior were established and enforced informally but rigorously. In this context it is difficult to imagine gangs of teenagers passing around packets of heroin to be sniffed, as was happening among youth gangs in urban America.

Still another factor was the relative strength of the anti-alcohol movement in the two countries. In America the prohibitionist crusade was influential long before the Eighteenth Amendment outlawed alcohol at the federal level in 1920. By that time many counties and states were already dry. In such circumstances, where drinking was illegal or severely criticized, many persons must have turned to narcotics or narcotic-based patent medicines to get high while escaping legal difficulty or social censure. In Britain, the anti-alcohol movement supported temperance, not prohibition. Beer was cheap and readily available to the working classes, while the more well-to-do favored whiskey and wine. One did not become an object of opprobrium simply by taking a drink. In contrast to America, this must have meant that fewer persons indulged in the secret passion of drug-taking as a means of escape.

A recreational drug subculture, similar to that which exists today, was visible in American cities at least by the 1890s and perhaps earlier. In Britain, it did not fully appear until 1916, and then it was confined to a few areas of London. Compared to America, the addict population of Britain was tiny. At the height of the drug scare in Britain in 1923, there were fewer than 300 prosecutions for narcotic drug offences nationwide. Assuming, conservatively, that about half of these were against transient seamen and other foreigners, there were never more than 150 Britons prosecuted for drug offences in any single year. By contrast, in America between 1921 and 1940, there were never *fewer* than 3,000 narcotics prosecutions in any single year. In some years, there were more than 7,000. While prosecution statistics do not mirror exactly the pattern of drug use, a disparity of this magnitude is surely indicative of different-sized drug problems in the two countries.

The drug subculture in Britain was not only smaller than it was in America, but it was based on a different drug. The characteristics of cocaine users in London in the early 1920s were very similar to those of heroin users in New York and other eastern cities at the same time: they were young, working-class or criminal males and prostitutes. It is, however, extremely significant that the American drug subculture was based on morphia and increasingly on heroin, while the London subculture was based on cocaine, which is much less addictive. A user can crave cocaine, but he does not suffer the extreme withdrawal pain of heroin addict who is deprived of his drug. Put another way, it is easier for a cocaine addict to do without his drug than it is for a heroin addict to do without his.

All of these factors accounted for the different drug problems in America and Britain by 1930. The medical experience with opiates was roughly similar, as were the characteristics of medical addicts. By the early twentieth century, however, this group was fast dying off in both countries. Morphia users in Britain who were prosecuted for DDA offences in the twenties were the last tiny vestige of these middle-aged, middle-class, therapeutically addicted persons. They did not mix with the Chinese opium smokers in Limehouse or the cocaine-takers in the West End. (Indeed, I wonder if they even knew of their existence.)

Recreational drug use in America grew largely—although not exclusively—out of opium dens where Caucasians first learned to smoke from Chinese. By the 1920s they had switched to sniffing and injecting white drugs, especially heroin. When drug-taking became illegal, the addict population was large enough, *and addicted enough,* to be able to support a network of illicit drug suppliers and manufacturers. Recreational drug use, which had been partially underground for at least three decades, now became entirely illicit. Despite prosecutions it thrived.

In Britain, by contrast, the recreational drug subculture appeared much later and was much more fragile than it was in America. When the police crackdown came in the early twenties, and cocaine became both scarce and expensive, many cocaine users apparently decided that it was simply not worth the trouble and price to maintain their habit. The police offensive was successful. The market shrank, and the suppliers disappeared. While the odd opium smoker popped up, and a few elderly morphia addicts lingered into the next decade, Britain's drug problem was essentially solved by 1930.

Effects of the Addict Transformation on Theory and Policy

In America as in Britain, the disease model of drug addiction gained acceptance in the later nineteenth century. Although there were some variations, American and British medical men were agreed that morphinomania was a physical disease which afflicted "nervous" but otherwise normal persons. They stressed that, in most cases, the disease was inflicted by medical men who treated their patients incautiously with opiates. British, and especially American, physicians believed that most addicts could be cured within a few weeks and returned to normal life. Those few addicts who could not be cured—notably elderly patients and those with a terminal disease—should be maintained on their drug for the rest of their lives.

Through the first two decades of the twentieth century this theory was dominant in both Britain and America. In America, as the addict population changed from middle-aged, therapeutically addicted females to young, male "pleasure-seekers," so did the theory of addiction. Due largely to the influence of Lawrence Kolb of the Public Health Service, a new theory, stressing the psychopathy of drug addicts, challenged the older view:

> Pleasure was the key; the four abnormal types [of drug addicts] had in common a heightened receptivity to the euphoric effects of opiates, whereas normal persons experienced only relief of pain. The greater the degree of psychopathy, Kolb hypothesized, the more intense the euphoria produced. Opiates also had the effect of alleviating the feelings of inadequacy which plagued the abnormal or psychopathic user; they were a kind of psychic crutch which enabled inferior personalities to temporarily raise themselves to the posture of normal men. Feelings of inadequacy and unconscious pathological strivings persisted even after withdrawal, which explained why most non-medical addicts speedily relapsed.[18]

The success of this new theory, Courtwright argues, was in part a direct result of the emergence of the new addict: "Psychopathy connoted irresponsible, deviant, and often criminal behavior, which fit the hustling style of the emerging non-medical majority, but not at all the shame and reticence of previous generations of medical addicts."[19]

Kolb's theory of addiction was compatible with the growing consensus in favor of a hard-line enforcement policy. Older therapies, which stressed medical treatment, seemed woefully inadequate for the new entrenched addict population. Kolb and others argued for long-term involuntary institutionalization in hospitals and rural narcotics farms: "Addicts of the new breed were the type who seemed to belong in institutions, anyway; in contrast to the sedate nineteenth-century medical addict, they were prone, by nature and circumstance, to irresponsible and criminal behavior."[20] It is no wonder that Harry Anslinger, the legendary tough-guy director of the Federal Bureau of Narcotics, endorsed the psychopathic theory of addiction, and that the first American federal narcotics hospital (at Lexington, Kentucky) was constructed along the lines of a prison.

Kolb's theory of addiction never caught on in Britain because the kind of addicts which it described were never very numerous there and were rapidly disappearing by the late 1920s. The older theory of addiction went unchallenged and provided the conceptual framework for the Rolleston Committee's Report of 1926.

Narcotics Policy and Addict Populations

The liberal reformers' view of the history of drug policy and its results in Britain and America needs re-examination. As David Courtwright has shown, the Harrison Act did not cause the sudden transformation of the American addict population. Indeed, that had been underway from the mid-1880s. Although the Harrison Act probably strengthened the connections between narcotics addiction and the urban underworld, these connections were firmly in place long before 1914. The increasingly hard-line American enforcement and treatment policy during the 1920s was less the cause than the effect of the emerging criminal-addict.

As Eric Josephson has recently noted, the differences between the (American) criminal model and the (British) medical model of drug addiction have been overemphasized.[21] Both the DDA and American drug legislation provided for close control over the manufacture and sale of narcotic drugs and stiff penalties for illicit trafficking and recreational drug use. They differed primarily in that drug maintenance was provided for medical opiate addicts in Britain but not in America. First, it is worth noting how close the British came to emulating the American model. Malcolm Delevingne, the prime mover of British drug legislation, was antipathetic to maintenance. Only when he was confronted by the solid opposition of the members of the Rolleston Committee to this position did he back down. Second, we should not credit the Rolleston Committee's members with any ideological commitment to a liberal drug policy. Above all, they were medical men who were defending the professional prerogative of the physician to exercise control over the drugs he administered. Finally, the Rolleston Committee was able to defend this position because drug addiction—both medical and recreational—really was waning, as they reported. By 1926, the period of acute concern about narcotic drugs was over in Britain. Thus in Britain as in America, drug policy was less a cause than it was an effect of the addict population. Put simply, narcotic drug maintenance was accepted in Britain in the 1920s because the addict population was small, elderly, and dying off.

One can make a plausible and perhaps even convincing case for heroin maintenance in present-day America. But one cannot expect that this policy will produce the same results in contemporary America as it did in Britain in the 1920s. The British drug policy of the twenties was the result of a political compromise that was unique to postwar Britain, and it was designed to serve an addict population substantially different from that of America in the 1980s.

Notes

1. David Musto, *The American Disease: Origins of Narcotic Control* (New Haven: Yale University Press, 1973), p. 214.

2. Some of the proponents of this liberal critique include Rufus King, *The Drug Hang Up: America's Fifty-Year Folly* (Springfield, Ill.: Charles C Thomas, 1972); "Narcotic Drug Laws and Enforcement Policies," *Law and Contemporary Problems*, 22 (Winter 1957);

Charles E. Terry and Mildred Pellens, *The Opium Problem* (New York: The Committee on Drug Addiction, 1928); John A. Clausen, "Early History of Narcotic Use and Narcotics Legislation in the United States," in *Contemporary Social Problems*, R. K. Merton and R. A. Nisbet, eds. (New York: Harcourt, Brace, Jovanovich, 1961); Howard Becker, *The Outsiders* (New York: Free Press, 1963); Edward M. Brecher, et al., *Licit and Illicit Drugs* (Boston: Little, Brown, 1972); Edwin M. Schur, *Narcotic Addiction in Britain and America: The Impact of Public Policy* (Bloomington: Indiana University Press, 1963); Alfred R. Lindesmith, *The Addict and the Law* (Bloomington: Indiana University Press, 1965). I am indebted to David Courtwright for some of these references.

3. David Courtwright, *Dark Paradise: Opiate Addiction in America Before 1940* (Cambridge, Mass.: Harvard University Press, 1982).

4. Courtwright, p. 20.

5. Courtwright, pp. 43–46, and Musto, pp. 69–73.

6. H. Wayne Morgan, *Yesterday's Addicts: American Society and Drug Abuse, 1865–1920* (Norman: Oklahoma University Press, 1974), p. 8.

7. Courtwright, p. 38.

8. John Frisch, *Another Slavery in America: A Synoptic View of Opiate Dependence* (unpublished manuscript, 1979).

9. Courtwright, p. 47.

10. Courtwright, pp. 52–54.

11. Courtwright, p. 41.

12. Musto, p. 91.

13. Courtwright, p. 53.

14. Courtwright, pp. 58–59, and Musto, p. 33.

15. Courtwright, p. 52.

16. Courtwright, p. 97.

17. Courtwright, p. 68.

18. Courtwright, pp. 134–135.

19. Courtwright, p. 136.

20. Courtwright, pp. 138–139.

21. Josephson made the point in discussion at the National Institute on Drug Abuse Conference on the History of Narcotic Drugs, Philadelphia, June 1981.

A Note on Sources

The most important sources for this study were the articles published in the pharmaceutical and medical press. The former consists, for the most part, of two journals, the *Pharmaceutical Journal*, begun in 1841 as the organ of the Pharmaceutical Society of Great Britain, and the *Chemist and Druggist*, begun in 1859 to reflect the views of druggists politically opposed to the dominant Pharmaceutical Society. While the controversy was resolved in 1868, the orientation of the two journals remained different. Generally, the *Pharmaceutical Journal* tended to publish articles on pharmacology and the scientific interests of the profession, whereas the *Chemist and Druggist* concentrated on the business side of pharmacy, with a plethora of information about prices and articles on such subjects as the economics of patent medicines. Both journals have an extensive subject index. However, I felt that it was necessary to look through every issue, since much of the best material came from unindexed articles or candid letters to the editor which discussed the conditions of trade, or even personal problems. The two journals yielded valuable information on such topics as prices and market conditions of opiates, political issues, the history of the profession, and changes in prices. Some of the information I gathered I could not use, including a wealth of data about patent medicines or pharmaceutical politics in the nineteenth century. I doubt that I will ever write on these topics, but I urge other enthusiasts to look into them.

Medical periodicals were another important source of information. They were especially useful for the topics covered in Chapters 3, 4, and 7. I used the *Index Catalogue to the Surgeon-General's Library* to assemble a basic bibliography of articles relating to narcotic drugs. Because of their prominence I searched every issue of *Lancet* and the *British Medical Journal*.

A second major source was government statistics and reports that were published in the *Parliamentary Papers*. The statistical data, gathered from annual reports in the *PP*, provided answers to such basic questions as how much opium did Britain import and export (Figs. 1 and 2) and did the poison legislation affect opiate poisonings (Tables 5 and 6)? Parliamentary "Blue Books," those exhaustive reports on various aspects of life and work in Victorian Britain, provided useful information about the everyday use of opiates, most of which is presented in Chapter 4. There is a subject index to the *Parliamentary Papers* in the Government Documents Room of the British Library. It points the researcher to such reports as the 1857 Select Committee on Poisons, or the Opium Commission reports of 1894–95. But references to opiate use are scattered throughout less obvious reports, and finding them is often a matter of patience and luck.

A third major source was the collection of government manuscripts held at the Public Record Office, Kew. The records of the Rolleston Committee are all together in four files (MH 58/275–78), except for one file still held at the Home Office (HO 45/408/10A). Most of the other records relevant to narcotic drugs are scattered throughout the HO 45 series. Some of these can be traced through the subject index at the Public Record Office. Other Home Office records are still closed, especially those which contain confidential reports on domestic or international drug trafficking. When they are opened near the end of the century, they will probably shed new light on the topics I covered in Chapters 10 and 11. Still there are sometimes ways to circumvent the system. In the wake of the Humphrey prosecution in 1923, Malcolm Delevingne of the Home Office communicated the particulars of the case to his colleagues in the Foreign Office. While copies of his correspondence are closed in the HO records, they are open in the FO records. Likewise the British reports on DDA prosecutions to the League of Nations' Opium Advisory Committee are missing after 1923. However, I was able to consult them at the UN Library in Geneva.

Finally, I had my share of fortune, both good and bad. In the category of major disappointments was the material I expected to find but did not find in local and county archives. I had hoped to locate enough case notes from local doctors that I could generalize about the use of opiates in general practice. However, I found few, and they were nearly illegible. I did locate some interesting manuscripts, but often they were so odd that it was difficult to generalize from them. For example, one county archivist in Wales showed me a temperance pledge in Welsh, circa 1910, abjuring opium as well as alcohol and tobacco. I did not pursue this lead by checking other temperance literature, although in retrospect I probably should have. One sort of record that exists in abundance in county archives is prescription books from nineteenth-century chemists, often in multi-volume sets. These record the prescriptions dispensed by a particular chemist's shop over a period of years, and often decades. If I had had the time, I would like to have analyzed some of them to find out, for example, if the percentage of opiate-based prescriptions was rising through most of the century and falling from the 1880s, as I suspect was the case. A person with patience and a calculator could learn a great deal about grassroots changes in nineteenth-century materia medica and therapeutics by analyzing these records.

On the other side of the ledger, I had several strokes of unexpected fortune. Miss Jones, a member of the staff at the Pharmaceutical Society Library, led me to a treasure trove of eighteenth- and nineteenth-century price lists and "prices current," which allowed me to plot changes in the wholesale and retail prices of opiates. An elderly gentleman with whom I had the good chance to take tea one day told me about the Whiffen & Sons' manuscripts in the London County Council archives. And an advertisement in a London Underground station for "Collis Browne's Mixture" led me to Mr. Wilson, the managing director of the firm, who kindly furnished me with sales figures on "Dr. J. Collis Browne's Chlorodyne," the most important opiate-based patent medicine of the late nineteenth and early twentieth centuries.

These are only the major sources that I found and was able to exploit. There are undoubtedly others which I missed or did not fully appreciate which will provide raw materials for future researchers.

Appendix

Table 1.
Wholesale Prices of Opium and Opiates, 1726–1902

Year	Turkish Opium (shillings/lb.)	Morphia Salts (shillings/oz.)	Tincture of Opium (shillings/lb.)
1726	12/–		
1776	12/–		
1793	12/6		
1805	23/–		
1816	27/–		
1822		144/–	
1825		60/–	5/–
1831	22/6	23/–	
1832			4/–
1836	27/–	15/–	4/8
1838	17/–	11/–	
1840	16/–	12/–	
1859	25/6	13/6	4/8
1866	20/–	12/8	5/–
1873	32/–	14/6	
1880	20/–	10/6	
1888	9/–	4/6	
1890	13/9	6/3	
1902	11/–	5/6	

Sources: "[Drugs] Prepared and Sold by Matattias Sarfati, Chymist, at the Van-Helmont's Head, in Little Britain," London, 1796 (Pharmaceutical Society Library); "Inventories of Drugs, 1776–1794" (Pharmaceutical Society Library); "Price Lists Sent to Samuel Glover, 1804–1816" (Leeds Municipal Archives); "Invoices Supplied to Jacob Anthony, Druggist and Chemist, Bedford, 1829–1839" (H. E. Chapman Collection, Pharmaceutical Society Library); "Catalogue of Drugs, Chemicals . . . with prices," London, 1836 (Pharmaceutical Society Library); "Prices Current of R. E. Dear, Chemist and Pharmaceutist," London, 1839, 1840 (Pharmaceutical Society Library); Hearon, McCulloch & Squire, "Prices Current of Drugs, Chemicals and Pharmaceutical Preparations," London, April 19, 1859 (Pharmaceutical Society Library); Allen & Hanbury's "Price Book of Drugs, 1846–1866" (Pharmaceutical Society Library; Allen & Hanbury's "Price List," July 1871, and September 1873 (Pharmaceutical Society Library); "Exchange Column" and "Trade Reports," Chemist and Druggist, 1880–1884 and 1887–1889; W. Kemp & Sons, "Price List of Specialties," Horncastle, September 1890 (Pharmaceutical Society Library); C. R. Harker, Stagg & Morgan, "Prices Current for June 2, 1902," London (Pharmaceutical Society Library); "Price List of T. Morson, 1822," Chemist and Druggist, March 5, 1887; Allen, Hanbury's, and Barry, "Cost Price Book, 1824–1844" (Pharmaceutical Society Library); "Catalogue of Drugs and Chemicals, Prepared by Gascoyne & Hill, Druggists," London, 1825 (Pharmaceutical Society Library).

Table 2.
The Opium Crop in the Turkish Empire, 1864–1889

Year	Yield (baskets)	Smyrna Prices During Season (piastres)	
		Highest	Lowest
1864	3400	140	111
1865	4350	130	94
1866	1350	160	122
1867	3000	170	120
1868	1600	390	146
1869	3500	295	180
1870	4300	270	130
1871	8500	200	130
1872	4400	220	170
1873	3150	260	165
1874	2430	274	130
1875	6300	145	122
1876	3250	190	137
1877	9450	138	122
1878	6050	145	120
1879	4300	250	135
1880	2100	250	135
1881	11000	135	103
1882	4500	135	90
1883	6970	115	85
1884	5400	115	90
1885	7400	95	80
1886	7600	164	63
1887	1800	180	71
1888	7300	100	62
1889	5000	NA	NA

Source: C&D, March 22, 1890, 424.

Table 3.
Retail Prices of Opium and Opiates, 1696–1912

Year	Opium (per oz.)	Laudanum (per oz.)	Battley's Laudanum (per oz.)	Morphia Salts (per scruple—1/24 oz.)
1696	9d.			
1767	1/–			
1776	1/–			
1777	10d.			
1779	1/–			
1784	10d.			
1823	3/6	8d.		
1853		8d.	2/6	
1860		6d.		
1875	6/–	8d.		1/6
1880	4/–	6d		1/6
1882	4/–	6d.	2/–	2/–
1885	4/–	6d.	2/–	1/6
1896	2/–	6d.	2/–	8d.
1900	1/6	3 1/2d.		
1909	2/9	6d.	2/–	8d.
1911	1/9	3 1/2d.		
1912	2/9	4d.		8d.

Sources: Gideon Harvey, *The Family Physician and the House Apothecary,* London, 1696 (Pharmaceutical Society Library); Fochaber Bills, 1737–1784, 2 vols. (Pharmaceutical Society Library); "Catalogue of Genuine Drugs, Chemicals, etc. Sold by John F. James," Sheffield, 1823 (Pharmaceutical Society Library); Edinburgh Chemists Association, "Retail Price List," 1875 (Pharmaceutical Society Library); Liverpool Chemists Association, "Dispensing and Retail Price List," London, 1880, 1885, 1896, 1909 (Pharmaceutical Society Library); Manchester Chemists and Druggists Association, "A List of Retail Prices," London, 1882 (Pharmaceutical Society Library); Giles, Schacht & Co., "Cash Price List of Pure Drugs and Medicines," London, 1900 (Pharmaceutical Society Library); "Price List of Montague Folkard, Dispensing Chemist," York, 1911 (Pharmaceutical Society Library); Ferris & Co., "Cash Price List," Bristol, 1912 (Pharmaceutical Society Library); Joseph Goddard, *The Chemist's Counter Companion,* London, 1853 (Pharmaceutical Society Library); "Account Book of Morris E. Morris, Chemist, Druggist and Grocer, of Portmadoc, Wales, 1860–1863" (National Library of Wales).

Table 4.
Sales of "Dr. J. Collis Browne's Chlorodyne," 1871–1920

1871–1899 (home and export sales)

1871	£28,415	1886	31,152
1872	32,375	1887	31,698
1873	36,349	1888	30,929
1874	34,427	1889	30,779
1875	40,431	1890	32,052
1876	37,472	1891	31,043
1877	32,348	1892	30,132
1878	32,087	1893	26,196
1879	35,216	1894	24,433
1880	32,662	1895	24,872
1881	34,325	1896	25,535
1882	34,034	1897	27,526
1883	34,657	1898	26,745
1884	34,000	1899	25,851
1885	32,601		

1906–1919 (home sales only)

1906	£17,400	1913	17,000
1907	16,800	1914	18,000
1908	17,400	1915	21,800
1909	16,800	1916	23,200
1910	16,800	1917	28,800
1911	18,200	1918	42,800
1912	17,000	1919	53,000
		1920	50,600

Source: Private letter from Mr. C. D. Wilson, Managing Director, J. T. Davenport, Ltd.

Table 5.
Accidental Poisonings, 1840–1926

Year	Total Accidental Poisonings	Total Accidental Opiate Poisonings	Opiate Accidents as a Percentage of Total Poisonings	Opiate Poisonings Under Age 5
1840	188	56	29.7	42
1852	364	123	33.7	
1853	386	125	32.3	
1854	374	152	40.6	
1855	358	140	39.1	
1856	408	163	39.9	
1863	357	126	35.2	
1864	399	134	33.5	
1865	340	120	35.2	
1866	351	114	32.4	
1867	363	158	43.5	
1868	371	141	38.0	58
1869	348	101	29.0	39
1870	326	90	27.6	29
1871	349	96	27.5	39
1872	363	102	28.0	40
1873	324	108	33.3	27
1874	404	103	25.4	36
1875	377	116	30.7	39
1876	414	111	26.8	32
1877	418	110	26.3	24
1878	494	132	26.7	36
1879	517	144	27.8	36
1880	487	131	26.2	32
1881	268	104	38.8	33
1882	274	97	35.4	22
1883	277	104	37.5	30
1884	222	72	32.4	20
1885	247	107	43.3	22
1886	223	92	41.2	23
1887	244	104	42.6	22
1888	252	108	42.8	20

Table 5. Continued

1889	249	99	39.7	21
1890	249	97	38.9	16
1891	270	112	41.4	20
1892	270	103	38.1	17
1893	278	107	38.4	16
1894	307	111	36.1	16
1895	309	117	37.8	18
1896	312	103	33.0	11
1897	325	131	40.3	11
1898	275	93	33.8	14
1899	302	95	31.4	10
1900	358	92	25.6	11
1901	317	69	21.7	12
1902	261	84	32.1	10
1903	255	95	37.2	12
1904	289	78	26.9	4
1905	261	64	24.5	8
1906	269	77	28.6	7
1907	262	73	27.8	6
1908	257	56	21.7	3
1909	227	61	26.8	9
1910	222	48	21.6	2
1911	245	63	25.7	6
1912	241	53	21.9	2
1913	238	57	23.9	3
1914	224	50	22.3	6
1915	166	25	15.0	3
1916	129	14	10.8	0
1917	129	20	15.5	5
1918	137	27	19.7	4
1919	123	18	14.6	1
1920	116	23	19.8	4
1921	136	15	11.0	1
1922	121	15	12.3	2
1923	111	15	13.5	1
1924	106	15	14.1	0
1925	161	10	6.2	0
1926	111	8	7.2	0

Source: Annual Reports of the Registrar-General.

Table 6.
Suicidal Poisonings, 1840–1926

Year	Total Suicidal Poisonings	Total Opiate Suicides	Opiate Suicides as a Percentage of Total Suicides
1840	161	19	11.8
1852	88	23	26.1
1853	122	24	19.6
1854	95	28	29.4
1855	108	32	26.6
1856	140	37	26.4
1863	121	19	15.7
1864	153	28	18.3
1865	134	22	16.4
1866	128	18	14.0
1867	135	28	20.7
1868	137	35	25.5
1869	142	17	11.9
1870	151	27	17.8
1871	131	11	8.3
1872	138	21	15.2
1873	162	42	25.9
1874	149	25	16.7
1875	155	36	23.2
1876	175	30	17.1
1877	168	32	19.0
1878	215	35	16.2
1879	247	43	17.4
1880	215	36	16.7
1881	228	40	17.5
1882	228	32	14.0
1883	264	32	12.1
1884	250	47	18.8
1885	280	53	18.9
1886	280	42	15.0
1887	246	52	21.1
1888	324	62	19.1

Table 6. Continued

1889	260	48	18.4
1890	276	65	23.5
1891	327	55	16.8
1892	299	59	19.7
1893	368	67	18.2
1894	500	85	17.0
1895	578	73	12.6
1896	467	66	14.1
1897	501	63	12.5
1898	491	58	11.8
1899	514	72	14.0
1900	449	72	16.0
1901	483	60	14.4
1902	496	62	12.5
1903	515	59	11.4
1904	600	79	13.1
1905	676	90	13.3
1906	536	60	11.1
1907	530	63	11.8
1908	583	66	11.3
1909	556	46	8.2
1910	534	43	8.0
1911	514	50	9.7
1912	554	52	9.3
1913	522	41	7.8
1914	506	41	8.1
1915	324	30	9.2
1916	245	15	6.1
1917	196	5	2.5
1918	218	13	5.9
1919	256	14	5.4
1920	314	16	5.0
1921	375	16	4.2
1922	433	7	1.6
1923	417	10	2.3
1924	411	6	1.4
1925	466	6	1.2
1926	606	9	1.4

Source: Annual Reports of the Registrar-General.

Table 7.
Home Consumption of Dangerous Drugs, 1924–1929

Year	Raw Opium* (lb.)	Morphia and Salts (oz.)	Cocaine and Salts (oz.)	Medical Opiates (lb.)	Diacetyl-morphine (oz.)
1924	15,822	18,849	8,873	†	4,055
1925	N.A.	N.A.	N.A.	N.A.	N.A.
1926	8,748	19,211	9,032	2,041	4,206
1927	8,773	19,215	9,319	2,216	4,715
1928	8,281	18,283	9,319	2,070	3,818
1929	8,301	20,215	9,059	2,139	2,764

*Includes opium used to manufacture opiate products, ca. 7/8 of total; assumes 11.5% opium.
†Included with raw opium.
Source: Home Office report, PRO, HO45/14213/482142.

Table 8.
Opium Alkaloid Manufacturing, T. Whiffen & Sons, Ltd., 1893–1923

Year	Morphine Quantity (oz.)	Price (£)	Codeine Quantity (oz.)	Price (£)
1893	94,326	17,662	7,522	4,272
1894	137,978	29,870	9,495	4,863
1895	144,516	28,425	8,459	4,139
1896	109,903	23,728	10,207	5,002
1897	148,204	31,861	11,538	6,094
1898	111,856	21,826	7,254	3,928
1899	190,009	41,475	11,538	7,869
1900	198,758	45,796	10,860	6,570
1901	200,224	47,064	11,643	6,811
1902	258,439	49,870	11,227	5,459
1903 to 1908:	Ledger books missing			
1909	233,143	77,071	24,813	12,113
1910	203,243	72,252	24,992	11,664
1911	185,385	71,488	7,914	4,315
1912	244,994	141,150	20,684	15,319
1913	377,578	174,240	12,831	8,191
1914	497,801	208,194	19,545	14,390
1915	572,975	397,284	55,182	61,356
1916	650,305	468,944	64,509	64,306
1917	333,765	326,628	86,853	88,035
1918	100,020	129,006	71,984	79,519
1919	296,994	257,130	60,539	72,392
1920	433,025	347,734	34,566	41,617
1921	53,490	31,177	18,497	10,123
1922	57,080	21,057	8,040	4,502
1923	In April, 1923, morphia production was halted.		2,493	1,592

Source: London County Council Record Office, Whiffen Ledger Books, B/WHF/86–89, 77.

Table 9.
Exports of Drugs and Medicinal Preparations, 1868–1909

1868	£497,900	1889	£ 971,415
1869	582,676	1890	1,060,379
1870	614,515	1891	1,053,436
1871	720,830	1892	1,013,231
1872	734,086	1893	945,483
1873	676,269	1894	973,894
1874	660,461	1895	1,048,310
1875	694,197	1896	1,122,201
1876	643,292	1897	1,133,085
1877	694,329	1898	1,103,934
1878	777,745	1899	1,155,637
1879	784,811	1900	1,262,685
1880	814,412	1901	1,339,970
1881	938,765	1902	1,368,545
1882	935,293	1903	1,408,537
1883	922,649	1904	1,382,374
1884	893,184	1905	1,464,598
1885	842,725	1906	1,549,471
1886	814,213	1907	1,735,119
1887	869,083	1908	1,543,872
1888	932,154	1909	1,718,086

Source: "Annual Accounts of Trade and Navigation," *Parliamentary Papers.*

Index

A.S.F.: *The Story of a Great Conspiracy.*
   See Rhode, John.
Acetylsalicylic acid ("aspirin"), 103,
   211
Addiction, degeneration and, 94–
   95; modern civilization
   and, 94; cures for, 96–97,
   190–191, 193; dangers of,
   208; definition of, 204; disease theory of, 92–105;
   medical definitions of, 192;
   psychological predisposition to, 93–94
Alcock, Sir Rutherford, 90
Alton Locke (1850). *See* Kingsley,
   Charles.
Allbutt, Dr. Thomas Clifford, 85,
   92, 94, 95, 97
America, narcotic drugs in, 201–
   220
Anglo-Chinese Agreement of 1907,
   129
Arsenic Act (1852), 69
Aspirin. *See* Acetylsalicylic acid.

Balta Limon, Treaty of (1838), 13–
   14
Barbiturates, 103, 211
Battley's Syrup, 18, 39n

Belgravia, satire of De Quincey's
   Confessions published in, 7
Bermondsey, 28
Birdwood, Sir George, 90
Birmingham Daily Post, 27
"Black Drop," 39n
Blackwood's Edinburgh Magazine, sat-
   ires of De Quincey's *Con-
   fessions* published in, 7
Bluegate Fields, 52
Bolton, Deric, 152
Botanic medicine, 25–26
"Broken Blossoms." *See* Griffiths,
   D. W.
"J. Collis Browne's Chlorodyne." *See*
   Chlorodyne.
Buchan, William, 25
Burke, Thomas, *Limehouse Nights*
   (1917), 119

Campbell, Sir George, 90
Carleton, Billie, 135–136, 141n, 172
Cannabis, 96–97
Cerebrasthenia, 94
Certificate system, 135, 154, 156–
   157
Chang, Brilliant, 168–171, 178
Chemist and Druggist, 28, 31–32
Chemists, patent medicine sales

238

East India Company, 11
Edinburgh Committee for the Sup-
    pression of the Indo-
    Chinese Opium Traffic,
    148, 150–151
Edwin Drood, The Mystery of. See
    Dickens, Charles.
Eliot, Sir Charles, 158

Fen district, opium consumption in,
    48–51
"Frailty" (1921), 125
France, drug smuggling and, 156–
    157, 160

Garraway's Coffee House, 16
General Medical Council, attempt to
    restrict sale of laudanum
    by, 29–30
Gentleman's Magazine, 31
Germany, drug smuggling and,
    156–157, 160; as illicit
    cocaine source, 176–177
"Godfrey's Cordial," 33–34, 42
Griffiths, D. W., "Broken Blossoms"
    (1919), 124

Habitual Drunkards' Act (1879), 88
Hague Opium Conferences (1911–
    1914), 129–130
Hahnemann. *See* Irregular prac-
    titioners.
"Hall's Coca Wine," 34
Harrison Act (1914), 202, 210–211
Herbalism, 24–26
Heroic therapies, 23–24
Heroin, 96–97, 123–124, 179, 191,
    216–217
Hill, John, 25
"Human Wreckage" (1924), 128n
Humoral theory of disease, 23, 101
Humphrey, H. M. F., 155–160,
    162n
Hunter, Dr. Charles, and the hy-
    podermic syringe, 80

Hypodermic syringe, 79–80, 100,
    207–208

Inebriates' Act (1898), 88, 199n
Inebriety, Society for the Study and
    Cure of. *See* Society for the
    Study and Cure of Inebri-
    ety.
Inebriety or Narcomania. See Kerr, Dr.
    Norman.
Infanticide, 44–46
Institutionalization of drug addicts,
    88
Irregular practitioners, 23–24

Japan, international drug traffic
    and, 149–151, 157–158,
    162n
"J. Collis Browne's Chlorodyne." *See*
    Chlorodyne.
Jennings, Dr. Oscar, 83, 93, 96, 97,
    100–101
Jordan, Kate, "The Grey Land of
    Drugs," *Pearson's Magazine*
    (1916), 97–99
Josephson, Eric, 219

Kane, H. H., *Drugs that Enslave,* 208
Kempton, Freda, 168
Kerr, Dr. Norman, *Inebriety or Nar-
    comania* (1894), 87–89, 102
Kingsley, Charles, *Alton Locke*
    (1850), 50
Kirkdale Gaol, opium use by in-
    mates in, 47
Kolb, Lawrence, 218–219

Lancashire, herb trade in, 25–26;
    opium use in, 43, 46
Laudanum, 18, 23, 39n
Laughter of Fools, The. See Mills, Lady
    Dorothy.
Laurier, John, 156–157
Lawton, Walter, 93, 96
League of Nations, 164, 180n

DATE DUE

DEC 1 6 2004			
DEC 0 2 2004			